THE ECONOMIC
DEVELOPMENT
OF CHINA

An East Gate Book

VICTOR D. LIPPIT

THE ECONOMIC DEVELOPMENT OF CHINA

M. E. Sharpe, Inc.
Armonk, New York/London

For Rose and Jules Lippit

East Gate Books are edited by Douglas Merwin
120 Buena Vista Drive, White Plains, New York 10603

Copyright © 1987 by M. E. Sharpe, Inc.

Available in the United Kingdom and Europe from M. E. Sharpe,
Publishers, 3 Henrietta Street, London WC2E 8LU.

Library of Congress Cataloging-in-Publication Data

Lippit, Victor D.
    The economic development of China.

    Includes bibliographies and index.
    1. China—Economic policy. 2. China—Economic conditions. 3. Social
classes—China—History. 4. Elite (Social sciences)—China—History.
5. Saving and investment—China—History. I. Title.
HC427.L486   1987   338.951   86-20410
ISBN 0-87332-403-X
ISBN 0-87332-404-8 (pbk.)

Printed in the United States of America

Contents

Preface

This book has taken shape over many years. I began writing it in the 1970s, planning a work that would sum up my long interest in the social and economic changes taking place in China. Since these changes are continuing and actually intensifying, however, the subject matter of the book became a moving target. Under these circumstances, it became difficult to arrive at any final assessment of economic development in China and therefore to complete the project I had begun. While it is true that any assessment must be tentative, however, I believe it is still possible to present an integrated framework, a perspective on the Chinese economy and society that makes it possible to reevaluate on an ongoing basis the changes taking place. This is the thrust of my effort here.

My initial perspective as I considered the Chinese economy in the 1960s was strongly colored by the events transpiring in the United States; this is probably always the case when someone in one culture attempts to interpret circumstances in another. For me in the 1960s, the image of the United States was one of a national preoccupation with material gain, the existence of widespread poverty despite immense national wealth, the reality of discrimination, and the willingness to use military power to advance the interests of capitalism. The academic establishment in Chinese studies seemed comfortable with this state of affairs and consistently prepared to denigrate Chinese efforts to create a new society based on the precepts of socialism. Particularly striking about the establishment's efforts was an almost complete unwillingness to consider China's efforts at social change in its own terms.

Perhaps under these circumstances it was inevitable that radical scholarship in the United States would emphasize a more balanced and favorable assessment of China's attempt to construct a new society. I myself strongly identified with this critical literature. It seemed to me impossible to dismiss China's efforts to create a society in which personal gain was not the primary motive force of individual activity, one in which concern for and commitment to the welfare of others would take center place. Yet with the death of Mao Zedong in September 1976, followed in short order by the arrest of the "gang of four" and—two years later—the initiation of the reform program, the structure of Chinese society and the nature of China's approach to development were transformed dramatically. The Cultural Revolution's emphasis on "serve the people" was replaced by the implicit injunction to "serve yourself" and the explicit slogan "it's all right to get rich first." This shift in orientation, complemented by such drastic institutional changes as the introduction and rapid spread of the market system, forced all the radical students of the Chinese economy to reconsider their position. In particular, the question of whether or not China was carrying out any form of transition to socialism came to the fore, and with it the very meaning of socialism.

I have long been dissatisfied with the conventional presentations in comparative economic systems textbooks that treat socialism as an economic system characterized by state ownership of the primary means of production. It seems to me preferable to think of socialism in terms of the relations of production more broadly conceived, relations of which ownership is merely one aspect. More specifically, it seems that each economy or economic system is characterized especially by its class structure and the way in which the dominant class or classes dispose of the economic surplus. Socialism is an economic system characterized by the ascendancy of those classes that work for a living (as opposed to those classes supported primarily by their ownership of property or authority over others). Socialist economic development, then, is simply economic development that advances the interests of working classes especially, and the transition to socialism means the deepening authority of these classes in all spheres of social activity. I would suggest that this framework affords a useful perspective for considering the dramatic changes that have taken place in China, one that makes possible an on-going reassessment as new developments occur.

Above all, then, this book considers the economic development of China from the perpective of class interest and class structure. In presenting the argument, I have found it necessary to develop at some length the concept of a "statist" social formation with a dominant bureaucratic class. As the text will make clear, despite the spread of the market system in China, I regard statism as a far more probable alternative to socialism than capitalism. The type of society that ultimately emerges in China will depend in large measure on whether the bureaucracy comes to constitute a distinct class. I believe it is too early to reach a conclusion concerning this, but I do attempt to specify the criteria that can be used in an on-going reassessment.

Part II of the book, initially meant to provide historical background for the rest of the volume, was published independently in *Modern China* (vol. 4, no. 3, July 1978) and reprinted in Philip Huang, ed., *The Development of Underdevelopment in China* (Armonk, N.Y.: M.E. Sharpe, 1980). In *Modern China* it served as the basis for a symposium, with critical assessments provided by historians and economists, and in the 1980 book I added my own afterword to these. I believe that many valid points were raised in the symposium, but in reconsidering my work after these years, I find that I remain convinced of the substance of my argument and have decided to leave it essentially as I initially presented it. Some sections in part III initially appeared in *The Transition to Socialism in China* (Armonk, N.Y.: M.E. Sharpe, 1982), which I co-edited with Mark Selden. These sections have been rearranged to fit the logical development of the argument in the book.

I am indebted to the Committee on Research at the University of California, Riverside, for financial support during work on various stages of the manuscript, and to many people for their constructive criticisms over the years. To Professor Ishikawa Shigeru I owe a special debt for his influence on my early approach to the Chinese economy. The suggestions and criticisms of Joseph Esherick especially, but also of Jerome Ch'en, Linda Grove, Philip Huang, James Parsons, and Irwin Wall, were of great help in completing part II. For critical comments on part III I am indebted to Bob Pollin, Mark Selden, and Howard Sherman, all of whom read parts of the manuscript. I also owe a great deal to Professor Zhang Yunling of the Chinese Academy of Social Sciences for information on recent developments and many lively discussions concerning economic reform in China. Perhaps most of all I am indebted to my graduate students in the Economics Department at the University of California, Riverside. Drawn here by the rich tradition in political economy, they have challenged my thinking as much as I have challenged theirs.

PART I
THE ANALYTICAL FRAMEWORK

1. Class Structure and the Development Process

When Europe was still in the Middle Ages and prevailing opinion held the world to be flat, China passed through a prolonged period of rapid economic expansion and technological development, emerging with a culture of unparalleled sophistication. Yet China's economic lead was frittered away, and while the Industrial Revolution brought sustained economic development to the West, nothing comparable took place in China. Rather, by the nineteenth century, China had become one of the most underdeveloped countries in the world. It persisted in this state until the middle of the twentieth century, when the Chinese revolution swept new classes into power and a period of sustained economic development was initiated.

Both the failure of Chinese development to be carried through in earlier centuries—despite favorable initial conditions—and the successful initiation of the development process in the middle of the present century require explanation. This is to be found above all in the key role played in the development process by the dominant classes and the use they make of the economic surplus. Almost every society generates a surplus, an output in excess of the customary consumption requirements of its ordinary members. The dominant groups or classes in the society dispose of this surplus in a manner calculated to serve or promote their own interests. Where those interests coincide with the objective requirements of economic development, development proceeds; where those interests conflict with the objective requirements of development, development is blocked. When development proceeds, it is capable of following a number of alternative paths, depending on which classes are predominant. That is to say, if the dominant classes find development to be in their interest, they shape the process in ways that reflect that interest. In short, economic development is a class-specific process.

Although class structure and the attendant pattern of surplus use typically play the most significant role, development prospects are also influenced by such factors as resources, technology, and international conditions, and in some cases they are determined by the actions of foreign powers and the international economic system they have created. The most clear-cut case of this is colonialism, where the dominant classes in a less-developed country are replaced by a foreign power which shapes the colony's economic activity to reflect the interests of its own dominant classes. Even in the case of colonialism, the most clear-cut case of development being blocked by external forces, questions of class structure and surplus use come to the fore, since the dominant class interests of the mother country replace those of the colony, and since the process of surplus extraction and disposition encompasses the core of colonial economic activity. Where direct colonial rule is not present, imperialism and the capitalist world economic system can nevertheless affect profoundly the prospects for development in less developed countries, and the course of development if it does take place. Where this is the case, however, it is still necessary to examine the domestic class structure and the use of the surplus it determines as well as the impact of the world system. Methodologically, moreover, it is important to examine the two in this order because the impact of the world system can be appropriately clarified only after the character of the domestic system with which it interacts has been established.

The analysis of class structure and surplus use gives this study of the economic development of China its unity. The book is divided into three parts. Part I lays out the analytical framework that underlies the study as a whole. Much of the discussion in this part, therefore, does not deal directly with China, but elaborates the categories of analysis. Those who are less concerned with the theoretical framework can proceed directly to part II, which considers the reasons for China's development failure prior to the middle of the twentieth century; those whose interests are limited to the postrevolutionary period can proceed directly to part III. Although I have sought to make the three parts complementary and thus give the book its structural integrity, I have sought at the same time to make each of the three parts comprehensible in itself, so as to meet the needs of those whose interests are more specific. The topics in this chapter (part I) include the concepts of class and surplus, economic development, modes of production, social formations, and the transition to socialism. Part II turns to the development of underdevelopment in China, attempting to clarify the reasons for which China, once one of the most advanced societies in the world, became by the nineteenth and early twentieth centuries one of the most underdeveloped. There, developing the argument through an extensive critique of earlier theories, I argue that the class structure and associated patterns of surplus use bear primary responsibility for underdevelopment.

The major part of the book, part III, is devoted to an analysis of economic development in China since the founding of the People's Republic in 1949. There I argue that the critical change was the replacement of classes with a hostile or ambiguous attitude toward development or the changes needed to bring it about (such as land reform) by classes with a clear interest in development. The classes favored by development in contemporary China are composed of people who work for a living, and for the most part they have shaped the development process to reflect their interest. Much of the discussion in part III is meant to document this by showing that, in general, the characteristic features of China's post–1949 development can be grasped most readily as an expression of the class interests of those who work for a living.

The relation between the development process and the interests of the dominant class is invariably a complex one, however, embodying various contradictions and affected by a host of related factors, including among others international ones and historically determined initial conditions. The most important contradiction is that posed by a vanguard party and strong state, necessary on the one hand to provide leadership and protect the mass class interests, but at the same time capable of defining and asserting an independent interest that conflicts with theirs.

To analyze this and other contradictions, and to provide the basis for a comprehensive assessment of China's economic development in the modern period, this chapter sets out the basic features of socialist economic development; that is, development that reflects the interest of workers, peasants, and indeed all those doing socially useful work. This provides a benchmark against which it is possible to assess the actual economic record and clarify the contradictions that have emerged in the course of Chinese development. As the discussion in part III makes clear, Chinese development has on the whole reflected the interests of those who work, but there have been notable deviations which if left uncorrected would have threatened the entire socialist project.

The Concept of Class

Throughout the book, the conception of class plays a central role, for I assert that in the last analysis it is dominant class interests that blocked development prior to 1949, and (a new set of) dominant class interests that promoted and shaped the development process after 1949. By class I refer in the first instance to the economic relations into which people enter as a consequence of their participation in the production process, including its characteristic ownership patterns. Common usage is sometimes a satisfactory indicator of class status, sometimes not. Thus, for example, the identification of capitalists as the private owners of the means of production and of workers or the proletariat as those who must sell their labor power in order to live is fairly straightforward. The term "middle class," on the other hand, has no clear reference to economic roles and thus is avoided here.

Sometimes, however, popular terminology is convenient to use even though it fails to isolate the critical elements that distinguish classes. Thus the terms poor, middle, and rich peasant, for example, appear to be based on income, and at one level of analysis they indeed are. At the same time, however, poor peasants can be identified as those whose farm income is inadequate to meet their subsistence, and who must supplement their income to a considerable extent by selling their labor power, full or part time, or engaging in handicraft production. Since the term "poor peasant" incorporates this economic role, it is useful for class analysis. Similarly, middle peasants are those with sufficient land to occupy them fully or nearly so, while rich peasants have more land than they can farm themselves and thus hire one or more full-time laborers to assist them. Landlords, by contrast, do not engage in labor, but derive the greater portion of their income by renting out their land to others. In each of these cases, a production relation underlies the common usage of the term.

Thus the concept of class must first of all be based on economic relations entered into as a consequence of the production process and the system of ownership that surrounds it. To be useful analytically in identifying distinct groups in the population and grasping their behavior, however, it must go beyond these relations. For example, dominant classes are characterized by the development of mechanisms to transfer class status from one generation to the next. Thus inheritance is an important mechanism in perpetuating capitalist class status. In some societies elite educational institutions fulfill the same function. Unless such mechanisms for intergenerational transmission of class status exist, the concept of class loses much of its descriptive and analytical power.

In analyzing post–1949 China, it is important to grasp the role of the cadre-bureaucrats—those with access to the power and resources of the state—in this context. Nominally they serve as representatives of the working classes—composed of workers, peasants, and all those doing socially useful work—but in practice they naturally tend to develop distinct interests of their own. As will be seen later, this creates one of the principal contradictions in the transition to socialism, but from the standpoint of class analysis the critical questions are whether the cadres develop mechanisms for intergenerational maintenance of class status, whether they will free themselves entirely from the authority of those whom they nominally represent, and whether they divert a significant share of the surplus they control to serve their own purposes. As I will argue later, these conditions for class formation have not yet been met in contemporary China. Thus the bureaucracy can be identified as a potential class-in-the-making, but one which has not yet emerged as a distinct class. Indeed, when and if it does so, the transition to socialism in China will be cut short.

In general, to clarify the potential of the bureaucracy as a class, we need only keep in mind the central role any bureaucracy, whether in China or in another less-developed country, can assume in the process of economic reproduction. Even though it is not directly involved in economic production, a substantial share of the economic surplus passes through its hands in the form of taxes, profits of state enterprises, state fees, and bribery. The members of the bureaucracy are often in a position to divert these revenues to their own purposes. Their situation can be likened to that of merchant capitalists who also find a substantial share of the surplus flowing through their hands. Like merchant capitalists, the bureaucrats bear a definite relation to the production process without direct involvement in it. Just as merchant capitalists can appropriate much of the surplus by virtue of their position in the circulation process, in their case by differential pricing, so the bureaucracy can appropriate the surplus it controls, using such means as high salaries or expense accounts, establishing new enterprises or other state activities, accepting bribes, and so forth. Even if the bureaucracy directs the surplus into what it perceives, from its class perspective, as proper public projects, however, its distinctive relation to the production-circulation process remains, and so too, therefore, does its class status.

One final clarification of the concept of class I will be using here is in order. I have spoken of class as being defined in the first instance by the characteristic relation to the production process. Class membership also involves the acquisition of a set of values, way of perceiving the world, and various cultural accoutrements, although considerable diversity exists and can be tolerated about the norm. More significant, when society is divided quite clearly into those who produce the surplus and those who appropriate it, the appropriators may engage in a variety of activities without changing their class status.

In imperial China, it was not unusual for far-sighted families to prepare some sons to enter trade and others to enter the bureaucracy by passing the requisite examinations. Despite their different activities, it would be quite improper to ascribe different class status to the brothers involved. In similar fashion, members of the bureaucracy who enriched themselves in office and used the funds thus acquired to purchase land or establish pawnshops did not thereby change their class status. In imperial China—and the argument here will be developed much more fully in chapter 4—the social structure brought about a thoroughgoing interpenetration of the various elite class roles, and mobility among them. Thus, although a specific relation to the production process determines class status in the first instance, the multiplicity of roles that the appropriators can assume and the ease of movement among these roles may make it most meaningful to group the appropriators of the surplus in a single class. As we will see, this approach is certainly warranted for late imperial China.

The Surplus and Development

The dominant class or classes are, by definition, those who control the disposition of the surplus. Some uses of the surplus, especially investment, promote economic growth, or an expansion of economic output over time. Economic development refers to the process whereby accumulation, consisting of both saving and investment, and technological change become institutionalized. That is, institutional mechanisms become established that regularly channel a portion of the surplus into accumulation. In capitalism, the corporation fulfills this function. Pursuing profits and propelled by competition, it regularly sets apart a portion of the cash flow generated by profits and depreciation for reinvestment. Because involvement in this process does not depend on the particular individuals involved, it can be said to be institutionally determined. In like fashion, in the socialist or statist societies (the distinction between the two is clarified below) where the accumulation process is directed by the state, a proportion of state revenues is regularly set aside for reinvestment, again irrespective of the particular individuals who may be involved.

Economic development requires certain favorable conditions, but, of equal importance, it takes place only when the dominant classes perceive it to be in their interest to routinize the process of capital accumulation and technological change. They need not, of course, be conscious that this is in fact what they are doing, just as individual capitalists pursuing profit may have no idea or even interest in the fact that they are contributing to the development process. In imperial China, the gentry class which controlled the state was so much the beneficiary of the existing order that it tried at all costs to defend it rather than promote the reforms that would have contributed to the development process. As the discussion in part 2 shows, a substantial surplus existed in prerevolutionary China, amounting to at least 30 percent of national income. The critical determinant of the development of underdevelopment, then, was not a shortage of capital, but the disposition of the surplus by the dominant class in ways that failed to advance the development process.

When the People's Republic was established in 1949, China's per capita income was approximately U.S.$60 (in 1957 prices; Perkins 1975, 134). At that level, it was impossible to meet the needs and aspirations of the working mass of the population, which had assumed dominant class status as a result of the revolution. It was only natural, then, that in implementing reforms and institutional changes that reflected its class interest, it would attempt to institutionalize the accumulation process, routinely channeling a significant share of the surplus into capital formation. This process is documented in part III, but by far the greatest concern there is analysis of the relation between the class interest that spawned development in China and the characteristic features of the development process that emerged. Economic development is possible under a variety of regimes distinguished by their predominant classes, and we can expect the nature of the development process to differ sharply among systems with differing class structures. Most of part III is devoted to analyzing the specific nature of Chinese development as a case study in socialist economic development, clarifying on the one hand how the dominance of people who work for a living shapes the development process in a manner quite divergent from the characteristic features of capitalist development, and on the other how the bureaucratic structures that revolutionary societies tend to spawn can modify the process in ways inimical to mass class interests.

Economic development, then, is a class-specific process both in the sense that whether it occurs depends above all on the interest of the dominant class, and in the sense that if it occurs, it does so in a way that reflects that interest. The analysis of the Chinese case, however, is complicated by the fact that the establishment of socialism is a historical process that does not end with the establishment of public ownership of the means of production but begins with it. Ultimately, the meaning of socialism as a socioeconomic system lies in the dominance of the working classes at every level of society, from the workplace to the state. Public ownership of the means of production is a necessary condition for this dominance but by no means assures it. Rather, the revolutionary expropriation of private capital ushers in a more or less prolonged period of transition to socialism, a period which continues as long as the prospects for the growing authority of the working classes remain viable. It is also possible, however, for the transition period to be cut short by the emergence and entrenchment of a bureaucratic class with a distinct interest of its own. This issue will be explored more fully in chapter 9, but here I would like to lay the groundwork for that discussion by elaborating the concepts of modes of production and social formations, and then discussing the various models of development based on these concepts.

Modes of Production and Social Formations

A mode of production refers to the distinctive relations, including ownership relations, into which people enter in production activity, and to a corresponding development of the forces of production, including such factors as capital, technology, and human skills. The relations of production, which define class status in the first instance, are the most important element specifying the mode of production. Most presocialist modes of production tend to be exploitative in that of the two primary classes, one tends to live off the surplus above its subsistence requirements produced by the other. Thus slave owners live off the surplus created by slaves, feudal lords live off the surplus created by serfs, and capitalists live off the surplus created by workers. Precapitalist modes of production are not always exploitative, however, and may not even have a dual class relation of this type. Petty commodity producers like independent farmers or artisans who produce goods (commodities) for sale on the market, for example, appropriate their own surplus. It is noteworthy, however, that the independent petty commodity mode of production has proven unstable historically, invariably giving way to the capitalist mode of production.

A social formation refers to the mix and interaction of modes of production in a given society, as well as to the institutions and activities that govern their interaction. It refers in short to the entire economic structure, with the varied modes of production at its core. The social formation defines the context of a specific mode of production, and in doing so it is capable of affecting profoundly its internal character. Thus slavery in the nineteenth-century United States differed from that in ancient Rome, for the former was profoundly affected by the capitalist environment in which it emerged and flourished. In naming social formations, the name of the predominant mode of production is usually used.

In addition to the modes of production I have noted, two others assume particular importance for the analysis of economic development in part III: the statist and socialist modes of production. The socialist mode of production requires public ownership of the means of production and has two additional defining characteristics: the direct producers control the work process and govern the disposition of the surplus both in an immediate sense—e.g., at the enterprise level—and in a class sense, at the national level. Thus a collective enterprise may or may not be included in a subset of the socialist mode of production. In the case of the Soviet *kolkhozy* (collective farms), for example, the collectives were set up from above as a means of extracting the surplus from the peasants and are rigidly controlled from above. For either reason, they could not be included in the socialist mode of production despite their collective form.

In fact, in the contemporary world, we would have great difficulty pointing to any specific example of a socialist mode of production. There is a good reason for this. As I have noted, socialism refers to a historical process of transformation, the possibility for which is ushered in with the establishment of public ownership of the means of production. What is commonly referred to as a "socialist country," therefore, is actually one in which the preconditions for a transition to socialism have been established; socialism remains at once a vision and a process of transition. Only when the working classes have established their authority throughout society, and at the enterprise and national levels in particular, will the socialist mode of production be established. In this sense socialism is a project on which the "socialist" countries have embarked.

That the end product of such a transition process will be socialism is by no means assured, for many contradictions are capable of aborting the process. In practice, the most significant contradiction has been that posed by the leadership role of a vanguard party and the state bureaucracy that is inevitably the product of successful revolution. Nominally, the party and bureaucracy rule on behalf of the working classes, in their interest. But as I have noted, by virtue of the positions of authority and economic control they assume, the cadres of the party-state are capable of emerging as a distinct class with their own interest. Even if they do not do so, but manage to sustain the socialist project, the predominant mode of production during the transitional period can most appropriately be termed "statist."

Thus the statist mode of production is one in which public or collective ownership is combined with bureaucratic authority over the production process. A statist social formation is one in which the statist mode of production predominates. According to this definition, both China and the Soviet Union are characterized by statist social formations. Many third world countries without socialist or communist governments are also characterized by statist social formations. Since the emergence of a capitalist class was severely hindered in most colonies, in the postcolonial era the state bureaucracy has naturally assumed a leading role in society and in the pursuit of development; this is especially true in Africa. In these cases, socialist revolution has not been the motive force underlying economic change, and the bureaucracy is relatively free to identify its own class interest with the national interest, and to privatize wealth in its own interest. Privatization, depending on the form it takes, may spur or hinder the development of the capitalist mode of production. The statist social formations thus cover a wide range of different situations and may be stable in form (e.g., the Soviet Union), indicate the possibility of socialist transition (e.g., China), tend toward privatization and capitalist development (e.g., Kenya and Brazil), or tend toward a privatization that is so extreme as to preclude the possibility of development (e.g., Zaire).

Economic development can proceed under a variety of social formations, statist as well as capitalist. In the modern era, even if the bureaucracy lacks a popular base, it typically must pursue development to sustain its legitimacy and enhance stability. If it is perceived as venal and not successfully pursuing development, it becomes subject to overthrow, as in a military coup. Thus even in this case, the self-interest of the bureaucrats, their interest in preserving the positions and system that nurture them, requires some effort to pursue economic development. For the analysis of development in post–1949 China, it is important to distinguish among the variety of statist social formations that may exist. Here I would like to distinguish among three principal types. I exclude from these three types the statist formation in which the bureaucracy acts in purely venal fashion, a type which tends to be extremely unstable in the modern world. The three types I would like to take up here include the statist social formation that is stable, that which tends toward capitalism, and that which tends toward socialism. The corresponding models of development are statist, capitalist, and socialist respectively.

The Soviet Union is an example of a stable statist social formation. Although the Soviet Union was founded with the intention of bringing about a transition to socialism, the project foundered and the bureaucracy assumed a distinct class role, appropriating a portion of the surplus for its own ends, defining the national interest in terms of its own class perspective, maintaining rigid control, and reproducing itself. The economic development process has been institutionalized—indeed that is a condition for legitimacy and thus stability in the modern world—and statist economic development reflects both the interest and the authority of the bureaucratic class. I will turn in the following sections to an elaboration of the statist—as well as capitalist and socialist—development models.

Historically, the state has always played an important role in capitalist development. This was true even in England, where control of the seas and the expansion of empire were significant. England, however, was an exception in that the bureaucracy did not have to play a direct role in the development process; the laissez-faire ideas of Adam Smith were indeed appropriate, in the main, for the era he ushered in. Most of the countries that played catch-up, however, were forced to allocate a greater role to the state, and thus to the bureaucracy. And the farther behind their starting position was, the greater the role that had to be allocated to the state to make catching up feasible. Thus the state played a central role when Germany and Japan initiated their development in the second half of the nineteenth century.

Since the gap between the advanced and less-developed countries is much greater today, the role of the state would on that count alone tend to be greater still. A variety of circumstances, however, intensify this effect. First, nationalism and development consciousness have magnified popular expectations, even while population pressures require speedy progress; initiative and action are necessary, and the magnitude of the problems requires the state to take the lead. Second, as I have noted, the indigenous capitalist class is typically weakly developed in former colonies, since economic development in the colonies was systematically frustrated and the most profitable activities were reserved for the mother countries. The colonial heritage also mandated an intensive period of institution-building, again requiring the state to take the leading role. Third, the capitalist world system has become so complex and sophisticated—to add to the rapaciousness that has always been present—that strong states have become necessary to protect the interests of nascent capitalists in the third world.

For all these reasons, laissez-faire is an outdated model of capitalist development for the less-developed countries today. Rather, capitalist economic development must proceed via a statist social formation in which the state, through the use of parastatal corporations and active manipulation of various economic levers, takes the lead; the widespread use of development planning in even the most conservative states is a reflection of this. Privatization typically plays an important part in early capitalist development as it proceeds under the aegis of a statist social formation. The bureaucracy uses its access to the power and resources of the state to carry out the process; methods range from the allocation of valuable real estate to themselves by highly-ranked military officers in Pakistan to the letting of lucrative contracts to well-placed individuals by government officials in Saudi Arabia. In the privatization process, government officials themselves and those closely connected to them tend to be the leading beneficiaries. Where capitalist development is proceeding successfully, then, the bureaucracy does not establish itself as a distinct class but gradually merges into the capitalist class which it itself nurtures.

In socialist economic development too, the leading role of the bureaucracy is a transitional one. Here too, it is the strengthening of a discrete class with which it identifies that prepares the basis for its own disappearance as a class-in-the-making. Initially, the bureaucracy appears in a leadership role as the agent of the revolutionary classes. If it is successful in institutionalizing the accumulation process with its attendant technological change, and in creating conditions for the deepening participation and control of the working classes at every level of social activity, then socialism will be realized. From this perspective, Marx's vision of socialism entailing the withering away of the state is eminently sensible. Although it is carried out initially in a statist social formation, then, the character of socialist development is such as to reflect the underlying interest of the mass classes of working people.

In part III, I analyze contemporary China as a case study in socialist economic development. To provide the basis for this analysis, I attempt to specify abstract models of socialist, statist, and capitalist economic development in the sections that follow. Underlying these models is the conception of modes of production and social formations specified here. Although in each case a statist social formation prevails initially, in the cases of capitalist and socialist economic development the statist formation undergoes a process of transformation resulting in the establishment of capitalist and socialist formations respectively. Capitalist economic development is characterized by the emerging strength of the capitalist class, socialist development by the growing strength of the working classes, and statist development by the growing articulation of the bureaucrats' independent class interest. In all three cases, development is a class-specific process whose character is shaped by the interests of the dominant class.

Types of Economic Development

Socialist economic development is simply development carried out in ways that serve working people: workers, peasants, teachers, health workers, and all those whose primary economic role is participation in socially useful labor. The principal beneficiaries of capitalist economic development, by contrast, are those who own the means of production or the newly emerging class of owners. The history of economic development in the West is a history of capitalist development, and by abstracting the class-specific features of that history we can simultaneously arrive at the essence of the capitalist model and have our attention directed to the contrasting class-specific features of the socialist model. The model of socialist development that emerges from this analysis is a "pure" one and as such is not matched by the empirical reality of any particular country's experience. It is necessary, however, to develop the pure model in order to provide a benchmark against which the Chinese experience can be evaluated.

The procedure I follow here, then, is to begin by clarifying the distinction between capitalist and socialist economic development. The model of pure socialist development that emerges will provide the basis for assessing China's development experience. In two principal regards, I will argue, China has deviated from the socialist model: the failure of real wages and peasant incomes to rise significantly over two decades starting in 1957, and the failure of Chinese policy to deal satisfactorily with the persisting social and economic hierarchy.

These failures are closely related to the fact that socialist economic development is carried out within a statist social formation and is always confronted with the possibility that the cadres and bureaucrats will develop an interest and outlook that effectively distinguish them from ordinary working people, and will use their access to the power and resources of the state to define a development path that deviates from the pure socialist model. In the extreme case, when the cadre-bureaucrats come to constitute a distinct class, a statist development model will result. But even though a distinct class does not form, the pure socialist model can be modified in a statist direction, resulting in a development practice that incorporates elements of both models. The Chinese experience, in fact, represents just such a case. To clarify the assertion that Chinese development, although predominantly socialist, incorporates statist elements as well, a brief elaboration of the statist model will be helpful. I do not mean to embark on a detailed presentation of the capitalist, socialist, and statist development models here, but merely to provide the basic framework that underlies the analysis of China's actual development experience in part III.

Capitalist Economic Development

Since the main contours of development everywhere reflect the interests of the dominant classes, the early stages of development in capitalist countries characteristically produce these general features: (1) growing inequality; (2) the perpetuation and even intensification of poverty in a large part of the population; (3) substantial unemployment and underemployment; (4) neglect of the people's welfare within the limits set by the need to assure the reproduction of labor and the preservation of social stability; (5) large-scale displacement of population and the exploitation of the countryside to the advantage of the urban economy; (6) a hierarchical ordering of society and the labor process with the subordination of the direct producers to the owners of capital and land.

These general features of early capitalist development, it should be emphasized, are characteristic tendencies; they are not universal, and certain ones change as the development of capitalism progresses. Thus the growing systemic requirements of a developing capitalist economy eventually include a more educated labor force and a great increase in technical and professional manpower. These requirements usually reverse the tendency toward growing inequality after development has reached a certain point. Further, the nature of development in a particular country may occasionally create a countervailing force relatively early in the course of development. If a sizable portion of the labor force is drawn from agriculture into industry, for example, national income distribution may appear more equal despite a growing gulf between workers and industrialists simply because the gulf between peasants and industrialists is larger still.

While these reservations should be kept in mind, the features of capitalist development itemized above are indeed the norm, as the empirical evidence presented below will indicate. In the 1960s, a number of writers observed that per capita income growth was not a satisfactory indicator of economic development, that what was really critical in development was declining poverty, inequality, and unemployment (see, for example, Seers 1973). Although this proposition expresses a worthy humanitarian critique of the widespread failure of third world development to deal with these critical social issues, it misses the point that all these shortcomings are systemic features of capitalist economic development. In the early stages of capitalist development, for reasons which are systemic rather than coincidental, working people are often the victims rather than the beneficiaries of social change.

If, on the other hand, the dominant classes are composed of working people, then each of these capitalist development characteristics will be replaced by its opposite. That is to say, socialist economic development is characterized by growing equality, disappearing poverty, shrinking unemployment-underemployment, sharply improved popular welfare, relatively balanced urban-rural development, and the sharp curtailment of social and economic hierarchy. The point to be stressed is that despite the rhetorical appearance of this listing, each of the elements follows quite naturally from the class-specific nature of the development process, as the class in power implements policies that serve its own interest.

A capitalist class will try to direct to itself as large a share of the national income as it can, consistent with maintaining the ability of the system to reproduce itself. Since this class constitutes a small proportion of the population, any degree of success will imply widening income disparities. Further, insofar as income is being channeled mainly to those who already have more than their share, reductions in poverty are likely to come about slowly, if at all. Finally, social hierarchy is an essential element securing the authority and control of the capitalist class and the bureaucracy with which it is allied. Unemployment and the threat of unemployment also enhance the authority of the capitalist class by weakening the position of the direct producers and, not incidentally, their wage demands as well.

There is ample theoretical and empirical support for the position that economic development is a class-specific process. In his discussion of primitive accumulation, for example, Marx (1961, part 8) shows that for capitalist production and reproduction to get under way on a regular basis, it is necessary to form concentrated clumps of capital capable of financing investment, on the one hand, and a class of people bereft of the means of self-support—peasants deprived of land or artisans of tools—on the other. Capital and wage labor form the poles of a unity necessary for capitalist development to proceed.

In his classic article "Economic Development with Unlimited Supplies of Labour," W. Arthur Lewis (1963) approaches the question of capitalist accumulation from a perspective that is quite different. Combining methods of neoclassical economic analysis with the class perspective of the classical period, he shows that as long as surplus (unemployed or underemployed) labor[1] exists, the capital accumulation process will tend to channel the increment in national income disproportionately to the capitalists, while real wages remain flat. Whether Marxian or neoclassical analysis is used, poverty, unemployment, and

---

1. Surplus labor is formally defined as labor whose marginal product is zero. That is, if a simple rearrangement of the work process can sustain output at the previous level when a worker withdraws, then surplus labor can be said to have been present. In practice, the concept of surplus labor is usually extended to cases in which the marginal product of labor is very low.

inequality would appear to be intrinsic elements in early capitalist development.

With the exception of a few special cases,[2] these theoretical findings are amply confirmed by empirical analyses of early capitalist development. Irma Adelman (1979), who has carried out the most extensive studies on the relationship between income distribution and economic growth, writes:

> The relationship between levels of economic development and the equity of income distribution is . . . asymmetrically U-shaped, with more egalitarian income distributions being characteristic of both extreme economic underdevelopment and high levels of economic development. Between these extremes, however, the relationship is, for the most part, inverse: up to a point, higher rates of industrialization, faster increases in agricultural productivity, and higher rates of growth all tend to shift the income distribution in favor of the higher income groups and against the low-income groups. (p. 314)

In a study of seven Asian countries—Pakistan, India, Bangladesh, Sri Lanka, Malaysia, Indonesia and the Philippines—which together account for about 70 percent of the rural population of the nonsocialist developing world, the International Labour Office (1977, 9–15) noted worsening distribution of income and declining real income of the rural poor to be persistent tendencies over a period ranging from ten to twenty-five years.

> In each case . . . it was found that the proportion of the population below the "poverty line" has been increasing over time. . . . In most

---

2. In small countries where a labor-intensive industrial export sector develops rapidly, the shift of a large share of the labor force from agriculture to industry may reduce inequality for the reasons elaborated in the text. In such cases, moreover, industrialists tend to be powerful relative to landowners, and they may be able to bring about a genuine land reform, which will be to their interest insofar as it raises agricultural productivity, lowers agricultural prices (and thus the wages they must pay), and extends rural markets. In effect, eliminating rural claims on the surplus enhances their prospect of obtaining a larger share. These factors may have been operative in Taiwan and South Korea, both of which have among the most equal income distributions of the less developed countries. In the case of Taiwan, the fact that the elite class was composed of mainlanders bringing "liquid" wealth (they couldn't carry their land) when they occupied the island in the late 1940s, a class quite distinct from the Taiwanese landowners, facilitated land reform. As the text makes clear, however, growing inequality is the norm in the early stages of capitalist development. Even in the case of South Korea, which has been widely cited in the literature as an example of equitable development, subsequent data indicate a pronounced tendency toward greater inequality starting in the 1970s (Koo 1984).

of the countries for which measurements could be obtained real wages either remained constant or there appeared to have been a downward trend. (p. 10)

It is certainly not the case that the increasing poverty of many of the poor is mainly due to general stagnation in Asia, or, worse, economic decline. On the contrary, all but one of the seven countries surveyed have enjoyed a rise in average incomes in recent years, and in some instances the rise has been quite rapid. Only in Bangladesh have average incomes fallen, and the interesting question there is how, despite the decline in the average, the upper income groups were able to improve their living standards. In a sense, Bangladesh is the most dramatic illustration of what is happening in the rest of Asia: in countries where average incomes have increased, the poor have tended to become poorer and the rich richer; in Bangladesh, where average incomes have fallen, the rich have nevertheless become richer while the incomes of the poor have fallen faster than the average. (p. 15)

The results described here are not anomalous; they flow logically from the inherent nature of capitalist economic development.

Socialist Economic Development

The brief description of capitalist economic development presented here was meant to demonstrate the class-specific nature of the development process and also to provide the contrasting backdrop against which the discussion of socialist economic development can proceed most meaningfully. Socialist economic development can take place where the classes of direct producers (peasants and workers especially) and other working people are dominant. Such classes will be concerned with eliminating poverty, reducing unemployment, promoting equality, enhancing public welfare, and combating hierarchy *as a matter of their self-interest*, as a matter of course. These concerns will typically be incorporated in any development strategy they pursue.

Consider, by contrast, the exploitation of women and child workers in the early development of England, the United States, Japan, and (prerevolutionary) China, in all of which they constituted the majority of the factory labor force (for Japan and China see Lippit 1978, 68). In the case of Japan, the women factory workers were typically young women from farm families too poor to support them prior to marriage;

poverty forced them to work in the factories under appalling conditions. There was no particular reason for the capitalist class to protect them and every reason to exploit them. In a nation where the direct producers are dominant, however, such a situation would be untenable. The women and children in question would be the leading class's own women and children, and allowing their exploitation would be acting contrary to its own interest. Where socialist economic development prevails, therefore, we would expect to find women workers protected and child labor eliminated. The extent to which policies that reflect the interests of working people are actually implemented in the nominally socialist countries determines the extent to which their development programs can in fact be considered socialist.

In conventional usage, countries where the means of production are predominantly publicly owned are referred to as socialist. As indicated, however, extensive state ownership and a major state economic role are characteristic of the entire third world, and indeed the predominant social formation is a statist one. The critical question in determining the character of the development process is not the ownership system but the class structure of society, for as Paul Sweezy (1971, 4) has properly pointed out, public ownership is a juridical form and in itself cannot express fully the class relations that underlie it. The essence of socialism is ultimately the control by working people—whether engaged in industry or agriculture, or carrying out intellectual, service, or other socially useful tasks—over their own productive activity and indeed over their own lives. It is only in the sense of deepening control by working people and the shaping of economic activity to conform to their interests and those of the entire population that we can talk of a "transition to socialism" in countries where the means of production have already been socialized.

The general criterion for socialist economic development is whether the strategy pursued and policies implemented serve the class interests of the working people. As I have indicated, this implies that the pure socialist model of development will differ markedly from the pure capitalist model in each of the features enumerated. Socialist economic development, reflecting the class interest of the vast majority of the population who must work for a living, will have the following general features: (1) relative equality; (2) the elimination of poverty (the provision of basic needs); (3) virtually full employment; (4) significant improvement in people's welfare, reflected in rising real wages as well as improving social services; (5) accompanying industrialization with rural development so that the entire working population benefits from growth; (6) the sharp curtailment of social and economic hierarchy.

In China, most of these features of socialist economic development have been present. There are, however, two notable exceptions: the failure of people's real wages in industry and earnings in agriculture to rise appreciably over a period of two decades starting in 1957, a period in which substantial increases in agricultural and industrial production occurred, and the failure to curb social and economic hierarchy. These failures were of such importance, moreover, as to jeopardize the entire transition to socialism. The failure to improve living standards reflects both a faulty development strategy and the ability of the party and state leadership to impose its preferences over mass aspirations for greater material prosperity. The enhanced authority of the state and party leadership, unsuccessfully attacked in the Cultural Revolution, also underlies the new forms of hierarchy that have replaced traditional forms of class rule and state power in modern China. When a transition to socialism is not carried out successfully, as in the case of the Soviet Union, the resulting social formation is sometimes referred to as "state capitalism." I believe this terminology to be unfortunate since the system has little or nothing to do with the class relations and dynamics of capitalism. The most appropriate term for such a formation is "statist," and I turn in the next section to a brief description of the principal features of statist economic development.

As I have indicated, in the contemporary world, capitalist, socialist, and statist patterns of economic development are all likely to emerge from social formations that are initially statist (successful capitalist or socialist development transforms the social formation accordingly). Moreover, socialist development typically incorporates both statist and socialist elements, and its failure typically results in the pursuit of a statist development model. For these reasons, it is important to clarify the essential features of the statist model. As in the discussion of the capitalist model, highlighting the features of the principal alternative development models will bring out the essential features of the socialist model more forcefully, and clarify the way in which the features of all the models are tied to dominant class interests. This in turn will provide the basis for the discussion in part III of China's post–1949 development.

Statist Economic Development

For the reasons indicated earlier, the state must take a central role in

contemporary economic development. This in turn means that those with key state positions—and/or key party positions if there is a political party determining state policy—play a predominant part in the early development process. In such circumstances, the social formation is statist. Three distinct development models, however, can emerge from this formation. If authority is gradually transferred to an emerging capitalist class, a process in which the privatization of public wealth typically plays a key role, the result is capitalist economic development, and the bureaucracy gradually merges into the rising capitalist class. If the process is successful, a capitalist social formation emerges (the capitalist mode of production becomes predominant). If authority is gradually transferred to the mass class of direct producers, socialist economic development results, and the bureaucracy merges into this class. If the process is successful, a socialist social formation emerges. If, however, those with access to the power and authority of the state consolidate their position, establish an independent class identity, and reproduce themselves, then statist economic development results and the statist social formation is consolidated and assumes a stable form.

Statist economic development, then, is characterized by the emergence of the party-state bureaucracy as a distinct class, and its principal features are determined by the interests of this class. Of the three development models, hierarchy will be the most extreme in the statist case since political, economic, and social authority are concentrated in a single hierarchy. Income inequality will be more pronounced than under socialism but not as pronounced as under capitalism if development is to proceed. The greatest inequality appears under a statist formation in which almost all of the surplus is appropriated by the bureaucracy for personal use, but then capital formation and development cannot take place; such a formation characterized imperial China.

In the past, social formations characterized by the bureaucracy drawing off the lion's share of the surplus for its own use could be stable, but in the contemporary world they tend to be highly unstable. Since capital formation cannot proceed at an adequate pace, mass living standards are apt to deteriorate or at the best remain at levels felt to be unsatisfactory. Under these circumstances, the legitimacy of the state rulers will be undermined, and the consequence is apt to be pronounced instability, frequently marked by coups d'état. This of course is a common pattern in the third world, but since it cannot lead to development it is not of primary concern here. If the bureaucracy is to

maintain its authority and emerge as a distinct class, it must devote a substantial share of the surplus it controls to capital formation. Further, if it is to maintain its legitimacy, a certain amount of spending to assure the basic needs of the population will be necessary. The result is income inequality which is less than under capitalism but more than under socialism.

The principal attributes of the bureaucratic class under this circumstance are its access to the power and resources of the state, and its control over the technical expertise which a successful development effort requires. Under these circumstances, it reproduces itself as a class by assuring subsequent generations privileged access to state positions and technical expertise. This does not mean, of course, that no interclass mobility can exist. To the contrary, just as under capitalism, drawing the most talented and ambitious members of the working classes into the ranks of the elite class enhances the effectiveness and stability of the statist social formation.

Statist economic development, then, entails public ownership of the means of production, a strong hierarchy in which political, economic, and social authority merge into one, an intermediate degree of income inequality, and a much greater tendency for basic needs to be met than exists under the capitalist model. In this last respect it is akin to the socialist model, but the socialist model goes beyond the provision of basic needs much more readily, in the evolution of an open society as well as in material respects.

The other characteristics of the statist development model also derive quite naturally from the principal interests of the bureaucratic class. Virtually full employment, like the provision of basic needs, is a condition for stability and legitimacy and is likely to be pursued. Moreover, since the unemployed are apt to become charges of the state under the statist model, their presence simply drains off a portion of the surplus which the bureaucrats could otherwise use for capital formation, themselves, or both. A high level of capital formation is also to be expected under the statist model, since that expands the role and authority of the bureaucracy and since economic growth enhances its legitimacy, but because a hierarchically administered economy will tend to be much less efficient and innovative than either a capitalist or socialist one, the rate of growth will not be commensurate with the level of capital formation. Finally, the statist model will tend to stand in between capitalism and socialism as far as the incorporation of the entire nation in the development process is concerned.

In the statist model, there are two opposing tendencies in this respect. On the one hand, bureaucratic hierarchy tends to concentrate authority in the capital, and to a lesser extent in other major urban centers. On the other, maintenance of a strong state is an overriding imperative vis-à-vis other states, and this typically requires strengthening border areas and other strategic regions, developing resource-rich areas, and incorporating national minorities into the statist social formation. The net result is apt to be a speedier process of national integration than capitalist development entails. National integration may in fact be as rapid as under the socialist development model in terms of regional development, but the moderation of rural-urban inequality may come more slowly, approaching more nearly the capitalist model in this respect.

This brief discussion of alternative development models is meant to provide the setting for the analysis of Chinese development pursued in part 3. The discussion of capitalist development serves to highlight the class specificity of the development process and to provide a contrast against which specifically socialist features emerge more clearly. The discussion of statist development is more directly relevant to the Chinese case, because a statist social formation and mode of production prevailed initially—and still do. Moreover, if the transition to socialism falters in China, the most likely result will be consolidation of the statist mode of production and social formation. The bureaucracy will tend to take on the mantle of a distinct class which reproduces itself, and the development process as a whole will approach the statist model. Whether this happens or the socialist project is pursued depends on the manner in which the contradictions that arise in the transition to socialism are resolved.

The Transition to Socialism

As I have indicated, the essence of socialism lies deeper than state ownership of the means of production, for a variety of production relations are possible under the veil of state ownership. It is possible, for example, for the same hierarchical relations of production that characterize capitalism to exist in state-owned enterprises. Since socialism incorporates a concept of class interest that public ownership in itself may not express, it is clearly inappropriate to define socialism in terms of public ownership alone.

This is especially true if one considers the moral content that has been associated historically with the idea of socialism, which has evoked people's commitment not only because of their class interest— and at times in spite of it—but also because they saw fraternity, equality, and justice as intrinsic to socialism, because they saw socialism as a system in which the full potentialities of human beings could be realized. To define socialism exclusively in terms of juridical forms, ignoring this ethical thrust, does violence to the broader meanings with which history has imbued the term.

The transition to socialism is the process by which working people come to gain control over their own lives at the workplace and at every level of the economic, political, and social institutions that govern their existence. At the same time, it is the process by which rational social consciousness imbued with the spirit of justice comes to shape social decision-making and resource allocation. Both are made possible by the public ownership of the means of production; neither is guaranteed by it. The transition to socialism begins with a statist social formation and proceeds sucessfully only if a series of contradictions is overcome. I would like to indicate here four principal forms such contradictions may assume, noting as I do that under particular circumstances other contradictions may emerge more intensely. Progress in the transition to socialism is determined by how successful the resolutions to these contradictions, which repeatedly emerge in new form, prove to be.

The first contradiction is that between the immediate producers and society. As indicated, socialism requires the expression of the interests of the working classes at every level of society. Even if there is control of the workplace by the immediate producers, that cannot in itself assure that the broader class interest will find expression at other social levels and may actually prevent it. In Yugoslavia, for example, it is common for industrial workers to choose their own management and receive a substantial portion of their income as a share of the enterprise profits. They thus have a vested interest in minimizing hiring, and in pursuing relatively capital-intensive forms of technological change. Yet at a national level serious unemployment exists. The point to be stressed here is that control of the workplace does not assure that working class interests will find expression at other levels of society and may actually conflict with such expression. In short, there is a potential contradiction between the interests of the immediate producers at any particular workplace and the broader social interest.

It is my purpose here to indicate the principal contradictions rather than to specify appropriate resolutions, partly because chapter 9 takes up the empirical manifestations of these contradictions and partly because conditions change and the contradictions are constantly being recreated in new form. It may not be inappropriate, however, to indicate the broad framework within which this first contradiction must be resolved, for this will help to clarify the analytical approach. In the example I have presented, the broader social interest (which is also the broader class interest of the working people) must be embodied in central planning and the direct interest of the immediate producers in control over the workplace. A successful resolution of the contradiction between the two most certainly requires a mix of central planning and market allocation, the latter a necessary condition for investing the producing unit with real decision-making authority. As I shall argue more fully in part III, excessive centralization marked public policy prior to the post-Mao reforms, impeding the transition to socialism as well as generating serious economic difficulties.

The second basic contradiction stems from the fact that the consciousness that a socialist system may ultimately engender is also needed for the transition itself. Some revolutionary intellectuals and party leaders have a vision of society and a sophisticated consciousness that grasps the self and society simultaneously, that grasps the self in society. It is appropriate, indeed necessary, for them to take a leadership role in raising the consciousness of the rest of society, which is often limited to personal affairs and personal benefit. But there is no sharp line dividing such leadership from censorship and thought control, and the victims are working people as well as intellectuals.

Thus the second basic contradiction defining the transition to socialism emerges. On the one hand, it is incumbent on those with an advanced consciousness to assume a leadership role in propagating it via all the forms of social communication, including education, the press, the arts, and so forth. On the other hand, such activities are open to evident abuse; those who claim to be disseminating "correct thought" do so by virtue of their political and social power, which bypasses completely the question of the legitimacy of their ideas. Moreover, the ethical thrust of socialism, which is a quite inalienable part of the concept, mandates a respect for the individual, for free expression, and for equality, and an abhorrence of hierarchy, manipulation, and thought control, all of which conflict with the interests of the working classes in any event. Leadership is necessary, but thought control by a self-constituted elite is anathema to socialism.

The third contradiction is that between the leaders and the masses, between party cadres and the bureaucracy that public ownership of the means of production and the enhanced state power of a revolutionary regime tend to spawn, on the one hand, and the mass of the working population on the other. If this contradiction is not successfully resolved, it is possible for a cadre-bureaucratic stratum to form a distinct class, based largely on its preferential access to the power and resources of the state, in opposition to the classes made up of working people. The result will be a stable statist social formation, one which is distinct from capitalism but nevertheless aborts the transition to socialism. As indicated, elements in the formation of a cadre-bureaucratic stratum as a distinct class include (1) the appropriation of a significant share of the surplus for its own use, thereby widening differences between its interest and that of the direct producers, (2) the loss of control by working people over its activities, and (3) the development of institutional mechanisms that maintain the class status of its descendants. Events appear to have led in this direction in the Soviet Union. The situation in China is much more ambiguous; there the issue of new-class formation remains to be determined.

In China, cadre status has not by and large been a source of personal enrichment. It is true, on the other hand, that ordinary people have had little or no control over the selection and activity of cadres, and the tentative steps toward democratization that marked the earliest stage of the reform period in the late 1970s and early 1980s, including the popular election of factory and local government officials on a trial basis, appear to have been put on hold for the time being. It is still too early to tell whether this movement will be resurrected, although the powerful counterpressures to professionalize management and retain political control in an era of rapid institutional change militate against an early revival. At the same time, the reforms in education, especially the reinstitution of the examination system for admission to higher education, tend to favor children from educated urban households, including cadre households. Whether this will prove to be a mechanism for maintaining class status remains to be determined. Overall, whether a cadre-bureaucratic class will be formed in China remains an open question; the result may depend in large measure on the extent to which the efforts to encourage democracy are revived and prove viable.

The fourth contradiction, emphasized by Marx in his analysis of the dynamics of social change, is that between the forces and relations of production. Emphasizing equality and downplaying material incentives runs the risk of slowing economic development to such an extent as to endanger the entire transition process. Relying on modes of consciousness that are still incipient to motivate economic behavior may, by breaking the link between direct work effort and reward, be counterproductive, benefitting primarily those who are cynical or lazy, or who are simply not strongly motivated. Moreover, if the result is an unsatisfactory pace of improvement in people's material lives, popular support for the socialist project will be undermined. On the other hand, if compensation according to labor is emphasized, people's highly unequal natural endowments and social opportunities may spontaneously generate inequality and a new hierarchy of wealth and position. Thus, giving priority to developing the forces of production runs the risk of undermining socialist relations of production, whereas prematurely stressing socialist relations may undermine the development of the forces of production, threatening the viability of the socialist transition.

Once public ownership of the means of production has replaced private ownership, a necessary but surely insufficient condition for the achievement of socialism, the period of transition to socialism is defined especially by the four basic constradictions I have outlined, and progress toward socialism can be measured in terms of the resolutions that are themselves constantly changing in the course of development. To analyze the transition to socialism in China, it is necessary to examine how each of these contradictions has been resolved. Such an examination forms the core of chapter 9.

Conclusion

In this book I attempt to analyze the economic development of China from a class perspective. In part II, I argue that the underdevelopment of China took place during the imperial period because the dominant gentry class found the measures needed to bring about development to be inconsistent with its class interests. The decay of the old order and the inability to chart a new course involved a complex interweaving of domestic and foreign elements, but among these the simple fact that the gentry opposed those changes that would have infringed upon its dominant position stands out.

During the Republican period, which lasted from 1912 to 1949, new classes began to appear and the capitalist mode of production gained a foothold. Nevertheless, the old class interests remained predominant. The landlord-tenant relation persisted in the countryside, and the surplus generated there continued to be disposed of, for the most part, in an unproductive fashion. At the same time, the capitalism that emerged did so in close alliance with the power of the state bureaucracy, which on the one hand drew off part of the surplus and on the other diminished through its protection the need for vigorous competition and innovation. Some capitalist development proceeded during this period (see, for example, Rawski 1980), but it was not vigorous enough to raise per capita income during the first half of the twentieth century, despite a moderate population increase of about one-half of one percent annually. For the most part, the dominant classes still found the changes necessary to promote economic development to be a threat to their interests. Only with the establishment of the People's Republic in 1949 did classes with an unqualified interest in development come to power, and only from that time did development begin in earnest.

The analysis in part III examines the post-1949 development of China as a case study in socialist development. The general features of socialist development have been sketched in above; they derive from the class interests of the working classes as the dominant classes. These interests provide the benchmark against which the actual development record can be assessed, and the discussion of the main features of capitalist and statist development throws the socialist features into relief.

Chapter 5 presents an overview of modern Chinese development, a periodization, and a discussion of population. More than the other chapters, this one tends to be descriptive, providing the background for the more analytically oriented chapters that follow.

Chapters 6 and 7 examine industrial development and agricultural development respectively. Both chapters begin with an effort to lay out the way in which the general features of socialist development can be applied to the sector in question, and to the class interests of workers and peasants in particular. In both cases, the body of the chapter is made up of an investigation of the extent to which the development of the sector has conformed to these interests, and to the imperatives of socialist development generally. In each case, the analysis leads to an assessment that although sectoral development broadly conformed to the socialist model, substantive deviations in the direction of a statist model were present, deviations which if left uncorrected would have brought the socialist project to an end.

Chapter 8 examines economic reform in China in this light. The reform program, adopted formally at the end of 1978, can be viewed in part as an attempt to remove the deficiencies in socialist development revealed in the earlier chapters. These deficiencies can be viewed largely as a consequence of the party-state cadres and bureaucrats placing their own interests and priorities ahead of those of the working classes, not in any simple venal sense, but in the sense that their access to the power and resources of the state gave them a set of priorities and a view of the world that differed from those of the mass classes they purported to represent.

As chapter 8 indicates, the contradictions that gave rise to the reform program had to be resolved to maintain the socialist project, and the reform program effectively does so. Thus, for example, the overwhelming emphasis on capital accumulation at the expense of higher living standards and the leadership's arrogation of the right to define "correct thought" clearly infringed on the rights of the working classes and are incompatible with the socialist development model. The reform program corrects these in substantial measure. At the same time, however, it generates new contradictions that will have to be resolved in their turn if the transition to socialism is to be sustained. Thus, although incomes generally have risen strongly in the reform period, some have risen spectacularly, generating new forms of income inequality. Whether or not such newly emerging contradictions will be successfully resolved remains of course a matter of conjecture at this time, but it must be noted that any course of action will give rise to contradictions, so that the emergence of contradictions per se is not sufficient grounds for condemnation.

Chapter 9 examines China's development experience from the standpoint of the transition to socialism as a dynamic process. The focus here is on the particular forms that the contradictions that characterize the transition have assumed in China, and on the measures taken to resolve them. Socialist economic development assumes forms that reflect the material interest of the working classes, while moving at the same time toward their deepening assumption of control at every level of society, from the workplace to the state. The endpoint of a successful transition to socialism is the firm establishment of a socialist social formation, one in which the contradiction between the working classes and the party-state cadres who are supposed to represent them is resolved in favor of the former, who assume control over their own lives in a full sense. Although the issue of contradictions arises in the rest of part III, the focus there is more simply on the extent to which the characteristic features of Chinese development conform to the interests of those who work for a living. In chapter 9, by contrast, the focus is on the contradictions that have arisen in the socialist transition, and on the manner of their resolution.

In part II, then, I deal with the development of underdevelopment in pre–1949 China, and in part III with the economic development that began in the post–1949 period. The book gains its unity from a consistent evaluation of the development process from a class perspective, with the evaluation of the manner in which the dominant class blocked development prior to 1949 giving way to an assessment of the manner in which a new set of class interests both promoted development and shaped the process in the post–1949 period.

PART II
THE DEVELOPMENT OF UNDERDEVELOPMENT IN CHINA

2. The Historical Setting

The history of China has shown no development, so that we cannot concern ourselves with it any further.

—Hegel

During the Song dynasty (960–1279), an economic revolution swept over China. The development of wet-field rice cultivation in conjunction with a great southward migration led to sharply higher land productivity in agriculture. At the same time, rapid expansion in domestic and foreign trade accompanied urban growth, and for certain commodities the market became a national one. The growing commercialization of the economy led to increasing sophistication in the means of exchange, and by the end of the eleventh century paper money was used in much of China (Elvin 1973, 159). The entire Song period was marked by technological and organizational innovation, with the transmission of new ideas and techniques facilitated by the spread of woodblock printing, which came into general use early in the period (Elvin 1973, 179; Balazs 1972, 42).

The principal features of the agricultural revolution included improved soil preparation based on new knowledge, tools, and fertilizers, new seed strains that increased yields or made two crops possible by ripening earlier, the extension and improvement of irrigation and hydraulic techniques generally, and the increased specialization in production, including the development of crops other than foodgrains, that the growing commercialization of the economy made possible. The practical agricultural treatises that appeared with the spread of printing were read by the educated landowners and contributed to the dissemination of the improved techniques. By the thirteenth century, Chinese agriculture was among the most sophisticated and productive in the world.

In foreign trade, Song China exported a wide range of goods, including textiles, porcelain, tea, precious metals, lead, and tin, while importing incense, perfumes, spices, pearls, ivory, coral, amber, shells, agates, crystal, and other luxury goods (Balazs 1972, 63). Trade reached from Japan in the east to South Asia, the Near East, and Africa in the west. During the Tang dynasty (618–906), domestic shipping was already extensively developed; in the eighth century, the commissioner for salt and iron had ordered 2,000 boats built for service on the Yangzi with a capacity equal to one-third that of Britain's merchant fleet in the eighteenth century (Elvin 1973, 136). During the Song dynasty, improvements in ship technology made Chinese ships preeminent in foreign trade as well (Elvin 1973, 137), and the further development of river and canal shipping played a major role in the development of the national market.

By Song times the towns had become thoroughly urban in character, with merchants and artisans constituting the majority of the inhabitants. More striking, however, was the development of large cities and a sophisticated civilization of great complexity and specialization. The most developed city of all was Hangzhou, the capital from 1135 of the Southern Song (1127–1279), a city of which we have extensive detailed accounts by a number of contemporary observers.

In 1270, on the eve of the Mongol invasion, the population of Hangzhou exceeded one million (Gernet 1970, 38, 84). The two dozen trades included masons, carpenters, potters, brickmakers, weavers, tailors, gilders, lacquer workers, and makers of oil and candles (Balazs 1972, 90). Merchants specializing in luxury goods and the necessities of life were numerous and flourishing. A contemporary account of the city's teahouses explains,

> They make arrangements of the flowers of the four seasons, hang up paintings by celebrated artists, decorate the walls of the establishment, and all the year round sell unusual teas and curious soups. During the winter months, they sell in addition a very fine powdered tea, pancakes, onion tea, and sometimes soup of salted beans. During the hot season they add as extras plum-flower wine with a mousse of snow, a beverage for contracting the gallbladder, and herbs against the heat, etc. . . . At present, the teahouses lay out a display of flowers, in which are arranged curious pines, strange cypresses, and other plants. The walls of the room are decorated, and business is done to the click of clappers and the sound

of singing. Only porcelain cups are used, and things are served on lacquer trays. (Balazs 1972, 94)[1]

While the teahouses typically served as rendezvous points for off-duty officials and young men of wealthy families, there were also teahouses that served especially as meeting places for laborers, domestic servants, and artisans of the various crafts. For those more concerned with eating than with meeting, the city's elegant restaurants offered a wide range of choice, including restaurants for noodles and *jiaozi*, vegetarian restaurants, patisseries, inns and bars, pubs, low-class eating houses, and restaurants offering a choice among literally hundreds of elaborate Chinese dishes. At the end of the thirteenth century, in the words of Gernet (1970, 18), "In the spheres of social life, art, amusements, institutions and technology, China was incontestably the most advanced country of the time."

The contrast with the first half of the twentieth century could not be more striking. Some six and half centuries later, China was among the poorest, most underdeveloped countries in the world. In 1933, the entire modern sector accounted for some 7 percent of gross domestic product (GDP), with per capita product coming to slightly over U.S. $60 (Perkins 1975, 119, 125). Even this low per capita income figure can be highly misleading as an index of welfare, however, for it fails to take into account the gross inequalities in the distribution of income, the systematic exploitation of labor in the countryside and cities, unemployment, underemployment, and corrupt, ineffective government. All of these characteristic features of underdevelopment marked Chinese life in the century preceding the success of China's socialist revolution in 1949. In part II, I am concerned primarily with analyzing the process by which China, the world's most advanced country in 1270, became one of the world's most underdeveloped countries by 1949. In other words, I am concerned with the process of the development of underdevelopment in China.

To explore this process, I shall turn in the next section to a summary sketch of some principal features of China's economic history. This sketch is admittedly most cursory; its purpose is principally to provide a backdrop for the ensuing discussion of theories of underdevelopment,

---

1. This passage is from Wu Tzimu, *Meng-liang lu* (Account of the Gruel Dream), preface dated September 16, 1274. This book is the most important source of information regarding Hangzhou at the end of the thirteenth century, and it is extensively discussed in Balazs (1972, 82–100).

which appears in chapter 3. These theories fit into two main categories: Some of them are major theses in the literature of economic development that attempt to explain the phenomenon of underdevelopment, while the others have been articulated by China specialists—historians, economists, and others—seeking to explain the Chinese experience specifically. While the categories are not always clearly distinguished (China specialists have of course often made use of more general theories), I have found it convenient to distinguish three of the more general arguments from three of those developed in a specifically Chinese context. Some of the theories provide important insights, but none is adequate to account for the development of underdevelopment in China. Accordingly, I provide my own account in chapter 4, focusing on the class structure and use of the economic surplus in traditional Chinese society, and analyzing the role of Western expansion and imperialism as a contributory but distinctly secondary factor.

Chinese Economic History since 960:
A Thumbnail Sketch

During the late Tang (618–906) and Song (960–1279) dynasties, and into the early part of the subsequent period of Mongol rule (Yuan dynasty, 1279–1367), the Chinese economy expanded rapidly in what Elvin has termed China's "medieval economic revolution." I have already touched upon some of the agricultural, commercial, and demographic changes, including urbanization, that characterized this period. With the active encouragement and sponsorship of the state, this period was also marked by great advances in science and technology. Elvin (1973) provides the following summary.

> From the tenth to the fourteenth century China advanced to the threshold of a systematic experimental investigation of nature, and created the world's earliest mechanized industry. A few examples will illustrate the range of these achievements. In mathematics, a general technique was found for the solution of numerical equations containing any power of a single unknown. In astronomy, a new level of observational accuracy was achieved with the casting of much larger instruments and the perfection of hydraulic clockwork. In medicine, a start was made upon systematic anatomy with the dissection of cadavers; more precision was attained in the description of diseases; and a vast number of new remedies were added to the pharmacopoeia. In metallurgy, coal certainly (and coke possibly) was used for the extraction of iron from iron ore. In warfare,

gunpowder changed from a material for fireworks into a true explosive; and flame-throwers, poison gas, fragmentation bombs and the gun were invented. At the same time there was an increasing tendency to try to relate existing theoretical systems more closely with the mass of empirical information collected in the preceding centuries, most notably in pharmacology and chemistry. (p. 179)

In the fourteenth century, this rapid economic and scientific progress ceased for reasons that are not entirely clear. We do know, however, that continued technological progress did not require scientific knowledge beyond Chinese attainments of the time. The reason for the end of the medieval economic revolution, therefore, is to be sought in the weakening of the social, political, and economic forces that sustain invention and innovation.

Two factors contributing to the decline, which appears to have lasted until the beginning of the sixteenth century, were the disappearance of the frontier and the decline of foreign trade (Elvin 1973, 204-25).[2] As I have noted, substantial migration to South China, with a much greater productivity potential than the North, was associated with the rapid expansion of the medieval period. As the best lands in the South filled up, the stimulus provided by migration came to an end.

Another important stimulus was lost in the government suppression of foreign trade. Whereas in Song and earlier times the long arm of the government had extended into commercial affairs with the licensing of trade—both a means of control and an important revenue source—increasing restrictions during the Mongol period were followed by a complete ban on foreign trade from the early Ming dynasty (1368-1644). Although the ban was partially lifted in 1567, government policy throughout the Ming and subsequent Qing dynasty (1644-1912) was to suppress and restrict foreign trade as much as possible; while foreign trade did increase after the Opium War (1839-1842), it remained essentially peripheral to the Chinese economy throughout the imperial period.

Although the possibility of encouraging licensed trade as a source of revenue was not lost upon the government, the restrictions were designed to "starve out" the pirates that flourished along the coast, to prevent the smuggling of arms and the export of weapons technol-

---

2. Elvin also cites a change in the attitude of philosophers toward nature, but it seems more appropriate to regard this as a consequence rather than as a cause of economic decline.

ogy, and above all to prevent competing centers of power from being established along the coast. This latter concern was compounded by the absence of a strong imperial navy, which had been allowed to decline after the Grand Canal to Beijing was reconstructed in 1411 and the sea transport of grain eliminated in 1415. With the Yangzi basin grain necessary to sustain the capital moving north through the Grand Canal rather than along the coast, a strong navy became a luxury rather than a necessity. The restrictions on foreign trade severely damaged the economies of the principal trading centers, especially in Fujian province, gave rise to a flourishing smuggling industry, aided and abetted by the protection and financing of the local gentry, and foreclosed the possibility of receiving the stimulus that foreign trade sometimes affords to economic development through the transmission of new ideas and technology, investment demand, and the provision of a surplus for investment through the gains of exchange.

The renewed economic expansion between the sixteenth and eighteenth centuries opened new opportunities for the propertied classes in pawnbroking, moneylending, and urban real estate as well as in the expanding domestic trade. A contemporary commentator observed:

> There are one-fold profits in agriculture and it needs very great labour. Fools do it. There are two-fold profits in manufacture and it needs great labour. Those who have skilful fingers do it. There are three-fold profits in trading, and little labour is needed. Those who are prudent and thoughtful do it. There are five-fold profits in the (illegal) sale of salt, and labour is not necessary. Bad and powerful people do it. (Elvin 1973, 248)[3]

Despite this cynical observation, income from agricultural land remained the principal source of unearned income in the countryside. In the agricultural sector of the 1930s, land rent constituted 10.7 percent of national income, farm business profits or the surplus produced by annually hired labor above its own consumption 3.4 percent, and rural interest payments 2.8 percent (Lippit 1974, 76). While these percentages may well have been different in the eighteenth century, there is no reason to believe that the interest and profit income might have been higher relative to rental income at that time.

In keeping with the new sources of income, and attracted by the

---

3. Geng Ju, cited in Elvin (1973, 248). Elvin (248–49) suggests that elite income from landholding became relatively unimportant compared to other income sources in the late imperial period, but the impression he conveys is misleading. See the following discussion in the text and the quantitative estimates in chapter 4.

security as well as the amenities of urban living, by the eighteenth century most landlords of any substance had become urban residents. While the very largest lived in the larger cities, most lived in the provincial towns that grew up as regional market centers. "Their big, high-walled compounds enclosing many courtyards, replete with servants and hoarded supplies and proof against bandits, still dominate the old market towns" (Fairbank 1971, 26). Their homes symbolize their role in China's economic stagnation between the late eighteenth and early twentieth centuries, for insofar as the landowning gentry became a largely rentier class, divorced from productive activity, it is natural that innovation in the countryside languished. By comparison, the dynamic agricultural progress of early Meiji Japan and eighteenth-century England rested on a resident landholding class that was vitally concerned with improving the techniques of production.

By the eighteenth century, the class structure that characterized the first half of the twentieth century was, in the main, already established. For a population of 300–400 million, there were less than 20,000 senior government officials (Fairbank 1971, 29–30). This was possible only because local authority was for the most part in the hands of the gentry class. Narrowly defined, this class was made up of the one and a quarter million degree holders who had passed at least the lowest level of the state examinations (Fairbank 1971, 30), but its social and economic basis was landownership and such related activities as moneylending. Under the gentry-dominated landowning class (3 percent of the agricultural population),[4] the peasants could be divided into three classes: rich peasants (7 percent), middle peasants (20–30 percent), and poor and landless peasants (60–70 percent). The rich peasants, with more land than they could farm themselves, commonly hired agricultural laborers to work for them on a year-round basis. They often used the surplus generated by their farming activities to engage in trade, set up distilleries or other local enterprises, engage in money-lending, and so forth. The middle peasants typically had enough land to produce a subsistence income. The poor and landless peasants, numerically the largest group, often did not; their marginal existence during "ordinary" times left them highly vulnerable to the frequent natural and man-made calamities that wreaked havoc in the Chinese countryside, and their children's chances of surviving to maturity were typically less than even. While a

4. As the discussion in chapter 4 shows, practically all of the principal landowners had gentry status, and members of the gentry class owned about three-fourths of the land that was rented out.

number of scholars have contested whether or not there was actually a decline in living standards after the middle of the nineteenth century,[5] there is no doubt about the extremity of poverty in which the majority of peasants lived in the first half of the twentieth century.[6]

The seventeenth century and most of the eighteenth was a period of thriving economic activity, but stagnation was more characteristic of the economy from the end of the eighteenth century. During the nineteenth and twentieth centuries population continued to expand slowly, but the cumulative increases were quite substantial, with the number of Chinese increasing from perhaps 275 million in 1779 to 430 million in 1850 (Ho 1959,64) and 500 million in 1933 (Liu and Yeh 1965, 34–36). The major exception to the population expansion was caused by the more than 20 million deaths associated with the Taiping Revolution, the civil war which raged across much of China between 1850 and 1864.[7] During the nineteenth and first half of the twentieth centuries, moderate technological progress in Chinese agriculture made it possible for agricultural output approximately to keep pace with population growth. To some extent, the cultivation of new land also contributed, as Manchuria especially was opened to Han Chinese immigration after 1860, and in the early part of the twentieth century the migration became fairly substantial. Still, as a proportion of the total Chinese population, the number of migrants to Manchuria was quite small,[8] and for the most part China's good-quality arable land was being fully utilized long before the nineteenth century.

While the impact of the West was strongest in the nineteenth and twentieth centuries, consideration of earlier relations may help to clarify the nature of the impact. The first Europeans in the age of Western expansion to reach China were the Portuguese, who arrived at Guangzhou (Canton) in 1517. In 1519 a small Portuguese fleet which landed at Tunmen captured some slaves and bought others, concentrating on

5. On this issue see Myers (1970; 1977), Hou (1965), Murphy (1974), and Esherick (1972). The first three authors argue that imperialism did little damage to Chinese peasants; Esherick strongly objects.

6. For accounts of rural poverty in the twentieth century see, for example, Chen (1973), Fei (1945), Hinton (1966), Myrdal (1965), and Yang (1965).

7. Although the Taiping Revolution is usually referred to as the Taiping Rebellion, the usual term is clearly a misnomer, for this movement, seeking the transformation of society, clearly had both organization and ideology. I therefore use the term "revolution" whenever I refer to it.

8. The population of Manchuria, including foreigners, increased from 9 million in 1895–1900 to 20 million in 1916 and 31 million in 1930–31 (Sun 1969, 21).

adolescent youths and girls, as had proven so profitable in Africa. Evidently reflecting a popular belief, however, the responsible Chinese officials misunderstood the routine commercial practices of the Portuguese traders, believing that they acquired children in order to eat them (see, for example, Chinese official Gu Yan-wu, quoted in Franke 1967a, 29). From 1522 the Portuguese traders were forbidden to return to China, but as they and the merchants and officials they bribed found trade profitable, it could not be suppressed altogether. This pattern of the West achieving its purposes in non-Western countries by corrupting an elite social stratum and identifying that stratum's interest with its own would reappear in the twentieth-century era of neocolonialism. In 1530 Guangzhou was reopened to foreign trade, with the Portuguese excluded but effectively permitted to trade elsewhere.

I have already noted the Ming and Qing efforts to restrict foreign trade. The government saw in it a potential threat to the political order and, given the size of China and the extent of its domestic trade, felt little need to acquire things unavailable domestically. As the Qian Long emperor (1736–1795), responding to the English request for expanded trade relations, wrote to King George III: "If I have commanded that the tribute offerings sent by you, O King, are to be accepted, this was solely in consideration for the spirit which prompted you to dispatch them from afar. . . . As your Ambassador can see for himself, we possess all things. I set no value on objects strange or ingenious, and have no use for your country's manufactures" (Schurmann and Schell 1967, 107–108). The empire regarded trade as part of the tribute system, according to which nominal recognition of Chinese suzerainty by tribute-bearing emissaries was rewarded by the emperor's permitting a limited amount of trade. The Chinese court always regarded trade as a privilege rather than as a right.

For its own part, the Chinese government proclaimed the right to a monopoly over the limited foreign trade it did permit. It did not act directly itself, however, but assigned the right to trade to a group of Chinese merchants known as the "Cohong" (gong hang), who exercised it as agents of the government (Franke 1967a, 67). The foreign merchants who dealt with them, not allowed to reside in Guangzhou itself, were restricted to narrow areas outside the walls of the city. The foreigners were allowed to deal directly only with the so-called Hong merchants who, to a certain extent, were held responsible even for their behavior.

Prior to the nineteenth century the British Empire had an imbalance in its trade with China. As China exported much more than it imported, silver had to be sent to China to make up the difference. From the second half of the eighteenth century especially, English merchants discovered the profits to be made in exporting opium from British India to China, and the British actively promoted these exports to remedy the specie drain. In the nineteenth century opium exports expanded dramatically. In 1816, 3,210 chests of opium were imported into Guangzhou (each chest was about 100 catties or 110 pounds); in 1831, 16,500 chests were imported; and in 1838, 40,000 chests (Wakeman 1966, 32). By 1829, opium changed the balance of trade and silver began flowing out of China.

Since 1729 the imperial government had banned opium smoking, and in 1800 it banned importation of the drug. Despite such efforts, however, imports increased by leaps and bounds, with renewed Chinese efforts to put a stop to them leading to the Opium War of 1839–1842. British victory was followed by the Treaty of Nanjing (1842), according to which the Chinese were forced to cede Hong Kong to Britain and open Guangzhou, Xiamen (Amoy), Fuzhou, Ningbo, and Shanghai to foreign trade as "treaty ports." This was the first of a series of unequal treaties that the Western powers forced on China. It was followed by similar treaties with the United States, France, Belgium, Sweden, Norway, Portugal, Russia, and Prussia. Up to the 1860s the Western powers were interested mainly in extending trade; after that they were more concerned with colonial acquisitions, and by the end of the century it was as common to refer to "German China" (Shandong province) as to speak of "German East Africa" (Franke 1967a, 70).

The unequal treaties forced on China contained four main points. First, the extraterritoriality of foreigners was established, making them subject to their own law rather than to Chinese law. Second, the level of the customs duties that China could levy was restricted, making it difficult to protect nascent Chinese manufactures against foreign competition. Third, international settlements and concessions were created in the treaty ports and removed from the jurisdiction of Chinese authorities, while other Chinese territories (like Kowloon, opposite Hong Kong) were leased to foreigners, usually for ninety-nine years. Fourth, foreign ships were granted free movement in Chinese inland and territorial waters. After the Japanese defeated China in the Sino-Japanese War of 1894–1895, Japan won the right to establish manufacturing facilities in the treaty ports. The "most favored nation clause," which

Table 2.1

China's Exports, Imports, and Total Trade, 1871-1929
(US $ millions; commodity trade only; annual averages)

Year	Exports	Imports	Total trade	Per capita	% of world trade	Exports as % of GDP
1871-1884	$102.5	$106.2	$208.7	$0.58	1.3%	2.5%
1885-1900	110.2	143.5	253.7	0.66	1.3	—
1901-1914	201.0	293.8	494.8	1.19	1.5	—
1915-1919	521.2	570.8	1,092.0	2.47	—	—
1920-1929	619.6	799.0	1,418.6	3.01	2.4	7.3

Source: Dernberger (1975, 27).

the foreign powers forced upon China in their treaties from 1843, automatically extended this right to all the others, for this clause stipulated that any right the Chinese should grant to other nations in the future would automatically be extended to the signatory.

The impact of the West upon Chinese development and underdevelopment was many-faceted. As I shall discuss at some length in chapter 3, some scholars have attributed Chinese underdevelopment primarily to the impact of Western imperialism, while others have seen the Western impact as the primary stimulus to development. Here I would like mainly to indicate some of the background information that will be helpful in assessing the Western impact. First, it should be noted that insofar as the West had an economic impact in the nineteenth century it was exerted primarily through trade rather than through direct private investment. It was not until China's defeat in the Sino-Japanese War of 1894–1895 that direct foreign investment in the treaty ports became legal, and except for missionary houses foreigners were never allowed to own real estate outside the treaty ports. Also, foreign borrowing by the Chinese government was limited prior to the Sino-Japanese War, although indemnity payments resulting from the wars launched by the Western powers or imposed by force following attacks by Chinese civilians on foreigners at times put a serious strain on the imperial budget. This strain became steady and severe from the time of the Sino-Japanese War. Trade data appear in table 2.1.

After the Sino-Japanese War, direct foreign investment grew rapidly, with the annual average amounting to U.S.$47 million between 1902 and 1913 and increasing to $75.1 million between 1914 and 1930 (Dernberger 1975, 29). At the same time, debt service on largely nonproductive loans, combined with substantial indemnity payments as a consequence mainly of the Boxer "rebellion" in 1900, created steady pressure on the national budget and left little room for discretionary measures in support of industrialization. Between 1929 and 1934, loan and indemnity payments accounted for between 31.8 percent and 40.5 percent of national budget expenditures (Lippit 1974, 156).

While foreign investment expanded quite rapidly in the twentieth century and took a dominant role in a number of industries, Chinese-owned industry also expanded rapidly.[9] "By 1912, there were 20,749 Chinese factories employing seven or more workers. Even in 1933, after the peak of direct foreign investment, Chinese-owned factories in the modern manufacturing sector outnumbered foreign-owned factories by more than ten to one" (Dernberger 1975, 41). To evaluate the importance of foreign-owned factories by their relative number, however, would be highly misleading, because the average foreign factory was much larger than its Chinese counterpart. Even allowing for this, the data presented in table 2.2 indicate that Chinese industrial output was produced mainly in Chinese-owned firms in 1933.

Since all modern industry in China had been minimal at the turn of the century, the evidence indicates that Chinese-owned factories were not as a group replaced by foreign ones but grew apace with them. Since the industry in Manchuria was entirely foreign-owned in 1933, the figures for Chinese-owned industry in China proper that appear in table 2.2 also indicate the share of Chinese-owned industry in China as a whole, 66.9 percent. Over the entire period between 1912 and 1949, modern industry in China grew at an average annual rate of 5.6 percent (Chang 1969, 71).

Like the industrialization of the West and Japan, that of China before 1949 required a labor force forced to alienate its labor under abominable conditions merely to subsist. To sustain their labor force, employers as a group must typically pay a subsistence wage. While the wage is for an individual worker, however, the subsistence is for a family. The greater the participation of family members in the labor force, therefore, the less each individual worker must be paid. Moreover, as

---

9. The aggregate impact of this expansion, however, remained slight because the amount of modern industry to begin with was miniscule.

Table 2.2

Output and Number of Workers in Chinese- and Foreign-Owned Factories, 1933

	Gross value of output (Chin. $ millions)	Percent	Number of workers (1,000s)	Percent
China proper				
Chinese-owned	1,771.4	66.9	783.2	72.8
Foreign-owned	497.4	18.8	163.I	15.2
Manchuria	376.7	14.3	129.5	12.0
Total	2,645.5	100.0	1,075.8	100.0

Source: Feuerwerker (1968, 14).

mechanical power often reduces the physical strength required for productive activity, the growth of modern industry makes more feasible the use of female and child operatives. As elsewhere during the early stages of the industrial revolution, therefore, the typical factory operative in China during the first half of the twentieth century was not a man but a woman or child. Table 2.3 presents the data based on a comprehensive industrial survey of 1933. The case of an (industrial) tobacco worker in Shanghai, cited by Barnett (1941, 42–43), conveys clearly the sense in which workers could be paid a less-than-subsistence wage when the whole family worked. In 1936 the man in question worked nine and one-half hours a day and received 14.68 yuan per month, or about half of his family's expenses. His wife was employed in a silk-reeling establishment, working an eleven-hour day and receiving 10.90 yuan per month. One of his daughters, sixteen years old, worked an eleven-and-a-half-hour day in a cotton-spinning mill for 10.05 yuan per month. His younger daughter, nine years old and small for her age, accompanied his wife to work and in return for her food was permitted to serve an apprenticeship. "For 11 hours each day this tot stood upon a raised platform wielding a small brush in a steaming brazier full of boiling cocoons. Thus holding his family together in the one room which they occupied, this worker believed himself a lucky man. . . . The sum of his family's collective income in 1936 amounted to Chinese $35.63 each month or, in terms of American dollars, about U.S. $8.90. This was rather more than most of his working associates could boast."

Table 2.3

Employees in Chinese-Owned Factories, 1933

Men	Women	Children
202,762	243,435	47,060

Source: Feuerwerker (1968, 18-19); based on a survey by D. K. Lieu.

In general, conditions in 1936 were far better than they had been four years earlier, when the worldwide depression was at its worst, or than they would be four years later, when Shanghai reached the peak of a miniboom despite the outbreak of war, or because of it, as inflation pushed the real wages of workers to 55 percent of the 1936 level (Barnett 1941, 53). Quite directly, the situation of workers in Shanghai represented that of workers in China generally, for Shanghai held, in 1934, some 40 percent of the industrial capital of China excluding Manchuria (seized by the Japanese in 1931), employed 43 percent of the industrial workers, and produced 50 percent of the industrial output (Barnett 1941, 76).

Life in the countryside also posed its difficulties. A sophisticated European observer, the missionary Abbé Régis-Evariste Huc, after spending 1839 to 1851 in China and traveling throughout the country, wrote:

> At all epochs, and in the most flourishing and best governed countries, there always have been, and there always will be, poor; but unquestionably there can be found in no other country such a depth of disastrous poverty as in the Celestial Empire. Not a year passes in which a terrific number of persons do not perish of famine in some part or other of China; and the multitude of those who live merely from day to day is incalculable. Let a drought, an inundation, or any accident whatever, occur to injure the harvest in a single province, and two thirds of the population are immediately reduced to a state of starvation. You see them forming themselves into numerous bands—perfect armies of beggars—and proceeding together, men, women and children, to seek in the towns and villages for some little nourishment wherewith to sustain, for a brief interval, their miserable existence. Many fall down fainting by the wayside, and die before they can reach the place where they had hoped to find help. You see their bodies lying in the fields, and at the roadside, and you

pass without taking much notice of them—so familiar is the horrid spectacle. (Schurmann and Schell 1967, 30–31)

It may be that the appalling conditions of rural China a century later were no worse, but they were certainly no better. Life for a majority of the peasants remained marginal. Famine remained endemic. Bandits roamed the countryside and in some places were so well organized and powerful as to place a tax on the harvest. Given a succession of weak and corrupt governments, warlords dominated various regions; in such places as Sichuan they collected taxes many years in advance (Buck 1968, 328). The central government continued to rely heavily on tax farming for its revenues; in view of its weakness, those who obtained the rights would squeeze whatever they could obtain from the peasantry, remitting only a small percentage to the government (Chen 1973, 74). In much of South China at least, tenancy appears to have been increasing. Justice was a luxury of the well-to-do, and in every sense the poor and landless peasants were victims. Thus, by the first half of the twentieth century, China had acquired all of the characteristics associated with underdevelopment.

3. Theories of Underdevelopment

A number of theories have been advanced to explain the development of underdevelopment in China. Although some of them provide insights into the process, none is fully satisfactory. For treatment here, I have divided them somewhat arbitrarily into two main groups of three each. The first group includes general theories of underdevelopment, which I analyze in relation to the Chinese case, except that the first of these, the "preindustrial stage theory," has already been applied specifically to China by Eckstein, Fairbank, and Yang. The second and third theories in the group treat underdevelopment as a consequence of vicious circles that limit the supply of savings and the demand for investment, and as a consequence of the colonial and imperialist expansion of the West.

The second group of three involves attempts by China scholars to explain underdevelopment in China specifically. The first of these attempts to ascribe underdevelopment in China to a number of features of the Chinese social structure. Although Levy (1949, 350–65) puts great stress on the Chinese family system as an obstacle to modernization, the emphasis on social structure is not associated with a single thinker, and possibly because the case is so weak it has never been fully elaborated. Even so, many writers have emphasized one aspect or another of traditional Chinese social structure as a significant barrier to modernization, so it seems desirable to pay some attention to this issue in a unified fashion. The second theory in this group has received the most sophisticated elaboration. Elvin's theory of the "high-level equilibrium trap" has, moreover, proven so convincing that it has been accepted by many contemporary China scholars, including especially economists, and has even been treated by some as an established fact rather than as an hypothesis. It will be necessary, therefore, to analyze this theory in some detail in order to reveal the shaky grounds upon which it rests. Finally, possibly the most insightful of the theories of China's underdevelopment is that developed by Balazs over the course of his writings. Balazs attributes the failure of modernization in China to the constraints of a bureaucratic state and elite bureaucratic class stifling all private initiative. Despite the validity of many of his observations, his theory is too narrow and cannot explain such central issues as why the structure of the state failed to inhibit expansion in some periods while curtailing it drastically in others.

Preindustrial Stage Theory

According to a model developed by Eckstein, Fairbank, and Yang, the Chinese case can be fitted into one of two basic patterns of development, a pattern characterized by (1) traditional equilibrium, (2) the rise of disequilibrating forces, (3) gestation, (4) breakthrough or take-off, and (5) self-sustaining growth (Eckstein et al. 1975, 87–88). These authors argue that in the early nineteenth century China was in a state of "traditional equilibrium." The exogenous shock created by Western expansion in the nineteenth century, combined with population pressure and administrative decay, ushered in "a century-long process of disintegration, transformation and slow gestation within the traditional Chinese order," during which time "an acute degree of tension, in the minds of proud conservatives and later in the minds of modern patriotic Chinese . . . gradually built up to explosive proportions until the shackles of the old order were violently broken and the Chinese economy erupted at long last into [the] industrial take-off under totalitarian control which we are witnessing today" (Eckstein et al., 89–90). According to this stage theory, then, the social and economic institutions of the traditional order blocked development until the advent of the West, after a period of gestation and mental anguish, unleashed the forces of modernization.

Like other stage theories, this one is neither historical nor explanatory.[1] First, it is proper to inquire as to the meaning of a "traditional equilibrium." If it means "preindustrial" equilibrium, then the stages are tautological, for industrialization must be preceded by a period before industrialization and one leading up to it. Whether it does or not,

---

1. For incisive critiques of the misuse of stage theories in economic development see Baran and Hobsbawm (1973) and Griffin (1973).

the concept of traditional equilibrium belies the richness of change in "traditional" China. Chinese history is replete with equilibria and disequilibria and enormous economic changes—such as, for example, the commercial revolution in the medieval period, periods of active technological progress and others of relative stagnation, and so forth. Are all of these to be subsumed as part of the "traditional equilibrium?" If the theory is to be made historical, then it will be necessary to speak of "traditional equilibria" rather than a single equilibrium, and once this is done it will be more reasonable to argue that the first three stages have been repeated several times in Chinese history without proceeding to the fourth. A stage theory is of little value unless it can distinguish among stages unambiguously and unless it can clarify the logical necessity according to which each stage gives rise to the subsequent one; this theory fails on both counts.

Furthermore, the concept of "equilibrium" itself can be highly misleading. It can result from the dynamic tension of opposing forces or the absence of tension and opposition. The authors of the preindustrial stage theory imply the latter by suggesting that it was the growing tensions of the gestation period following exogenous shocks that led to industrialization. They strengthen this impression by incorrectly likening nineteenth-century China to Malthus's and Ricardo's model of a "stationary state," with a "population pressing against resources close to the margin of subsistence" (Eckstein et al. 1975, 91). In fact, as I will show below, the Chinese economy produced a considerable surplus above subsistence, and the control and use of this surplus was the central factor determining economic change in "traditional" China. By failing to grasp the role of the surplus and of the class structure associated with it, the authors of the stage theory not only miss the essential domestic forces contributing to underdevelopment in China but even obscure the impact of the West, which can properly be understood only in terms of its interaction with domestic forces.

Thus, the preindustrial stage theory does little to help us understand underdevelopment in China. By creating a category of "traditional equilibrium" that lumps China together with other contemporary underdeveloped countries, it denies a history to all of them. By treating underdevelopment as a characteristic of traditional society in China, it fails to grasp underdevelopment as an historical *process*; it cannot, accordingly, illuminate the process by which the world's most developed civilization became one of the most underdeveloped. Lacking any substantive explanation of the development of underdevelopment in

China and lumping all social forces into a traditional equilibrium inimical to growth, Eckstein, Fairbank, and Yang must explain modernization as a response to exogenous forces. Thus their theory of stages fails to go beyond its own initial assumptions.

The Vicious Circle of Poverty Thesis

The vicious circle of poverty thesis is another attempt to explain the phenomenon of underdevelopment generally. The theory has been stated most articulately by Nurkse (1964) in his classic work, *Problems of Capital Formation in Underdeveloped Countries*. Nurkse identifies two primary vicious circles, one limiting the demand for investment, the other the supply of savings. The poverty of the less developed countries is common to both of them. In poor countries, people's income is low and their purchasing power limited. This in turn limits the size of the market, making investment unattractive and limiting the demand for capital to invest. The limited amount of capital formation that results limits worker productivity and keeps incomes low, thus perpetuating the circle. On the supply of savings side, which Nurkse regards as more critical, low incomes limit the capacity to save, restricting the availability of capital for investment purposes. Again the limited capital stock per worker that results limits productivity and keeps incomes low, thereby perpetuating the circle.

While Nurkse's analysis does help to identify several critical problems of the development process, it explains neither underdevelopment in general nor the Chinese case in particular. It might first be noted that not everyone in poor countries is poor. Since one's ability to save depends, for the most part, on one's relative income standing within a referent group rather than on the absolute income level, even the poorest underdeveloped countries tend to have a substantial if usually untapped savings potential. On the demand for investment side, most countries have markets large enough to sustain at least some industrial development in such fields as brewing, baking, the manufacture of soap, matches, cloth, and so forth. The rise in productivity and incomes in such industries as these can help sustain the development of markets in other industries.

I have already noted the relatively extensive development of markets in premodern China. The typical farm family was by no means fully self-sufficient, and in this sense the often recreated image of China's premodern economy as a cellular one is somewhat misleading. In late imperial China as a whole, between 20 and 30 percent of agricultural output was marketed (Feuerwerker 1976b, 86), with the proportion rising to between 30 and 40 percent in the twentieth century (Perkins 1969, 115), with a much higher figure characteristic of certain regions. A number of industrial products enjoyed a national and even international market. "By the K'ang-hsi period (1662–1722), when Chinese porcelain 'had materially altered' the artistic tastes of the English aristocracy, the Ching-te borough (in northern Kiangsi) had about five hundred porcelain furnaces working day and night to meet the national and foreign demand" (Ho 1959, 201). In general, considerable regional specialization in production developed in premodern China, with interregional and local trade focusing on such staple commodities as grain, salt, fish, drugs, timber, hardware, potteries, and cloths, together with a variety of luxury goods for the ruling classes (Ho 1959, 198–99). During the late Ming and early Qing periods especially, the rise of interregional trade is attested to by the growing number of merchant guildhalls established in commercial centers. The lack of markets cannot have been a depressant on the demand for investment in premodern China.

At the same time, we know that poverty was not an absolute constraint on the ability to save in China. Ho Ping-ti (1959) cites the account of Xie Zhao-zhe, a Chinese official writing in 1602:

> The rich men of the empire in the regions south of the Yangtze are from Hui-chou (southern Anhwei), in the regions north of the river from Shansi. The great merchants of Hui-chou take fisheries and salt as their occupation and have amassed fortunes amounting to one million taels of silver. Others with a fortune of two or three hundred thousands can only rank as middle merchants. The Shansi merchants are engaged in salt, or silk, or reselling, or grain. Their wealth even exceeds that of the former. (p. 197)

In general, the late Ming-early Qing period was marked by the rise of great merchants. But the amassing of great fortunes was also an official prerogative and continued throughout Chinese history. According to Fairbank (1971),

> High office commonly meant riches. The favorite minister of the Ch'ien-lung Emperor, when tried for corruption and other crimes by that Emperor's successor in 1799, was found to have an estate worth in our terms of that period more than one billion dollars—probably an all-time record.

Another high Manchu, who fell into disfavor at the time of the Opium War in 1841, was found to have an estate of some 425,000 acres of land, $30,000,000 worth of gold, silver and precious stones, and shares in 90 banks and pawnshops. (p. 104)

Another way of grasping the savings potential of premodern China is to estimate the size of the surplus above the population's subsistence requirements. According to the estimates of Riskin (1975, 74), this figure was 27.2 percent of net domestic product in the 1930s, and the discussion in chapter 4 suggests that when allowance is made for certain hard-to-quantify factors that have been excluded from the estimates, the surplus was at least 30 percent of national income, again indicating that there was no absolute lack of savings capacity. Thus, it is clear that China's failure to develop vigorously between the ending of the medieval economic revolution and 1949 can be ascribed neither to the absence of markets nor to the absence of capital.

Colonialism and Imperialism

The emerging radical paradigm in development economics regards underdevelopment as essentially an historical process created by the imperialist-colonial expansion of the West. Unlike the orthodox paradigm, which treats trade, aid, and contact with the West as stimuli for development through the infusion of capital and new technology, the radical paradigm regards such relations as tending to promote underdevelopment, a consequence of the extraction of the resources and surplus of the less developed countries to serve the purposes of the advanced or advancing countries, the growth of technological, financial, and cultural dependency, and the support afforded elite classes opposed to the basic changes necessary for development.[2] Above all, the radical paradigm breaks sharply with the orthodox paradigm's tendency to deny underdeveloped countries a history (by treating them all simply as "preindustrial"), emphasizing by contrast that underdevelopment is an historical process. The concept of "development of underdevelopment," from which the title of part 2 is derived, stresses that underde-

---

2. A paradigm in any discipline provides the intellectual framework within which it is grasped, determines the types of research investigations that will be undertaken, and provides criteria for assessing the validity of research methods. Probably the best guide to the emerging radical paradigm is provided by the collection of essays in Wilber (1973).

velopment is not an inherent characteristic of preindustrial societies but one that has emerged as a consequence of specific historical forces.[3]

In this sense, I believe that the radical paradigm has much to offer students of economic development. Ultimately, however, in the form in which it has usually been articulated—treating underdevelopment as a consequence of the same historical forces that gave rise to development in the West—the radical paradigm cannot provide a sufficient explanation of the development of underdevelopment in China.

In many ways, the work of Paul Baran is the starting point of the counter-paradigm. In *The Political Economy of Growth* (1968, 145–46), Baran includes a description of the manner in which the promising development of eighteenth-century India was choked off by British colonial rule. He sees the process as characterized by a transfer of the economic surplus from India to England, India's inability under British rule to protect its own markets, severe restrictions on the import of technology, and exclusion from export markets in Britain and elsewhere. Writing in the same tradition, Frank (1973, 95) sees underdevelopment as "in large part the historical product of past and continuing economic and other relations between the satellite underdeveloped and the now developed metropolitan countries," while Griffin (1973, 69) argues that "the automatic functioning of the international economy which Europe dominated first created underdevelopment and then hindered efforts to escape from it." To what extent then, can underdevelopment in China be understood as a consequence of Western expansion?

I would like to argue here that although the imperialist-colonial behavior of the West (including Japan) was, on balance, inimical to Chinese development,[4] the primary role in the development of underdevelopment cannot be ascribed to it. This may be done most reasonably by first noting the ways in which Western actions contributed to underdevelopment in China and then arguing that the principal features of underdevelopment appeared and were sustained independently, for the most part, of the Western impact. The limited contribution of the

---

3. For an in-depth historical study showing how Western contact took the leading role in creating underdevelopment in Chile and Brazil, see Frank (1967).

4. Among those who take the contrary view that the foreigner was a necessary agent in China's modernization are Dernberger (1975) and Eckstein and Fairbank (1975). This contrary view is presented in the most extreme form by Elvin (1973, 315), who writes, "It was the historic contribution of the modern West to ease and then break the high-level equilibrium trap in China."

West to the development of underdevelopment in China is not because the intentions of the West were innocent—just the opposite is true—but because the process had deeper roots in the domestic economy.

There is no easy way to assess quantitatively the importance of the West's forcing opium upon China, but there can be no doubt that it did great harm. Opium was the leading import into China through most of the nineteenth century and was not edged out by cotton piece goods until about 1890 (Feuerwerker 1969, 52), by which time China was able to supply most of its own needs. Indeed, opium became the first major case of import-substitution based "development"; by the end of the century 10 percent of the Chinese population was smoking opium (Spence 1975, 154). Not only did the opium trade drain a substantial portion of the economic surplus out of China, the impetus it gave to organized crime and official corruption was, like the creation of a nation of addicts, hardly conducive to development. There is perhaps no more dramatic instance of the hypocrisy of Western proclamations of superior civilization than the opium trade the West foisted upon China, and it would be interesting to know what weights those scholars who treat the Western impact as conducive to development assign to it.

The aggressive opening of the Chinese treaty ports to trade and, from 1895, to investment is another way in which the impact of the West was quite visible. The removal of Chinese sovereignty from the treaty ports was of course humiliating, and the relations between Chinese and foreigners there were typical of colonized countries, but the treaty ports themselves had not shown signs of being development foci prior to the Western arrival, so it can hardly be claimed that the arrival hindered their development. To the contrary, such a major city as Shanghai, which prior to 1949 accounted for close to half of the output of China's modern industry excluding Manchuria, was an unimportant coastal trading center until the Treaty of Nanjing opened the way for its explosive growth from the middle of the nineteenth century. Any adverse impact of the trade and investment that the West forced upon China through the treaty ports, therefore, must have been less direct. Three possibilities that especially warrant mention concern the impact on domestic markets and handicraft production, the impact on the growth of Chinese-owned manufacturing establishments, and the financial impact of the Western presence.

It might first be noted that the "linkage" effects of treaty-port growth were limited—this growth did little to stimulate the economy of the interior. While China's principal exports remained mineral products and unprocessed agricultural products, both of which afford relatively little stimulus to the rest of the economy, the principal imports and treaty-port products finding their way to the countryside served mainly to displace handicraft products, thereby adding to rural distress. The largest handicraft industry of the nineteenth century, the spinning of yarn, was substantially ruined by the marketing of machine-made yarn. While specialized urban artisans were more likely to produce the luxury goods consumed by the wealthy, the handicraft production especially of everyday goods was largely a subsidiary activity of farm households. To the extent that it cut off the sources of cash income on which the peasantry depended, the Western impact must have contributed to the development of underdevelopment in China.

Recent Western scholarship, however, suggests that the Western impact on the Chinese countryside was not as damaging as some earlier observers had argued. Myers (1970, 207–10) finds that except for prolonged periods of poor harvests and war, living standards did not decline between 1890 and the 1930s in the parts of Hebei and Shandong he studied. In a more recent work (1977), he finds that they did not decline in China as a whole until 1920 (after which they deteriorated drastically and remained depressed for three decades). Perkins (1975, 121) observes that even in the 1930s imports (excluding textiles) potentially competitive with handicraft products amounted to less than 0.5 percent of gross domestic product (GDP), while domestic handicraft output was more than 10 percent of GDP. Esherick (1972), on the other hand, shows the extent of the disruption caused by imports in the handicraft cotton-spinning industry and points out that the development of such export cash-crops as silk and tea as alternative sources of cash income exposed the peasant households to dependency on a world market over which they had no control, a dependency brought home by the virtual disappearance of silk and tea exports in the twentieth century. On balance, we know that the total production of handicrafts did not decline severely—the expansion of some products offset the decline of others—although the earnings from handicraft production may have fallen since peasants were typically ready to work for very little to obtain the cash income they could not do without and since the availability of machine-made imports depressed the demand for their products. At the same time, however, the development of the treaty ports stimulated the demand for cash crops, which provided alternative sources of cash income. Moreover, the urban-rural terms of trade were generally favorable to the peasants between 1906 and 1929 (Buck 1968,

319). In making an overall assessment of the impact of imports and the treaty ports on rural development, then, their varied and often contradictory consequences must be recognized, and there is inadequate evidence to support a general theory of rural decline in response to the Western impact.

In Chinese manufacturing, a parallel argument can be made. Japanese textile firms in China, although vigorous competitors among themselves, did engage in collusion on prices and other matters through regular meetings in order to drive Chinese competitors out of business, while the foreign-owned utilities gave preference to foreign enterprises in providing power and other products (Kiyokawa 1975). As in the case of handicrafts, however, when the case studies and general observations are supplemented by the aggregate evidence, a rather contradictory picture emerges, for the Chinese firms as a group grew as fast as the Western ones. In large-scale manufacturing as a whole, for example, including firms with thirty or more employees and using power, the share of foreign firms was 35 percent in 1936 and that of Chinese firms, 65 percent (Hou 1965, 129). While we lack earlier figures with which to compare these, given the initiative taken by foreign firms in the establishment of most modern industries, it appears that Chinese firms were at least able to hold their own and may have increased their share of the total over time. This is not to deny that foreigners held a dominant role in the modern sector generally and especially in strategic areas like mining, heavy industry, and shipping, but simply to point out that this dominance did not preclude a comparable growth of Chinese-owned industry.

With regard to financial matters, the case against the foreign impact is much stronger. As has been true in the less developed countries generally, foreign firms financed much of their expansion with retained earnings and locally generated capital, and the new capital inflow was more than offset by larger remittances abroad of profit, interest, and capital. Moreover, payments by the Chinese government on foreign loans and indemnities consistently exceeded the proceeds from new loans. Thus, at least from the beginning of the twentieth century, the Western impact tended to drain the surplus out of China. The annual inpayments and outpayments on foreign investments in China appear in table 3.1. These figures suggest that the West was indeed extracting the surplus from China rather than providing fresh capital on a net basis. The critical question with regard to this, however, is whether the portion of the surplus that drained out of the country would have made a substantive contribution to development had it not done so. Since the amounts going abroad were an extremely small share of the total surplus—slightly over 1 percent in 1933, for example, based on table 3.1 and the 7.85 billion yuan estimate of the actual surplus that appears in a later section—and since a minimal share of the domestically retained surplus went into investment or development-related projects, it appears unlikely that terminating the foreign drain on China's resources could in itself have provided a major thrust for modernization.

In assessing the impact of Western colonialism and imperialism on Chinese underdevelopment, the effect of foreign control over Chinese tariffs and support for a government that hindered modernization must also be considered. An Englishman was placed in charge of the Chinese customs bureau from 1854, and tariffs were limited to 5 percent of the value of imported goods. Tariff autonomy was not fully regained until 1929, when the ratio of the actual import duty to total import value was 8.5 percent; it rose steeply thereafter to 29.7 percent in 1936 (Hou 1965, 108). It is evident that the tariff restrictions prevented the Chinese government from protecting nascent industries against foreign competition. Against this, however, must be weighed a number of considerations which in the aggregate suggest that foreign control of the customs was not seriously inimical to Chinese development.

While budgetary problems would have been magnified, there was nothing to prevent the Chinese government from subsidizing selected industries directly as a substitute for tariff protection until they were capable of meeting foreign competition. Furthermore, government corruption was endemic in Republican as well as Qing times; the honest administration of the customs under foreign control undoubtedly precluded a vast new source of corruption and smuggling, while providing a secure and growing portion of the national budget. It should also be noted that those countries, especially in Latin America, that have tried to base their development on an import-substitution strategy, relying on high tariffs to protect the new industries, have often run into severe problems; the protected industries have typically failed to become internationally competitive, remaining instead inefficient, high-cost producers profiting from their monopolistic-oligopolistic position and imposing excessively high prices on the local population. As I shall argue below, the nature of the traditional state involvement in the Chinese economy would have made such a scenario more than likely if infant-industry protection had been possible. Finally, and most decisively, China showed no signs of a vigorous industrial development

Table 3.1

Annual Inpayments and Outpayments on Foreign Investments in China, 1894-1936 (in Chinese $ millions)

Period	Inpayments			Outpayments			Inpayment-Outpayment ratios (percent)		
	Govt. loans	Direct investment	Total	Govt. loans	Direct investment	Total	Govt. loans	Direct investment	Total
1894-1901	21.3	—	—	20.9	—	—	101.9	—	—
1902-1913	61.0	52.8	113.8	89.2	69.3	158.5	68.4	76.2	71.8
1914-1930	23.8	73.6	97.4	70.9	138.8	209.7	33.6	53.0	46.5
1928	4.0	96.0	100.0	63.0	179.0	242.0	6.35	53.63	41.3
1929	0.0	170.0	170.0	79.1	198.5	277.6	0.0	85.6	61.2
1930	0.0	202.0	202.0	111.4	198.0	309.4	0.0	101.8	65.3
1931	—	—	43.6	135.2	87.2	222.4	—	—	19.6
1932	—	—	60.0	90.0	56.0	146.0	—	—	41.1
1933	—	—	30.0	93.0	24.0	117.0	—	—	26.6
1934	—	—	80.0	112.6	15.0	127.6	—	—	54.9
1935	—	—	140.0	107.4	55.0	162.4	—	—	86.2
1936	—	—	60.0	127.8	70.0	197.8	—	—	30.3

Source: Hou (1965, 99-100).

Note: The data exclude Manchuria after 1931.

policy prior to 1949. Tariff protection might have been justified only in the context of a concerted development strategy. In the absence of one, it is difficult to ascribe great significance to the lack of tariff autonomy as a cause of underdevelopment.

The question of the influence of foreign support for an anachronistic imperial government is also complex, but on balance the evidence does not suggest that such support was decisive in perpetuating the dynasty and thereby creating underdevelopment. A central issue here is the role of foreigners in suppressing the Taiping Revolution (1850–1864). The Taiping Revolution, supported by a utopian socialist ideology, sought to eradicate the scholar-official and landlord class, together with the Confucian ethos on which its authority rested. According to the Taiping program, private property was to be eliminated and land divided equally for use; men and women were to get an equal share (indeed, the Taiping Revolution was the first great movement to raise the issue of women's equality in China) and children under sixteen, one-half the adult allotment.[5] Each person was entitled to take from the harvest only what was required for his or her own subsistence—everything else was to go into the common granary. Other agricultural products and handicraft products were to be distributed in like fashion. Although the program could not be implemented under the conditions of civil war, its thrust was clear.

By contrast, Zeng Guofan, whose army defeated the Taipings, "certainly represented the interests of the landholding Hunan gentry, which strongly resisted the Taipings' revolution program—indeed, he had been able to set up and maintain his army only because of the material and spiritual support of the Hunan gentry" (Franke 1967b, 184). While there was at first considerable popular sentiment abroad in favor of the Taipings on account of their pseudo-Christian ideology, their revolutionary thrust and the character of their religious claims (Hong Xiuquan, the leader of the revolution, believed himself to be the son of God and the younger brother of Jesus Christ) soon led to a reversal of sentiment. Eventually, European and especially American mercenaries played an important role in the suppression of the Taipings. On the level of national policy, England and France came to oppose the Taipings for

---

5. For an account of the Taiping Revolution and of the Taiping program objectives, see Shih (1967) and Franke (1967b), "The Taiping Rebellion." Despite the title of his essay, Franke too regards the movement as a revolution rather than as a rebellion.

fear that their treaty gains of 1858—especially military reparations and the opportunity to reap opium profits (Taiping commandments banned opium smoking)—would be lost. If indeed the Taipings had had a viable program and the Western opposition had been decisive in their defeat, a strong case could be made on such grounds alone for assigning the responsibility for Chinese underdevelopment to the West.

Neither assumption, however, is correct, as the course of events shows. The Taiping Revolution got under way in Guangxi (South China) in the summer of 1850, with the main support provided by poor peasants and, to a much lesser extent, members of the proletariat, including several hundred charcoal burners, some thousands of mine workers, and coolies from Guangzhou who had lost their jobs as a consequence of the Opium War (Franke 1967b, 183). Unemployed pirates, deserters from the government, and a few businessmen, rich peasants, and scholars also joined the movement. The revolution rapidly gained strength, and in the spring of 1853 the Taipings captured Nanjing, southern capital of the Ming dynasty, after an eleven-day siege. There they temporarily established their capital. When they sent an army north to capture Beijing, the Manchu government prepared to flee, but the thrust fell short due largely to inadequate preparation and poor communications. At about the same time, Hong Xiuquan (who had had himself declared the Heavenly King) and other leaders entered into a life of excess—including high living, luxury, and many concubines—in direct opposition to the revolutionary code. In Nanjing, bloody internal conflicts developed, leading in 1856 to the deaths of some of the movement's most important leaders, their followers, and twenty or thirty thousand others. With the corruption and decay at the top, the revolution lost its élan and remained on the defensive from 1856 until it was finally crushed by the capture of Nanjing by Zeng Guofan's forces in the summer of 1864.

It is clear that although the Taiping Revolution was essentially a class conflict, the movement lacked class consciousness, and its religious mysticism, opportunism, and other extraneous elements undercut its socialist ideology and created the basis for its internal decay. The failure of the revolution must be ascribed as much to its internal contradictions as to the gentry-class opposition to its radical objectives. The West, of course, was not responsible for the internal contradictions, and although it supported the counterrevolution, its role in it was not primary. Thus, the perpetuation of the Qing dynasty and a government incapable of taking the lead in bringing about China's modernization which the defeat of the Taipings temporarily assured cannot be ascribed to the West.

After the Taiping Revolution, British diplomats feared nothing so much as the collapse of China's weakened central government. Such a collapse, they believed, would make it necessary for the British to step in and assume administrative control over most of China in order to keep it out of the hands of other foreign powers, and they believed that the costs of such administrative control would be out of all proportion to the benefits received (Franke 1967a, 89–90). Thus the principal aim of British policy became the preservation and strengthening of the central government. In the current age of neocolonialism, it has become clear that one of the basic factors contributing to underdevelopment is foreign sponsorship of governments and class interests inherently opposed to development. If the British had indeed been responsible for perpetuating the imperial regime, their role in China's underdevelopment would be established. In fact, however, revolutionary energies were exhausted for some time after the collapse of the gigantic Taiping effort and the loss of some 20 million lives in the civil war it brought, and there was no severe challenge to the central government until the end of the century. Thus, Western support for reactionary government in China was not decisive in inhibiting economic development.

In making an overall assessment of the impact of the West on the development of underdevelopment in China, one of the most basic questions to consider is whether China showed signs of a vigorous development cut short by the Western impact. Perhaps because the villainous intent of the West is so apparent, it is easy to ascribe excessive importance to the Western impact. Britain fought the Opium War in order to force opium—and anything else it wanted—on China. But if we look at the aftermath of the war, we find that Britain spent most of the remainder of the 1840s trying merely to negotiate entry into the city of Guangzhou for the purpose of trade (Wakeman 1966, ch. 1). Such facts must be kept in mind in order to realize that the foreign impact on the economic life of the Chinese was in many ways quite marginal. Foreigners were limited to the treaty ports (except for the missionaries) and could not own real estate outside of them. Until 1895 they could not set up manufacturing facilities even in the treaty ports. Foreign trade was a small share of China's national product (see table 2.1), and

Chinese always took the role of middleman in trade, keeping some of the gains of trade in Chinese hands. In the twentieth century a principal source of Chinese industrial capital—which, as I have indicated, held its own with foreign capital—was the profits obtained by the compradores, the Chinese who served as agents for Western firms. I do not mean to suggest here that the Western impact was unimportant, but merely that it should not be exaggerated.

The much more central issue is whether China would have developed in the absence of the Western impact. I believe that the evidence here is quite unambiguous: nineteenth-century China showed no signs of the economic vitality that might have made development possible. It is for this reason above all that the impact of the West cannot be assigned primary responsibility for the development of underdevelopment in China. In presenting in chapter 4 my own understanding of the development of underdevelopment in China, I will analyze in some detail the domestic forces responsible; let it suffice here to observe that they must be considered primary and the foreign impact secondary.

Social Structure and Underdevelopment

It has sometimes been argued that various aspects of Chinese social structure have contributed significantly to China's underdevelopment. The particularistic loyalties of the Chinese "family system," for example, have been regarded as fundamental obstacles to development (Levy 1949), as has the value placed upon classical learning and the scorn with which the elite regarded the practical-minded and the nouveau riche. The case is such a weak one that it would not warrant consideration were it not for the fact that such arguments crop up with embarrassing frequency in the writings of respectable scholars. Thus I would like here to present a few specific examples of the use and abuse of such arguments, and to indicate quite briefly the general grounds on which they must be rejected.

Ho Ping-ti (1959), in an otherwise sophisticated discussion of the shortcomings of China's traditional economy, writes:

> The lack of primogeniture and the working of the clan system proved to be great leveling factors in the Chinese economy. The virtue of sharing one's wealth with one's immediate and remote kinsmen had been so highly extolled since the rise of Neo-Confucianism in the eleventh and twelfth centuries that few wealthy men in traditional China could escape the

influence of this teaching. Business management, in the last analysis, was an extension of familism and was filled with nepotism, inefficiencies and irrationalities. These immensely rich individuals not only failed to develop a capitalistic system; they seldom if ever acquired that acquisitive and competitive spirit which is the very soul of the capitalistic system. (p. 205)

Now it might be noted that the family plays a central role in the business activity of many premodern societies, some of which have developed and others of which have not. Furthermore, essentially the same family system has existed in overseas Chinese communities, which have been noted for their business leadership throughout much of Southeast Asia, and remains strong if modified in modern Hong Kong and Taiwan, both of which have been growing quite rapidly.

In addition, without denying the importance of the family system, there are numerous instances of Chinese business organization transcending it when required by the scale of the activity involved. During the eleventh century, for example, the extensive coastal and international shipping trade was often carried on by several persons in partnership, by many small investors who provided capital to merchants engaged in international trade, or by large merchants who built up trading fleets of as many as eighty ships under delegated managers (Elvin 1973, 143–44). Another example is provided by the Shanxi banks, established during the eighteenth century for transmitting funds from one locale to another. The eight largest such banks had more than thirty branches each, enabling them to transmit funds from one end of the country to another; in the late nineteenth century they also set up branches in Japan, Singapore, and Russia (Elvin 1973, 296–97). Although dominated by a few powerful families, these banks were organized as partnerships with unlimited liability for all partners and profits distributed at three- or four-year intervals. Given the multiplicity of examples like these, it is clear that the family system did not necessarily curtail the scope or scale of business activity. It might be added that it is often as appropriate to think of the family arrangements as a convenience for carrying out business activities (family members might be more trustworthy or work harder than others) as to emphasize the possibilities of "nepotism, inefficiencies and irrationalities."

In addition to questioning the family system's supposed role as an organizational constraint on development, it is also proper to question its supposed role as a financial constraint. As numerous fortunes have been built up throughout Chinese history on the basis of official position or commercial activity, it is not at all clear why the same obligation to share with one's relations that failed to preclude the accumulation of fortunes should be blamed for their dissipation. Finally, Ho Ping-ti's suggestion that lack of acquisitiveness on the part of rich people played a role in the failure of China to develop a "genuine capitalistic system" is highly questionable.

In general, it is well to be suspicious of any arguments that assign the responsibility for China's failure to develop to the "wrong" values, lack of acquisitiveness, lack of entrepreneurship, lack of interest in technology, or other purported features of China's traditional social structure. China has always been filled with acquisitive people—great fortunes or even small ones were never built up by people lacking in acquisitiveness—and entrepreneurial talents have never been lacking. Furthermore, while the power and prestige of the scholar-officials were much greater than those of even the successful merchants,the initially symbiotic and ultimately still closer relationship between these two classes must be recognized and the pitfall of assuming that the values of one precluded those of the other must be avoided. The merchants used their wealth to acquire the education their progeny would require to enter the class of officials or, especially during the Qing dynasty when the always endemic corruption reached new heights, to purchase official titles or positions directly. Official status was valued in part because it protected one's family's wealth from the depredations of officials or provided the basis for accumulation via the common bribery and extortion, and in part because mercantile success depended on official connections.

Since the training of the scholar-officials and the examinations that certified them were in the classics, it is sometimes asserted that a lack of interest in technology resulted which undermined the possibilities of modernization. While it is true that inadequate attention was paid to matters of technology in late traditional China—inadequate from the standpoint of the demands of modernization—the low regard in which technology was held cannot properly be abstracted from the class structure and production relations of late traditional China, which awarded wealth, power, and prestige to an elite gentry class that had little or nothing to do with production itself. It is within this more basic context that the low esteem for technology must be grasped, a matter to which I will return in the next chapter.

The High-Level Equilibrium Trap

The most influential of the modern theories of underdevelopment in China is Elvin's theory of the high-level equilibrium trap (1973, ch. 17). Elvin's theory is essentially a variant of Schultz's argument in *Transforming Traditional Agriculture* (1964), where Schultz argues that "traditional" agricultural systems tend to reach a point of sharply diminishing returns to all available inputs. More investment does not take place because it is not profitable, and production remains stagnant. Such a traditional system cannot be transformed by marginal changes, but requires a package of "modern" inputs applied by a farm labor force with the education and skills needed to see the need for them and to apply them. Elvin is concerned with this transformation process only tangentially—when he argues that the West provided the exogeneous shock necessary to free China from the "high-level equilibrium trap" into which reliance on its traditional technology had led. His main concern is with explaining the development of underdevelopment in China in terms of the "trap."

According to Elvin, by late traditional times the big technological advances in traditional agriculture, transport, and so forth "had, as it were, already been used up" (p. 306). In agriculture,

> Yields per acre were very nearly as high as was possible without the use of advanced industrial-scientific inputs such as selected seeds, chemical fertilizers and pesticides, machinery and pumps powered by the internal combustion engine or electricity, concrete and so on. Furthermore, there was not enough suitable land to raise the yields per worker for the Chinese labour force as a whole by using either eighteenth-century British techniques, which depended critically on the interdependence of crop-raising and animal husbandry, or nineteenth-century American techniques of extensive, low per-acre yield, mechanized cultivation. Traditional inputs, whether in the form of irrigation works, fertilizer or labour, were also nearly as high as they could be without running into sharply diminishing, or even negative, returns. (p. 306)

Thus, Elvin claims that sharply diminishing returns for all available inputs characterized Chinese agriculture in late traditional times. Earlier advances had made Chinese agriculture quite sophisticated (and yields per acre were quite high) within the constraints of a premodern system, but the difficulty of further advance combined with the steady growth of population left the Chinese economy in a high-level equilibrium trap "that was almost incapable of change through internally-generated forces" (p. 312). Elvin understands the development of underdevelopment in China, then, as essentially the result of technological and resource constraints exacerbated by population pressures. Since his theory has had so much influence, I would like to indicate some of this before turning to a more formal exposition of his model and a discussion of the decisive reasons for rejecting his theory.

Dernberger (1975, 26) treats the high-level equilibrium trap thesis as a "given," and uses it to support his argument that the foreigner cannot have been the primary cause of China's agricultural problems. Without challenging his conclusion, I would like to note that the equilibrium trap theory rests on tenuous grounds and cannot be regarded as a given or the basis for rejecting alternative explanations of China's underdevelopment. In the same volume of essays, Perkins (1975, 120) accepts a variant of the equilibrium trap thesis in arguing that "China's traditional agriculture did not reach the complete stagnation of a 'high-level equilibrium trap' until after the mid-point of the twentieth century."

Elvin's formal exposition of the high-level trap is carried out with the aid of a figure reproduced here as figure 3.1. The curve OT shows how output would increase as labor inputs are added to a given quantity of land if the best premodern techniques were used; its curved shape reflects the diminishing returns to equal increments of the variable input, labor. The curves P_1, P_2, and so on reflect different levels of practice or technology in general use; they too reflect diminishing returns. At any given time, output can be increased by increasing labor inputs (as long as the output curve is still rising or the marginal product of labor is positive) or, more significantly, by improving the level of practice. OS shows subsistence requirements, assuming, not unreasonably, that these are directly proportional to the size of the labor force. When the labor force is OD, the actual level of output is DB, the actual surplus above subsistence BC, and the potential surplus AC. The existence of a surplus makes possible net investment which, together with changes in organization (Elvin cites commercialization and land tenure in particular) make possible a shift to a higher level of practice. This procedure can continue until E_T is reached, when there is no longer a surplus and when the best premodern methods are already in use. At that point the traditional economy will have exhausted its potentialities for internally generated development, it is caught in a trap. Elvin believes that by the late eighteenth century China was caught in such a trap, Dernberger ascribes it to the end of the nineteenth century, and

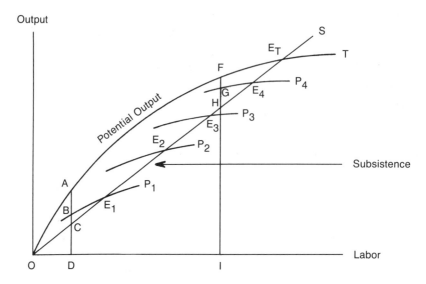

Figure 3.1: The High-Level Equilibrium Trap in Agriculture
Source: Elvin (1973: 313)

Perkins sees it as fully operative soon after the middle of the twentieth century.

Despite the impressive paraphernalia used in its exposition, the high-level equilibrium trap theory has several major deficiencies which render it more obscurantist than explanatory. Possibly the first thing that must be questioned is whether there is indeed such a sharp dichotomy between premodern and modern techniques as to create an unavoidable discontinuity in technological progress. The theory assumes an inverse correlation for the traditional economy between the level of technology and the possibilities for improving it, and Elvin's reference to "improvements in late traditional agricultural technology" reaching "a point of sharply diminishing returns" (p. 306) makes this quite explicit. The deficiencies in his argument are reminiscent of those of Malthus. The law of diminishing returns refers to changes in output as one or more inputs are increased and at least one held constant for a given technology; there is no law that can be applied to the rate of technological progress, and it is improper to speak of the best inventions having been "used up."

Second, the theory assumes a Chinese insularity that must in fact be explained. Many of the inventions and innovations of the West in the late eighteenth and early nineteenth centuries could have contributed decisively to Chinese economic progress. For example, James Watt's development of the steam engine came about through his efforts to improve upon the Newcomen engine for pumping out mines and forestalling flooding. Given the critical importance of water conservancy in Chinese agriculture, there was an obvious rationale for the adoption and adaptation of Watt's engine, the use of which would have provided clear stimulus to further industrialization. To speak of China as being in a trap, therefore, is highly misleading. Rather, we must ask why China failed to investigate and make use of the technology available in the West, why nothing even remotely akin to the veritable explosion of technological borrowing that characterized Meiji Japan, for example, took place.

One of the principal defects of the "trap" thesis is its assertion that the surplus above subsistence disappeared. As investment must come out of the surplus, and as new technology must typically be embodied in the form of new investment, the elimination of the surplus had it occurred would assuredly have hindered development. In fact, however, the surplus was not eliminated. As I have shown elsewhere, using the property share of national income as a proxy for the surplus, the surplus generated in the agricultural sector alone came to at least 16.9 percent of national income in 1933 excluding taxes, and 19.0 percent including taxes paid by the owner-operators of farms (Lippit 1974, 76 and ch. 2). The surplus here includes land rent (10.7 percent of national income), the surplus produced by annually hired labor above its own consumption (3.4 percent), and rural interest payments (2.8 percent), but it excludes the special levies of the government, the depredations of warlords and bandits, and so forth, all of which were considerable but which are difficult to quantify with any precision.

In an excellent study, Riskin (1975, 74) has shown that the capital share generated in the industrial sector amounted to an additional 8.2 percent of national income, so that the property share or surplus for the economy as a whole came to some 27.2 percent of national income in 1933 (or 7.85 billion yuan out of a 1933 net domestic product of 28.86 billion yuan; Liu and Yeh, 1965, 66). The proportion of surplus increases to 36.8 percent if the potential surplus, including the output foregone due to unemployed and unutilized resources, is calculated. Further analysis presented below suggests that if the conservative bias in the estimates of Riskin and myself is recognized (especially the exclusion of those components of the surplus that are not readily quantifiable), then the surplus in nineteenth-century China cannot have been less than 30 percent of the national income. Since the surplus was so large, it is clear that the Chinese economy was by no means "trapped." Indeed, the central question we must ask is why, given the substantial investment potential indicated by the size of the surplus, so little investment, modernization, and technical progress actually took place. This question can be answered only by examining the class structure and uses of the surplus in late traditional times, a task to which I shall turn in chapter 4.

There is no evidence to show a declining surplus in the first half of the twentieth century and nothing to prove a secular decline between Song or early Ming and late traditional times. What little evidence there is, in fact, suggests that the size of the surplus did not change very much. For example, the share of rent in the agricultural output of tenant farmers is an indicator of the size of the surplus. Ordinarily, the tenant must receive at least a subsistence income, and the surplus remaining defines the maximum limit of the rental share (the rental share may be smaller than this maximum if the number of people willing to work as tenants is limited in relation to the landowner demand for their services). If the surplus were declining over time, one would expect to find a secular decline in rent levels. However, in Song times the serfs and tenants paid about 50 percent of the harvest as rent (Balazs 1972, 120), a figure which held through Ming and Qing times (Perkins 1969, 20), and indeed right through the first half of the twentieth century (Lippit 1974, 45–63). While the rental evidence cannot be considered conclusive, it strongly suggests that if anything the agricultural surplus tended to remain roughly constant over time.

Finally, the high-level equilibrium trap theory seems to put an excessive burden on agriculture (and, to a lesser extent, transport) as the leading sector in modernization. While the importance of the agricultural sector should be recognized, this sector is by no means necessarily or even usually the leading sector in modernization. Changes in the industrial sector can bring about the modernization of agriculture as well as of industry, and the trap theory diverts attention from this central point. Elvin does argue correctly that the organization of many of the principal handicraft activities as part-time activities of rural households tended to discourage innovation by making supply highly elastic at low prices. This was not, however, an absolute barrier to innovation, as the eventual mechanization of spinning proved, and many industries were not so organized. There is, moreover, no sense in which urban-based or new industries would have been subject to the trap. There is no reasonable basis, therefore, for applying the concept of a trap to the industrial sector. And if progress in the industrial sector could have led to the transformation of the agricultural sector, then the agricultural sector and the economy as a whole can scarcely be considered to have been "trapped." Far from clarifying the development of underdevelopment in China, then, the high-level equilibirum trap theory has diverted attention from the central issues. It is not correct to assert that invention and innovation were precluded by technological constraints and population pressures in late traditional China; rather we must be concerned with the nature of the economic, social, and political forces that interacted to preclude development.

Balazs's Theory of the Bureaucratic State

According to Balazs, the failure of industrial capitalism to develop in China despite highly favorable conditions—China was ahead of the West technologically and scientifically until the time of the Renaissance—was due to the stifling effect of the bureaucratic state. Balazs writes (1972, 11) that "Chinese ingenuity and inventiveness . . . would no doubt have continued to enrich China and would probably have brought it to the threshold of the industrial age, if they had not been stifled by state control. It was the state that killed technological invention in China." He understands the inhibiting role of the state in the context of class relations, viewing the dominant scholar-official class, a class which "possessed every privilege, above all the privilege of reproducing itself, because of its monopoly of education," as "the embodiment of the state, which was created in [its] image—a hierarchical, authoritarian state" (pp. 16–17). This was a state so strong that the merchant class

> never dared to fight it openly in order to extract from it liberties, laws, and autonomy for themselves. Chinese businessmen almost always preferred to reach a compromise rather than fight, to imitate rather than branch out on their own, to invest money safely in land and carry on the permitted form of usury rather than risk putting their money into industrial enterprises. Their abiding ideal was to become assimilated, to be part of the state by becoming—or seeing their children or grandchildren become—scholar-officials themselves.
>
> Every time the merchant class succeeded in attaining some degree of liberty, or arrogating to itself some right, or securing an advantage, the state intervened, curtailed the liberty, and arbitrarily took over, wiping

out the advantages gained. The merchant class for its part . . . always chose to haggle rather than fight. . . . . Whenever a new invention (printing, bills of exchange, paper money, water mills) made its appearance in circles which the scholar-officials regarded as hostile, they sooner or later seized it in order to profit from it at the expense of the inventors, who were dismissed from the scene. As a result of this recurring process the scholar-officials and the merchants formed two hostile but interdependent classes. There was an interpenetration, a symbiosis, between them: the scholar-official became "bourgeoisified," while the merchant's ambition turned to becoming a scholar-official and investing his profits in land. Their common ground was that peculiarly Chinese phenomenon, corruption, and their normal reciprocal relationship might be described as one of bully-squeeze. (pp. 23, 32)

It will be clear from the foregoing passages that Balazs's understanding of the development of underdevelopment in China is quite different from that of the other authors I have discussed. His theory makes important contributions to our understanding of the development of underdevelopment in China, and I would like to comment on these briefly before turning to a critique of his analysis.

Balazs is correct in calling our attention to the primacy of internal factors inhibiting development, in perceiving that these were primarily social rather than technological, and above all in grasping the importance of class relations. In considering the stability and perpetuation of any economic system, possibly the first question that must be asked is "Who benefits from it?" When one speaks of "China" as though it were integral in every respect one is in a sense creating a metaphysical entity, for "China," like other countries, is or has been composed of groups and classes with sharply differing perspectives and interests. In explaining why China did not develop, we must recognize the possibility that development might not have been advantageous to the dominant classes or groups, that development did not take place because these did not *want* development to take place. Indeed, if a dominant class felt, as the Qian Long emperor stated in his memorial to King George, that it had everything it wanted, it would be quite natural for it actively to oppose development and development-related measures as threats to its position. As Baran (1968, 3–4) succinctly states, "Economic development has always been propelled by classes and groups interested in the new economic and social order, has always been opposed and obstructed by those interested in the preservation of the status quo." The principal merit of Balazs's theory is in calling to our attention the central role played by the class structure of traditional China in preventing modernization. His description of the scholar-gentry class helps to explain its interest in preserving the traditional system.

> The Chinese official—the dominant, central figure of the old regime—may have found a certain amount of material security in having a country estate and useful kinship relations, for this enabled him to be educated, and facilitated his passing the examinations and attaining a career in the service of the state. But it was only by being in office that he was able to make full use of his privileges, for then he no longer had to pay taxes and was exempted from corvée and, usually, from military service. The mere fact of being in office guaranteed to officials and their descendants the monopoly of education that provided such an inestimable source of prestige amidst a sea of illiterates. It also conferred special rights which in practice amounted to complete immunity before the law, in a country where the ordinary subject was deprived of all legal rights. . . . Moreover, official status allowed those who enjoyed it to enrich themselves by every means, legal or illegal, and to acquire new lands, or enlarge the family estate. The combination of these factors enabled the scholar-official gentry to continue in office and perpetuate themselves as the mandarinate that remained the ruling class until recent times. (p. 154)

Balazs shows, moreover, how the dominant class created and used the bureaucratic state for its own purposes, thereby stifling the forces and initiatives that otherwise would have tended to promote development. In traditional China the state had its finger in practically every pie. The trade in staples (salt was the most prominent) was organized as a system of monopolies with residual ownership vested in the state; merchants acquired the rights for particular regions from the state and ensured their trade by paying off regularly the officials responsible. The ownership of rental housing, shops, warehouses, and so forth and urban real estate generally was divided between private individuals and the state. Foreign trade, like the domestic trade in staples, was the prerogative of the state, and the merchants who engaged in it, although accumulating among the largest merchant fortunes in China, did so as agents of the state. Because the leading merchants in both domestic and foreign trade were protected monopolists, they were not impelled to reinvest their profits in new enterprises or to protect their positions, and thus the fortunes that were accumulated did not serve to promote development.

The contribution of Balazs to our understanding of the forces that promoted underdevelopment in China, therefore, is a substantial one. His presentation does, however, have a number of defects. These can be considered most conveniently under four distinct headings: (1) his understanding of class structure is not entirely correct; (2) his image of private forces as promoting development and the state as hindering it is overdrawn; (3) he does not consider sufficiently the impact of Western colonialism and imperialism; and, above all, (4) he fails to grasp the development of underdevelopment as an historical process. Why, for example, did not the bureaucratic state inhibit development during the Song dynasty as well as during the Qing dynasty?

Balazs talks of a distinct merchant class and a separate scholar-official class, and although he recognizes explicitly an "interpenetration" or "symbiosis" between the two, they remain in his view "two hostile but interdependent classes." As I show in the next chapter, however, by late imperial times there was in fact a single dominant elite class, the members of which sometimes served as officials, sometimes engaged in commerce or money lending, sometimes derived substantial revenues from landowning, and sometimes combined these activities. The difficulties China encountered in modernization in the late imperial period should be understood not as a consequence of the cooptation of a potentially progressive merchant class, but as a consequence of a single dominant class firmly wedded to the existing order of which it was the principal and indeed sole beneficiary; this argument is spelled out in greater detail in the following chapter.

When Balazs (1972, 102) writes that "the bureaucracy was perfectly satisfied with traditional techniques" or sees the state bureaucracy as completely inimical to private initiative, he is clearly overstating a basically accurate perception. The overstatement, however, conceals a number of basic questions. In certain historical periods the bureaucracy did not suppress entrepreneurship—why? In the modernization process in other countries, the state has often taken a leading role; why was this not true in China? One simply cannot accept a unicausal theory of development based on private initiative or a theory that fails to recognize the positive potential of the state's role in development. Another weakness of Balazs's theory lies in his failure to recognize the part played by imperialism in China's failure to modernize, an impact which, as I have argued, although secondary, cannot be neglected entirely.

Perhaps the most important weakness in Balazs's theory is that it is simply not historical. Balazs does not make a distinction between periods of progress and periods of stagnation. He does not recognize the process of China's becoming underdeveloped as an historical process. The state is always evil, always a "totalitarian Moloch of a state" (p. 17). Essentially the same state, however, contributed to making China—or at least failed to hinder China from becoming—the world's most "advanced" nation until the Renaissance in the West. Balazs's theory, therefore, leaves one without an explanation of the historical forces bringing about the development of underdevelopment in China.

4. Class Structure and the Development of Underdevelopment

In this chapter I would like to present my own understanding of the development of underdevelopment in China. To do so it is necessary first to clarify the class structure and relations of production that existed in late imperial China. Although my focus is on the nineteenth century, the structure with which I am concerned has, quite obviously, much deeper roots, and I will try to indicate these where possible.

The class structure of late imperial China is marked by the common class identity of the various elite groups. Discussions of the merchant class, landlord class, government-official class, and of the gentry as an educated class tend to obscure this central fact by drawing the class lines in the wrong way. In fact, there was one dominant class, the gentry in late imperial China, drawing its income from the surplus produced by the peasants, artisans, and workers above their own subsistence requirements. Landowning, moneylending, mercantile activity, official position, and so forth were different means of garnering this surplus, not the demarcations of distinct classes.

Since the Song dynasty the gentry had enjoyed a substantial income from office and landownership. Income from business activity, always present in some measure, also became of great importance in the late imperial period. From about 1700, wealthy gentry families

> began to put more and more of their money into pawnbroking, so that control of rural credit was by the 19th century a major source of gentry wealth.

Merchants and gentry had long been informally connected, and the division of urban society into mercantile and gentry spheres was already a fiction by the 18th century. Prominent lineages had members in both groups, and commercial pursuits were a surer road to gentry rank than simple land-holding. (Wakeman 1975a, 27, 234)

And gentry status, formally indicated by a degree received upon passing an examination or through purchase, was a prerequisite to holding office. Thus, although its members were engaged in different activities, there was one dominant class. This class was divided into two fairly distinct strata, one, rooted in the countryside, composed mainly of the lower gentry, and the other, distinguished by its large-scale activities and high income, composed of the upper gentry: officials, large merchants, large landowners, and so forth.

Officialdom was the principal path to fortune in imperial China. The average income of the 23,000 office holders in late nineteenth-century China was more than 5,000 silver taels per year (Chang 1962, 42; a tael is one-sixteenth of a catty or a little more than an ounce and in the 1880s was worth on the average U.S.$1.28). The average county magistrate (there were some 1,500 of them) received 30,000 taels per year, the average provincial governor 180,000 taels (Chang 1962, 31–32). This compares to an average income of 10 taels per year for an average laborer (Chang 1962, 101). To put these figures in perspective,[1] if an average laborer in the United States today earns $12,000, the average official received an amount comparable to $6 million annually, a magistrate $36 million, and a provincial governor $216 million—tax free of course. Of this income, only about one-nineteenth was salary; the rest came from unauthorized taxes and surtaxes, and from bribes (Chang 1962, 10, 42).

Of all the activities open to the gentry, the holding of office was not only the most distinguished career but was also almost the only way to amass a large fortune. In imperial Chinese society it was taken for granted that officeholding and wealth usually went together. There was a common saying, "May you be promoted in office and become rich."

It was not only the high officials . . . who gained high income from office. We know from materials in local gazetteers and clan records that

---

1. This is especially desirable because of the widespread fiction created in the literature that income differentials were not very great in traditional China. See, for example, Rhoads Murphy (1974, 46).

virtually all officials were able to acquire large sums. . . . An official career was regarded by the officials themselves and by all others as much more profitable than other occupations. (Chang 1962, 7–8)

The scale of official corruption thus was so huge that it not only afforded those concerned a life-style marked by extravagant luxury, it created as well enormous and concentrated pools of liquid capital for investment.

Some of this capital was used to acquire large landholdings. The net returns were some 5–10 percent of the purchase price, about half of what alternative "investments"[2] could bring (Feuerwerker 1976b, 82), but the status and security afforded by landownership and the self-satisfaction it afforded the owner made land a desirable purchase for men who could consume on a grand scale and engage in more lucrative investments at the same time. Thus Governor General Li Hongzhang's amassing of hundreds of thousands of acres of land and innumerable silk stores and pawnshops (Wakeman 1975a, 193), while unusual in scale (this noted "reformer" was regarded by late-nineteenth-century contemporaries as the richest man in the world; Chang 1962, 130), was not unusual in mixing official position with landowning, mercantile interest, and moneylending.

Indeed, returns on land investment were too low to permit the amassing of large estates by the reinvestment of rental receipts and too low as well to assure the position of the commoner landlords, who were subject to the squeeze of local officials and their underlings. The escape from taxation of the powerful gentry households increased the pressure on the other landowners. Moreover, in years of bad harvest, the full rent (normally half the crop) was difficult to collect. Under these circumstances, landowners of any size would seek the protection of gentry status, either by having their sons pursue the "regular" examination route or by the purchase of a degree.[3] Thus, although not all members of the upper gentry had extensive land holdings, all large landowners tended to be members of the gentry. And smaller landowners too, wherever their resources permitted, also sought the protection and advantage of gentry status. About one-third of China's farmland was owned by landlords, and while precise quantification is difficult, it

---

2. I am using the term "investment" here in the colloquial sense rather than in the economist's sense of capital formation.

3. Other measures included a suitably arranged marriage, the adoption of a promising scholar, and false registration.

appears that about three-fourths of this was owned by members of the gentry (Chang 1962, 144–45), who thus held about one-quarter of China's farmland.

Big business too was a gentry preserve, at least by the late imperial period. In the first place, the principal source of the substantial capital funds needed was official position, and in the second, official connections were of paramount importance in business success. The most profitable merchant activities, including especially the salt trade and foreign trade, were run as state-licensed monopolies. A substantial share of the profits was raked off by the officials charged with supervising these activities, and by the emperor and his family. Good official relations were necessary to secure and maintain the monopoly rights, and to keep the official rake-offs from assuming ruinous proportions.[4] In a society where the commoners could not ordinarily even gain audience with the officials, therefore, gentry status was essential for success in and maintenance of big business operations. It is not surprising then that "the records show that in the main the business administrators and the suppliers of capital in the salt trade were members of the gentry," and that despite the formal exclusion of gentry members from brokerage activities, "it was an open secret that hong merchants (foreign traders) were gentry" (Chang 1962, 158, 165).

The ownership of financial enterprises was also almost exclusively in gentry hands. Here, in addition to securing protection from the most rapacious officials and acquiring the necessary rights, official connections were necessary to secure government deposits. In the pawnshops, Shanxi banks, and native banks, the ability to deal with officials was of paramount importance, and the principal capital providers and managers were mainly gentry members.

The arrangements in the salt trade show how the interests of the officials (and the emperor in the most profitable businesses) and the gentry-merchants interpenetrated (Wakeman 1975a, 49–50). The salt commissioner was typically an imperial household official who paid off his palace superiors to obtain his post. The emperor expected expensive

---

4. James Polachek (1975, 211–13) tells the story of a wealthy moneylender who in 1854 advanced a loan secured by a stolen official stamp. The local magistrate saw the opportunity to raise funds for the local militia and fined him 10,000 taels. The outraged moneylender sought the protection of the noted reformer Feng Guifen, who promised to fix his case if he would give 2,500 taels to Feng's relatives to endow a public mortuary. This case demonstrates the arbitrariness of the fines levied, the lack of legal recourse of citizens, and the importance of relations with (and payoffs to) officials for self-protection.

presents from him, and if these were not forthcoming in sufficient magnitude the emperor could fine him heavily, or worse. His inducement to squeeze as much as possible was great, therefore, but it was tempered by his knowledge of the capital needs of the merchants, whose bankruptcy would halt the flow of salt revenue to the imperial household. These relations, which can perhaps best be expressed by the term "bureaucratic capitalism," reveal clearly the interdependence of the official and commercial interests. When industrial enterprises were initiated from the end of the nineteenth century, moreover, the major ones (limited in number) were almost exclusively the province of officials and those with close official connections. As Ho Ping-ti (1959) states,

> Even in the late Ch'ing and early Republican period the few new industrial enterprises launched by the Chinese were almost invariably financed by bureaucratic capitalists. In the cotton textile industry, for example, out of a total of twenty-six mills established between 1890 and 1913, nine were established by active and retired high officials, ten by mixed groups of officials and individuals with official titles, and seven by the new breed of treaty-port compradores, practically all of whom had official connections. It is common knowledge that after the founding of the Nationalist government in 1927 a few top-ranking bureaucrats who enjoyed Chiang Kai-shek's confidence exerted ever more powerful control over the modern sector of the national economy through the incomparably superior apparatus of four major modern banks. (p. 206)

In rural China, the constellation of activities raking off the surplus in the late imperial period was much the same as in industry, except that the activities were carried out on a much smaller scale. The rural (usually lower) gentry tended to be made up of smaller landowners and moneylenders, lower retired officials, and so forth. Some engaged in mercantile activities, but in contrast to gentry-dominated big business, these were no more than a minute fraction of the innumerable petty traders and small businessmen of China; when they did engage in such activities, however, they enjoyed a distinct advantage over their commoner competitors.

Rural gentry were more likely to be engaged in activities like tax collection, teaching, the handling of legal affairs, and the management of semipublic activities. As tax farmers, they had an opportunity to profit handsomely from locally imposed surtaxes, which increased markedly over the course of the nineteenth century, often reaching several times the land tax remitted to the central government. Furthermore, as the local farmers paid their taxes in copper cash while the central government received the taxes in silver taels, the local gentry also stood to profit by manipulating the exchange rate between the two. Most of the local gentry served as teachers, averaging an income of about one hundred taels, or as managers of public works projects, clan affairs, and so forth, in which capacity they received slightly more. Again comparison can be made with the ten-tael income of the average laborer, and it should be noted that such local gentry income was often combined with income from landholding, moneylending, and so forth. At the start of the nineteenth century, 1.2 percent of the Chinese population were members of the gentry, and by the end of the century the proportion had risen to 1.9 percent (Chang 1974, 140–41).

Above the direct producers in late imperial China, then, there was one elite class with two distinct strata skimming off the surplus which the peasants, artisans, and workers produced above their own subsistence requirements. The upper stratum was composed of high officials, big businessmen, and big landowners. The local stratum, much larger in number, dominated village life. The lowest level of central government authority in the countryside was the county magistrate, responsible in the nineteenth century for administering a district with typically some 250,000 people. This he could do only with the cooperation of the local gentry, thus inevitably involving them in tax-farming and other semioffical activities. The local gentry role expanded still further during and after the Taiping Revolution, when the gentry took the leading role in organizing and maintaining the local militia. At both levels, therefore, there was a complete interpenetration of public office and private interest.

The maturing of bureaucratic capitalism in late imperial China was highly inimical to technological progress and economic development. The path to wealth was becoming or paying off an official, and neither new technology nor fixed capital was protected against official rapacity. The profitability of big business depended on monopoly and of all business on official connections. At the same time, the relations of production in both industry and agriculture, marked by the divorce of the merchants from productive activity and of the landlords from the land, further inhibited technological progress.

Mercantile profits were in distribution, and merchants tended to remain ignorant of the production processes for goods they traded. The major wholesale cotton cloth dealers of Suzhou, for example, had nothing to do with production; they paid labor contractors a fixed price per piece rather than hire labor directly (Wakeman 1975a, 42). Under these circumstances, the merchants remained largely ignorant of the techniques of production and were hardly in a position to improve them. In agriculture, the movement of substantial landowners to urban areas between the sixteenth and eighteenth centuries continued a process long under way and climaxed the demise of the estate system. Progressive, "improving" landlords who took an active interest in farm management and technique disappeared. Increasingly in the nineteenth century, landlord bursaries, often invested with police powers to arrest recalcitrant tenants, took over the task of rent collection for absentee landlords. Even where landholdings were both substantial and geographically compact, the land was divided into small parcels and let out to separate tenants. The landowner, typically supplying no more than the land and sometimes the farm buildings, had nothing else to do with production and became a pure rentier. This pattern of production relations governed even the small landowners remaining in the countryside, and they too became purely parasitic.

Thus in both industry and agriculture, the production relations of late imperial China were marked by a fairly complete separation between large-scale owners and production processes. The path to profit was not the improvement of production but command over the social processes whereby the direct producers were relieved of the surplus they produced. The ruling class was the gentry class divided into two main strata, one composed of officials, large landowners, large moneylenders, and substantial merchants, the other, dominating the countryside, composed of smaller variants of these. Both levels carried out certain administrative and social operations necessary to keep Chinese society functioning. The system worked well from the standpoint of the gentry, providing them with wealth and status; there was no reason why they should want to change it, and indeed they did not want to do so.

The failure of China to experience substantive economic development (in a modern sense) prior to the twentieth century must be grasped in this context. The dominant gentry class was almost purely parasitic, marginally involved when involved at all in the processes of production. At the pinnacle of a society in which power, wealth, and education meant everything, it had everything. With the dominant class opposed to modernization or development and the threats to its position that social change would entail, it is natural that such change did not come readily.

To the extent that class structure accounts for the failure of China to develop economically in the late imperial period, the impediment posed by population expansion in the face of limited resources provides an inadequate explanation. Ascribing underdevelopment to population increase in the face of resource constraints, as Elvin (1973) and many others do, is a hopelessly unsatisfactory approach, confusing secondary factors with primary ones; it is somewhat like ascribing an automobile accident to a tree when a driver drives into one. As the misunderstanding about the role of population pressure is widespread, however, I believe it worthwhile to pause briefly here to place the population issue in the context I have just outlined. I do not wish to argue that population growth created no difficulties, but merely that the population growth rate was modest and that the central issue is why the moderate levels of capital formation and technological progress necessary to raise output more rapidly than this modest rate were not forthcoming.

The population of China increased from 270 million in 1770 to 410 million in 1850, and after a sharp fall brought by the Taiping Revolution increased again to 430 million in 1913 (Perkins 1969, 16). These estimates are perforce crude ones, but they are satisfactory for revealing rough orders of magnitude. In the period of most rapid growth, 1770 to 1850, population grew at a rate of 0.5 percent per year. This is not a particularly rapid rate of growth and contrasts with rates in excess of 2.5 percent annually for many third world countries today and a rate of 2.1 percent in China itself between 1953 and 1973 (Banister 1977, 35). Some expansion in the cultivated area—which increased from about 950 million mu in 1770 to about 1,210 million mu in 1873 (Perkins 1969, 16)—did take place as well as some capital formation in the form of water conservancy projects and so forth, so the rate of technological progress needed to assure growth in per capita output was indeed quite modest. Yet even this modest rate of progress—or the industrial capital formation that could in part have substituted for it—proved unattainable, not because the best innovations were "used up," but because the social and class structure discouraged the development of new ones.

The reasons for this I have already indicated: the elite class had little to do with actual production, and the path to riches was through connections and corruption rather than through innovation and capital formation. Moreover, the dominant Confucian ideology, precisely because it integrated the system and justified the exploitation at its core, could only discourage the scientific learning and outlook necessary to technical progress. The inhibition of innovation caused by China's socioeconomic structure is evident everywhere, but the following example, drawn from the sphere of China's international economic relations, is especially pertinent because it touches on the failure of China to borrow foreign technology as well as to develop its own.

The years between 1770 and 1850 were the period encompassing the industrial revolution in England, but there was no group in China with an active interest in investigating and importing the new technology. This can be understood only in the context of a dominant class divorced from production and comfortable in the knowledge that, in the words of the Qian Long emperor, "we possess all things." Moreover, the restrictions on foreign trade, which reflected in part the monopoly-rake-off mentality of China's elite, also hindered the possibilities of technological borrowing. This was shown clearly when a limited number of Chinese ports were opened to foreign trade between 1685 and 1760. Most of the trade was carried on by the English, and although they could buy at different ports, they often had to buy from one of the "king's merchants," monopolists who dominated several ports after buying a monopoly trading license from one of the emperor's sons (Wakeman 1975a, 119–120). Guangzhou was the only city that could resist the monopolists, so more and more of the trade went there. The Cohong or foreign trade guild there, however, also held monopoly privileges, and its monopoly profits were in turn siphoned off to an extravagant extent to the "hoppo" or customs officer. When an Englishman (James Glint) attempted to protest to the Qian Long emperor, the emperor responded by limiting all trade to Guangzhou, an edict which remained in effect from 1760 to 1833. The English traders did not realize that the hoppo was a member of the imperial household, and that the illicit income he received was being split with the emperor. Survival in the world of commerce for the members of the Cohong, then, as for Chinese in any profitable activity, depended on their official relations and had little or nothing to do with their knowledge of the conditions of production. Under such circumstances, innovation was hardly likely to be forthcoming.

The dominant Confucian ideology reinforced the social mechanisms inhibiting innovation. The entire hierarchical ordering of Chinese society was supported, justified, and indeed integrated by the social philosophy of subservience and status embodied in Confucian thought. As Balazs (1972) states:

After much hesitation, the officials adopted the Confucianist doctrine as being the ideology that best expressed their way of life, since, in spite of preaching respect for others, justice and reciprocity, these virtues were reserved for relations between educated people, whereas for the ordinary subject, the cardinal virtue was absolute obedience. Its unalterable aim was to maintain the status quo of the social hierarchy. Ancestor worship, divested of its earlier religious character, geared the social mechanism, regulating every detail of social relations. Respectfulness, humility, deference, docility, complete submission and subordination to elders and betters—these were the dominant features of the Confucian ethic that helped to cement the hierarchy, creating a patriarchal, paternalistic world in which gradations of rank, from the sovereign downward, were marked by the reciprocal relations of favor and obligation, and individual rights, initiative, and liberty were entirely lacking. (p. 155)

What is especially important to note here is that this ideology, so hostile to the development of free scientific inquiry, was consciously fostered "to maintain the status quo," to perpetuate a system of privilege.

Classical education was the proper, indeed only, education for elite status in Chinese society, and the examination system helped to insure the thorough inculcation of the values it embodied. Since classical education defined elite status and was completely integrated into the social structure, there was no space left for scientific or technical learning. The image of itself that Confucian ideology fostered in the gentry class was, moreover, inconsistent with the needs of modernization. As Wakeman (1975a, 31) observes, "Landholding suited the upper gentry's image of itself in retirement—benovolent gentlemen farmers composing poetry at their villa windows while loyal tenants toiled patiently in the distant fields." And Ho Ping-ti (1959, 205) points out that "technological inventions were viewed as minor contrivances unworthy of the dignity of scholars." Morever, since any effort to change the content of education threatened to make obsolete the learning to which the members of the elite had devoted much of their lives, and to make obsolete as well the whole system of status on which their positions depended, their committed resistance to educational reform until the very end of the nineteenth century can be readily understood. In this respect too the class structure of traditional Chinese society was inimical to economic development. It is to this structure, then, and to the relations of production associated with it rather than to population growth that one must look for an explanation of the development of underdevelopment in China.

To consider directly the causes of underdevelopment, some further clarification of its meaning is in order. There is no evidence to suggest that per capita national product in the nineteenth century was very different from that in Song China, and good reason to believe that it was not very different, especially as per capita agricultural product appears to have remained about the same, or at least to have shown no clear secular trend, between 1400 and the early twentieth century (Perkins 1969, 14–15). The principal referent for underdevelopment then, in China as elsewhere, is not the decline over time in a country's per capita product, but its per capita product in relation to the rapidly growing per capita products of Western countries from the nineteenth century.

Underdevelopment, however, involves more than just a low production in relation to other countries; it would be improper, for example, to speak of Japan in the first half of the nineteenth century as underdeveloped despite a per capita product low in relation to that of England. Underdevelopment implies as well a relationship of inequality between the less developed country and more developed ones. This relationship is expressed in the following ways. First, the advanced country wields military and political power over the underdeveloped country, limiting the autonomy of the latter and placing its citizens in an inferior position. Second, the relationship between them tends to contribute more to the growth of the advanced country than to the development of the underdeveloped one. Third, and possibly most important, the relationship creates or strengthens classes in the underdeveloped country whose interest is more closely tied to the activities of the advanced country than to the development of their own country or to the welfare of their countrymen. Fourth, the underdeveloped country tends to be thrown into a state of financial, technological, and cultural dependency on the advanced countries. And fifth, disarticulation appears in the economy of the underdeveloped country in the sense that progress occurring in one sector of the economy does not readily stimulate changes elsewhere; key sectors of the economy are tied to developments abroad more closely than they are to other domestic sectors. Thus, insofar as the growth of the treaty ports stimulated a demand for imports rather than local manufacturing, or the movement of the gentry with their capital to the cities led ultimately to capital flight abroad rather than urban development, the Chinese economy manifested disarticulation.

In all of the respects enumerated, inequality in the relations between China and the West played an unmistakable role in the underdevelopment of China. But to recognize the importance of this relationship and to assign it primary causal responsibility are two different things. China became an underdeveloped country during the course of the nineteenth century as its economy remained traditional and it was forced into a subservient and dependent relationship by the West and Japan. To understand China's underdevelopment in this way, however, does not mean that the West and Japan took the leading role in creating underdevelopment. Rather, to determine the principal factor, it is necessary to address the more general question, why did economic development fail to take place in China?

Had China's economic progress continued prior to or during the industrial revolution in the West, China would not have become underdeveloped. And the principal barriers to economic progress in China were not foreign but domestic. The Chinese economy in late traditional times produced a substantial surplus above the subsistence needs of the population; why was not this surplus invested? The discussion above concerning class structure and relations of production has already, I believe, provided most of the answer. Yet the issue is of such central importance that some further discussion of the size and mode of utilization of the surplus is in order.

In the agricultural sector, as noted above, the most readily quantifiable components of the surplus, expressed as a proportion of net domestic product in the 1930s—and nineteenth-century figures would not have been very different—were 10.7 percent for land rent, 3.4 percent for farm business profits, 2.8 percent for interest payments, and 2.1 percent for taxes paid by owner-farmers, totaling in all 19.0 percent of the national income (Lippit 1974, 76). These estimates are themselves based on conservative assumptions and exclude the graft payments to local officials and their underlings, special levies (including military exactions) and surtaxes, and the exactions of bandits, all of which properly form a part of the surplus. While these are not precisely quantifiable, it can be estimated with a high degree of confidence that in the rural sector alone, at a very minimum, 25 percent of the national income (38 percent of the income generated in the rural sector, on the assumption that this amounted to 65 percent of the national income) represented a surplus above the subsistence needs of the population. In the urban sector, the profits generated by mercantile and banking activities, including the enormous monopoly profits in the salt trade and foreign trade, income from urban real estate, and the graft income of senior officials and the emperor cannot have accounted for less than an additional 5 percent of national income, so that the surplus in China as a whole cannot have been less than 30 percent of the national income. While Riskin (1975, 74) estimates an actual surplus of 27.2 percent for 1933, his estimate excludes the massive illicit payments that characterized Chinese society right through the Republican period, so it is fully consistent with the 30 percent minimum estimated here. The point here is not to provide a precise estimate of the surplus, however, but merely to show that it was quite substantial, sufficient to have sustained a high rate of capital formation without depressing the living standards of the population.

Another way to examine the size of the surplus is through the estimates Chung-li Chang (1962) provides of the income of the gentry in late-nineteenth-century China and of the size of the national income. He estimates the gross national product (GNP) at 2,781 million taels (p. 296) but in relying on official data for the area of cultivated land understates the total by a fourth and income generated in the agricultural sector by a like amount (Feuerwerker 1969, 2; Perkins 1969, 16). Feuerwerker corrects Chang's estimate accordingly to get an 1880s' GNP of 3,339 million taels. This would correspond to a net national product of about 3,228 million taels, if depreciation was the same 3.3 percent share of gross product in the 1880s that it constituted in 1933 (Liu and Yeh 1965, 68). Against this figure can be compared the income of the gentry, almost all of which represented surplus (although not all surplus income went to the gentry). Table 4.1 indicates gentry income by source.

According to the information provided in table 4.1, the gentry, which constituted 1.9 percent of the population, received 719 out of the 3,228 million taels of the net national product generated in the 1880s or some 22.3 percent. This figure, however, does not include the entire surplus; most notably it excludes the emperor's income, income from urban real estate, the income of nongentry landlords, the profit income of rich peasants, the income from nongentry moneylending, nongentry mercantile profits, and the incomes from graft and extortion of yamen underlings (who lacked both gentry and official status). If the estimates of the size of the surplus are approached in this way, again it would appear that 30 percent of national income is the minimum conceivable level.

The uses of the surplus included primarily luxury consumption (including conspicuous consumption), the purchase of land, ceremonial expenditures, the military expenditures necessary to defend the empire

Table 4.1

Total Annual Gentry Income in the Late Nineteenth Century According to Source (in millions of taels)

Service income		
Officeholding	121	
Gentry services	111	
Secretarial services	9	
Teaching	62	
Other services	9	
Total service income		312
Income from landholding		293
Income from mercantile activities		114
Total		719

Source: Chung-li Chang (1962, 197).

Note: Chang estimates an income from landholding of 220 million taels, based on the assumption that gentry landowners held one-fourth of the land under cultivation. However, since his estimate of the amount of land under cultivation is too low, I have adjusted upward the rental income by one-third in the same manner that the income generated in the agricultural sector was adjusted upward in calculating the GNP.

against the foreigners and against the Chinese, and expenditures on classical education (with a net social utility that may well have been negative). The direct exactions of imperialism did not amount to very much before the turn of the century and even then they never amounted to more than a very minor share of the total surplus. Capital flight, which also absorbed a share of the surplus in the twentieth century, was not important in the nineteenth. Given the class structure and production relations of late imperial Chinese society, there was little or no incentive to invest the surplus productively.

This class structure was not always the same. Between the decline of the aristocracy in the late Tang dynasty and the increasing consolidation of gentry authority during and after the late Song, space existed for innovative merchants and landlords, and in the context of the favorable exogenous conditions provided by an expanding frontier, urban growth, and increasing domestic and foreign trade, these took a leading role in propelling forward China's medieval economic revolution. During the Song dynasty, merchants still existed as a class distinct from the scholar-officials, and in the countryside, rich peasants and improving landlords held a position unequalled before or since (McKnight 1975, 99). Many estates were run, at least in part, as large-scale production units, and it was not unusual for landowners to be reading treatises on agriculture and seeking to improve cultivation. In the cities, official control over markets collapsed, prototype merchant and craft guilds arose, and a city bourgeoisie with its own new culture appeared (Shiba 1975, 42). As later, it was wealth that mattered, but the road to wealth was not necessarily through corruption and monopoly, and at least some of the recipients of the economic surplus were concerned with improving production techniques and developing new or improved products. There is some evidence of renewed agricultural development in Ming times (Eberhard 1971, 248–250) and the late-Ming/early Qing period was marked by the rise of great merchants (Ho 1959, 197–201), but the further development in the same period of absentee landlordship, continuing a long historical trend, and its functional equivalent in the parcelization of estates limited further agricultural development.

As for the great merchants, their behavior was not very different from that of their contemporary European counterparts in early capitalist development. From Dobb's (1975) description of the latter, the parallel is evident:

> One feature of this new merchant bourgeoisie that is at first as surprising as it is universal, is the readiness with which this class compromised with feudal society once its privileges had been won. The compromise was partly economic—it purchased land, entered into business partnerships with the aristocracy, and welcomed local gentry and their sons to membership of its leading gilds; it was partly social—the desire for inter-marriage and the acquisition of titles to gentility. . . . The degree to which merchant capital flourished in a country at this period affords us no measure of the ease and speed with which capitalist production was destined to develop, in many cases quite the contrary. . . . The needs that merchants and usurers served were largely those of lords and princes and kings. These new men had to be ingratiating as well as crafty; they had to temper extortion with fawning, combine avarice with flattery, and clothe a usurer's hardness in the vestments of chivalry. In the producer they had little interest save in his continuing submissiveness and for the system of production they had little regard save as a cheap and ready source of supply. . . . To acquire political privilege was their first ambition: their second was that as few as possible should enjoy it. Since they were essentially parasites on the old economic order . . . their fortune was in the last analysis associated with that of their host. By the end of the 16th century this new aristocracy . . . had become a conservative rather than a revolutionary force; and its influence was to retard rather than to accelerate the development of capitalism as a mode of production. (pp. 121–22)

I have quoted Dobb at length because this striking parallel is of quite some importance in understanding the role of the Chinese merchants. The primary impetus for capitalist development in Europe came from producers accumulating capital, going into trade, and then reorganizing production free from guild restrictions (Marx 1962, 318–31; Dobb 1975, 123); the rise of great merchants, although it contributed to the growth of commodity production, did as much to forestall capitalist development as to further it. In the context of Chinese society, Confucian scruples were easily overcome in practice and successful merchants readily assimilated into the gentry class, becoming defenders of the status quo in much the same manner as their European counterparts. As for the rise of independent capitalist producers, there was simply no space for it in Chinese society. When the bureaucratic capitalist enterprises were nationalized in 1949, the enterprises owned by the "national bourgeoisie," smaller businessmen who had suffered like the peasants and workers from the joint domination of bureaucratic capitalism and imperialism, were left in private hands; in all they accounted for only 20 percent of the capital stock (Mao 1974, 268), testimony to the weak position of competitive capitalism at the end of the Republican era.

By the eighteenth century, absentee landlordism was the rule and gentry-merchant distinctions largely a fiction. There was no elite division to create a space where the forces of development—or the peasants and workers for that matter—could breathe. The examination system became totally irrelevant to the problems of society, with the candidates for office discouraged from discussing even current affairs from the late eighteenth century (Chang 1974, 176). Corruption, always present, grew to reach extraordinary proportions in the nineteenth century. In 1727, the Yong Zheng emperor had ordered expansion of the purchase system (of the titles for gentry status) because he was aware of the extent of the corruption in the examination system (Chang 1974, 115). In the nineteenth century, meddling in examinations by high officials to favor their relatives became common (Chang 1974, 186), and by late Qing times, according to Feng Guifen, "Malpractices in examination [were] practiced by seven or eight out of ten men. Only one case in several years has been punished according to law" (Chang 1974, 190).

The corruption existed at every level of Chinese society, permeating it to its core. Illegal surcharges which the gentry in their role as tax farmers imposed on the peasants reached as high as 250 percent in the nineteenth century while tax revenues reaching the government remained constant (Wakeman 1975b, 15). Corruption had always been a way of life in China, but in the nineteenth century it reached unprecedented proportions, not to be exceeded until the first half of the twentieth century.

> Public office had always been a major source of private income in late imperial China. How much more so was private office, especially when it included such lucrative pursuits as arms-buying with accompanying salesmen's rebates, or railway building with accompanying contractors' kickbacks. Governor-General Li Hung-chang, for example, amassed hundreds of thousands of acres of land, innumerable silk stores, and pawnshops across the empire. A common saying at the time alleged that "every dog that barks for Li is fat." . . . [T]he Chinese warships [in the Sino-Japanese War of 1894–1895] lacked explosive warheads for their naval shells because Li's purveyor, his son-in-law Chang P'ei-lun, had pocketed the money and bought hollow warheads from Krupp instead. Other associates had taken similar liberties. Torpedoes turned out to be filled with scrap iron instead of gunpowder and the munitions bags of Weihaiwei with sand instead of explosives. (Wakeman 1975a, 193)

The formula for early industrialization in China, *guandu shangban* (offical supervision and merchant management), applied in companies organized under Li and those like him, extended the corruption and embezzlement of offical and local Chinese life to the limited corporations of the industrial era.

The emperors of China had always been wary of allowing too much authority to devolve upon the local gentry. The Taiping Revolution in the middle of the nineteenth century, however, could only be defeated by allowing the local gentry to organize and head local militia, financed by special levies and surtaxes which they themselves administered. After 1864, local rebellions or unrest, foreign military pressure, and the weakness of the central government forestalled the demobilization of the local militia that would otherwise have been in order (Wakeman 1975a; 1975b). This was the situation out of which grew the warlordism that marked the first half of the twentieth century. Moreover, from being an extension of government in the countryside, the local gentry gradually became the government; there was no longer any check on the gentry's exploitation of the peasants. From collecting for their own pockets as much as two and one-half times the legal taxes in the nineteenth century, they came to collect as much as ten times in the twentieth century (Chen 1973, 74). Local police often became private militia, and "as control fell almost entirely into the hands of the local elite, taxes and rents, public and private, fused together" (Wakeman 1975b, 23).

The problem of the development of underdevelopment in China must be grasped in this context. Meaningful distinctions between officials and those involved in commerce and moneylending *as separate classes* disappeared, with landownership, public functions, and commercial activities common to both. The members of the elite in late traditional China enjoyed a status that combined power, prestige, wealth, and intellectual self-gratification, and they derived tremendous satisfaction from their status. This elite truly felt itself to be an elite, and in the context of Chinese society, where personal relations are so important, the consciousness of elite status was constantly being reinforced through interaction with others. The intoxication of the elite with its own status is marvelously described in *The Scholars*, an eighteenth-century novel by Wu Jingzi. The following passage describes the impact on a scholar of fifty-four, who after failing the examination more than twenty times, passed both the local and provincial examinations in succession.

Fan Chin feasted his eyes on this announcement, and, after reading it once to himself, read it once more aloud. Clapping his hands, he laughed and exclaimed, "Ha! Good! I have passed." Then, stepping back, he fell down in a dead faint. His mother hastily poured some boiled water between his lips, whereupon he recovered consciousness and struggled to his feet. Clapping his hands again, he let out a peal of laughter and shouted, "Aha! I've passed! I've passed!" Laughing wildly he ran outside, giving the heralds and the neighbors the fright of their lives. Not far from the front door he slipped and fell into a pond. When he clambered out, his hair was disheveled, his hands muddied, and his whole body dripping with slime. But nobody could stop him. Still clapping his hands and laughing, he headed straight for the market.

With the wealth brought by his new status, the protagonist moved into a new house. After several days, his mother admonished the maids to be careful with the dishes because they "don't belong to us."

"How can you say they don't belong to you madam?" they asked. "They are all yours."

"No, no, these aren't ours," she protested with a smile.

"Oh yes, they are," the maids cried. "Not only these things, but all of us servants and this house belong to you."

When the old lady heard this, she picked up the fine porcelain and the cups and chopsticks inlaid with silver, and examined them carefully one by one. Then she went into a fit of laughter. "All mine!" she crowed. Screaming with laughter she fell backward, choked and lost consciousness. (Wu 1957, 65–77)

It was only natural that the beneficiaries of the traditional system would do everything in their power to preserve it.

Consider, for example, the elimination of corruption in government, which would have eliminated literally 95 percent of the income of government officials. Or consider the question of tax reform through the elimination of tax farming, which would have eliminated a major source of income for the local gentry. Among the most important of the reform issues, however, was that concerning the examination system, for the encouragement of scientific and technical studies was essential to Chinese development. But those who had invested the better part of their lives in a classical education, and increasingly those who had purchased degrees, were not about to see their investment in human capital—in themselves—made obsolete. They correctly perceived that their whole position would be undermined by the spread of technical learning.

The power of conservatism was shown most strongly during the Tongzhi reform movement of the 1860s. This was a time when China, having experienced two foreign invasions and a major revolutionary effort, might have been expected at last to begin taking determined steps in the direction of modernization. It was not prevented from doing so by the West, but by its own gentry class. While Mary Wright (1957, 312) is correct in saying that "The T'ung-chih Restoration failed because the requirements of a modern state proved to run directly counter to the requirements of the Confucian order," her statement might have been more to the point if she had added "and the class interest it represented."

A major step of the movement was the establishment of the Tongwenguan, a school to teach engineering, astronomy, and mathematics to students training for government service. Although the school survived various direct attacks in the 1860s it ultimately failed, in large measure because traditional learning remained the qualification for provincial office and the students neglected their Western studies to pursue traditional ones (Wright 1957, 248). As Franke observes (1967a, 103), ''In the 1860s the whole educated class in China still agreed that the traditional order should be preserved at all costs.'' The vast majority of the gentry members who violently opposed reform were convinced that change meant possible infringement on their own position and interests; they were of course correct, for the traditional order had an internal consistency that could not be preserved in a modern state.

The opposition to substantive reform came not only from the officials and the local gentry, but from the imperial rulers as well. The attempt of the Ming dynasty officials to prohibit foreign trade altogether and the subsequent restrictions on it were in the interest more of imperial security than national security, and of imperial income rather than of national income. During the nineteenth century a similar policy prevailed with respect to industrial development. The imperial government believed—correctly—that industrial development, where it took place, would strengthen local authority vis-à-vis its own, and might, in the extreme case, pose a threat to the dynasty itself. Thus it was hesitant to support the schemes for industrial development advocated by the self-strengtheners. Here, the effort at self-preservation by the dominant element within the dominant class thwarted efforts at industrial development.

Thus in China there were no distinct elements within the elite to champion development. Rather, there was a strong consensus in favor of preserving the status quo. The impact of Western imperialism on Chinese development must be understood within this context of a single dominant class hostile to development. In one sense, underdevelopment in China was clearly a consequence of the outward thrust of the West: the military intrusion of the West, the dependency and economic disarticulation that accompanied it, and the inequality manifest in extraterritoriality, loss of tariff control, and so forth are indeed constituent elements in underdevelopment. In a more basic sense, however, China set itself up as a victim for Western aggression when its own elite class successfully thwarted the forces of development. As Mao Zedong stated in 1937, ''The fundamental cause of the development of a thing is not external but internal. . . . The contradictions within a thing are the fundamental cause of its development, while its interrelations with other things are secondary causes'' (Mao 1968, 26; I have corrected the translation slightly to make the English read more smoothly).

As indicated, the direct impact on China of Western colonial-imperialist activity was mixed. The treaty ports were sources of new technology, centers for investment, facilitators of the development of Chinese as well as foreign enterprises, and were sources of moderate stimuli through linkage relations with the rest of the Chinese economy, to cite several of the favorable impacts. On the other hand, the Western intrusion forced opium on China, prevented a rational trade policy, damaged some handicraft industries, and diverted resources to defense and later to indemnities, among other negative impacts. These direct impacts are secondary, however. China became an underdeveloped country in the late imperial era because the interest of the gentry class was in preserving the status quo, because the economic and social changes associated with economic development would have undermined the social order that provided everything it wanted. And China remained an underdeveloped country in the first half of the twentieth century because the class structure and relations of production remained largely unchanged. As Balazs states, "The nationalist bourgeoisie of the Kuomintang equaled the officials of the Celestial Empire in corruption, nepotism, bureaucracy, and inefficiency, and it was only to be expected that this national-socialist police state should firmly restore Confucianism and inscribe the ancient Confucian virtues upon its flag" (1972, 117).

In the countryside of Republican China, power remained in the hands of warlords and an ever more corrupt gentry, while the bureaucratic capitalism used to pursue industrial development was merely a variant of the traditional use of state power to pursue private ends. Although the bourgeoisie of the Republican era cannot be said to have had a class interest actively hostile to economic development in the same sense as the imperial gentry had, their corruption and inefficiency, holdovers of the traditional order, continued to forestall it. Without denying the significance of its antecedents, unambiguous progress toward economic development in China began with the success of the revolution in 1949, when the class of direct producers, of workers and peasants, a class with an undiluted interest in economic development, gained authority.

I have argued here that while the concept of underdevelopment derives from the development and aggressive outward thrust of the West, the weakness of the Chinese response to this thrust and China's victimization by it reflect primarily the opposition to modernization by the dominant gentry class, which was the beneficiary of the status quo. This was a class that developed over the centuries by incorporating within itself all of the separate groups that lived off the surplus created by the direct producers. Even as it did so, eradicating the distinctions among the groups, it became more and more detached from production itself. In this sense, the development of underdevelopment in China is more properly attributable to the domestic class structure and relations of production than to external influence. As a consequence of both its objective interest and its self-image, the gentry class was committed to preserving the existing order. The development of underdevelopment in China, then, should be understood in terms of the emergence of a constellation of domestic forces inhibiting progress, into which constellation a rapacious West intruded.

PART III
ECONOMIC DEVELOPMENT IN THE SOCIALIST ERA

5. An Overview of Chinese Development in the Socialist Era

From the late nineteenth century, changes began to appear in China's social formation. The dominant classes remained, but new industrial entrepreneurs emerged as well, and although they still depended on bureaucratic relationships for the success of their enterprises—and indeed themselves were frequently no more than bureaucrats in new clothes—the commercial and industrial activity of the twentieth century generated a momentum of its own and began to redefine objective class interests. In the Republican period (1912–1949) industrial growth averaged 5.6 percent per year (Chang 1969, 71). As indicated in chapter 2, Chinese capitalists by and large kept pace with their foreign counterparts in the share of industrial output they controlled. The output of consumer goods produced in the modern sector increased, and even the producer goods sector was marked by a broadening of capabilities, including the emergence of an engineering industry (Rawski 1975).

Yet from the standpoint of the economy as a whole the changes were only marginal, and from that of the individual Chinese they were often not even that; national income growth averaging perhaps 0.7 percent per year just kept pace with population growth, yielding no discernible increase in per capita income in the first half of the twentieth century (Liu and Yeh 1965, 34–36, 80–85; Perkins 1975, 122). The growth of modern industry was from a miniscule base—the entire modern sector constituted about 7 percent of gross domestic product in 1933 (Perkins 1975, 119)—so even moderately high rates of increase of output left it a small share of national income at mid-century. In 1949, China remained predominantly rural and agricultural, with close to 90 percent of the population living in the countryside and about 65 percent of the national income generated in the agricultural sector (Liu and Yeh 1965, 66, 212).

The constraints on economic development in the first half of the twentieth century were both external and internal. A series of aggressions by Japan culminating in World War II created the most obvious external constraint. The internal constraints were more varied, but in addition to the civil war between the Communists and the Nationalists (the Guomindang), perhaps the most important among them was the perpetuation of the class interests and patterns of domination that had marked the imperial period. Income from land rent, usury, and government office dwarfed that from capitalist activities, and this meant that the same class interests hostile to development that marked the entire late imperial period continued to predominate. Government officials at all levels remained more concerned with the gains of office than with the honest, efficient administration necessary for economic development; landlords—not surprisingly—preferred protecting their rents to the land reform and other social changes that development would have required; and the warlords, personifications of the drive for power and personal gain that marked the traditional culture, pursued their own purposes to the detriment of reform. In short, the class interests opposed to development, although less monolithic than in the imperial era, continued to predominate throughout the Republican period; economic development—or the social change needed to assure it—was not in the objective interest of those who wielded power in society. Indeed, only with the establishment of the People's Republic of China on October 1, 1949, were classes brought to power with an unambiguous interest in economic development, and only subsequent to that date did Chinese development begin in earnest.

This chapter first spells out the macroeconomic dimensions of thirty-five years of Chinese development and then breaks this overall picture down by periods. This provides the basis for the subsequent discussion of the issues and contradictions that continually emerged in the development process, contradictions whose resolution was the condition for continued progress. The overview of Chinese development presented in this chapter is meant to form the basis for the more analytical treatment of the character and contradictions of Chinese development presented in the remainder of the volume.

Macroeconomic Performance

The People's Republic of China was established in 1949, but the period to 1952 was essentially one of rehabilitation of China's war-torn economy. During the rehabilitation period, output in both industry and agriculture rose quite rapidly from the sharply depressed 1949 levels, and by 1952 output was restored to pre–1949 peak levels in most industries. To avoid the artificial upward bias that basing long-term growth estimates on 1949 levels of output would entail, most such estimates take 1952 as the base year, and that is the procedure followed here; the figures for 1949 and 1952 that appear in table 5.1 indicate the rapid pace of economic recovery in the newly founded People's Republic but are a misleading indicator of long-term growth patterns.

The separate treatment for the 1978–1983 period reflects the adoption of the sweeping new reform program which was ushered in formally at the Third Plenum of the Eleventh Central Committee meeting of the Communist Party in December 1978. Because of the change in strategy that the new program brought, it is most revealing to look first at the growth performance from 1952 to 1978, and then to supplement this with an examination of economic performance during the reform era beginning in 1979. Table 5.1, therefore, indicates the level of output of major industrial and agricultural products in 1949, 1952, 1978, and 1983 and the growth rates first between 1952 and 1978, and then between 1978 and 1983.

The figures in table 5.1 accurately reflect the shift in emphasis from heavy industry to consumer goods and agriculture in the reform period from 1978 to 1983, a shift which took place in an effort to restore balance among the sectors. The slow growth in the energy sector shown for these years is misleading, however, since correcting deficiencies in this sector received great emphasis during the period of readjustment and reform. The reason for the slow growth in output is twofold. First, investments in the sector tend to have a long lead time before new output comes on stream, especially where major projects are involved. Second, emphasis on maximizing current output in the previous years was associated with a relative neglect of maintenance, exploration, and development work, which created adverse conditions for increasing output in the early years of the reform and readjustment period. Appreciably improved production increases in the energy sector began to appear in the mid–1980s, however, with coal production and crude oil

Table 5.1

China's Macroeconomic Performance: Main Indicators.[a]

Item	Unit	1949	1952	1978	1983	Average annual growth rate (%) 1952-78	1978-83
Gross output of industry[a]	bil. yuan	14.0[b]	34.3[b]	423.1[c]	608.9[d]	11.2[e]	7.9[e]
Gross output of agriculture[a]	bil. yuan	32.6[b]	48.4[b]	145.9[c]	312.1[d]	3.2[e]	7.9[e]
Major industrial products:							
Coal	mil. tons	32.4	66.5	617.8	715.0	9.0	3.0
Crude oil	mil. tons	0.1	0.4	104.1	106.1	23.4	0.4
Electricity	bil. kwh	4.3	7.3	256.6	351.4	14.7	6.5
Crude steel	mil. tons	0.2	1.4	31.8	40.0	12.9	4.7
Timber	mil. m³	5.7	11.2	51.6	52.3	6.1	0.3
Cement	mil. tons	0.7	2.9	65.2	108.3	12.8	10.7
Chemical fertilizer	ths. tons	6	39	8,693	13,789	23.1	9.7
Locomotives	units	—	20	521	589	13.4	2.5
Cotton & synthetic cloth	bil. m	1.9	3.8	11.0	14.9	4.2	6.3
Paper & paperboard	mil. tons	0.1	0.4	4.4	6.6	10.0	8.4
Bicycles	thousands	14	80	8,540	27,580	19.7	26.4
Sewing machines	thousands	—	66	4,865	10,870	18.0	17.4
Wrist watches	thousands	—	—	13,511	34,690	—	20.1
Televisions	thousands	—	—	517	6,840	—	67.6

Major farm products:							
Grain	mil. tons	113.2	163.9	304.8	387.3	2.4	4.9
Cotton	mil. tons	0.4	1.3	2.2	4.6	2.0	15.9
Oil-bearing crops^f	mil. tons	2.3	3.7	4.6	10.6	0.8	18.2
Sugar cane	mil. tons	2.6	7.2	21.1	31.1	4.3	8.1
Hogs^g	millions	57.8	89.8	301.3	298.5	4.8	(0.2)
Large animals^g	millions	60.0	76.5	93.9	103.5	0.8	1.8
Aquatic products	mil. tons	0.4	1.7	4.7	5.5	4.0	3.2
Farm machinery in use:							
Large & medium-sized tractors	thousands	—	0.6	557	841	30.0	8.6
Hand tractors	millions	—	—	1.4	2.8	—	14.9
Power-driven drainage & irrigation machines	mil. hp.	—	0.1	65.6	78.8	27.1	3.7

Sources: People's Republic of China, State Statistical Bureau (1979) *Main Indicators, Development of the National Economy of the PRC (1949-1978)* (Beijing, State Statistical Bureau); *Beijing Review,* Aug. 27, 1984, pp. 18-21 & statistical insert; Aug. 13, 1984, p. 17; May 14, 1984, pp. III-XI.

Notes:
a. Excluding Taiwan.
b. Calculated in constant 1952 prices.
c. Calculated in constant 1970 prices.
d. Calculated in current prices.
e. Calculated in comparable prices.
f. Groundnuts, sesame seeds, and rapeseeds only.
g. At year end.

production both rising 8 percent in 1984.

The development of energy and transport in Shanxi province, which has China's largest coal reserves and which together with the surrounding area is to be developed into the nation's largest energy-supply base, indicates the acceleration in output anticipated for projects already initiated. Shanxi's coal production, which was 121 million tons in 1980 and 159 million tons in 1983, is projected to reach 360–400 million tons by 2000, while its power output increased from 12 billion kwh in 1980 to 15.1 billion kwh in 1983 and is projected to reach 85–100 billion kwh in 2000. Provincial freight volume, which was 137 million tons in 1983, is projected at 270 million tons by 1990 and 400 million tons by 2000 (BR, Dec. 17, 1984, 24–26). Whether or not the targets for Shanxi are fully attained, it is clear that the quantitative results for the energy and transport sectors during the early part of the reform period are not an adequate indicator of the emphasis placed on these sectors or the output growth that can be expected over the last fifteen years of the twentieth century.

As table 5.1 indicates, the overall growth performance of the Chinese economy from the base year of 1952 has been extremely strong. The overall growth performance, however, tends to mask several acute problem areas, including especially the unevenness of the growth path, lengthy periods during which real wages and agricultural incomes failed to rise appreciably, falling rates of return on investment, the poor performance of the agricultural sector (prior to 1979) from the standpoint of labor productivity, and the considerable underutilization of capacity which tended to plague the industrial sector. The overall figures may also mask some critical achievements, however, including development of the machinery industry, institutionalization of the accumulation process, and the rapid growth in land productivity in agriculture. Analyzing the economic peformance by periods can help to clarify the long-term record.

In 1949, the new Communist regime inherited an economy that was in a shambles as a consequence of World War II, the civil war, and the mismanagement of its Guomindang predecessors. Output in both industry and agriculture had fallen precipitously from previous peak levels, and the classic hyperinflation of the late 1940s had rendered the currency virtually worthless, with barter widely replacing purchase as a means of exchange. Between 1949 and 1952, the new regime proved highly successful in restoring agricultural and industrial output to previous peak levels, bringing inflation under control, and restoring confidence in its new paper currency. Moreover, during this period the land reform, initiated earlier in the liberated areas, spread over the whole of China. Some 44 percent of China's land area was redistributed to the poor and landless peasants, constituting 60–70 percent of the peasantry, who were the beneficiaries of the reform. The result was the rough equalization of holdings on a per capita basis in each region, the end of surplus extraction by landlords and rich peasants, and the destruction of their authority.

At the end of World War II, the Guomindang had taken over the Japanese enterprises in China with the intention of selling them off to private investors as soon as conditions permitted, but as a consequence of the resumed civil war suitable conditions never emerged. Thus, even without widespread nationalizations, the new government immediately acquired a substantial portion of China's industrial capacity. The state sector accounted for 34.7 percent of the total industrial output value in 1949, the joint state-private sector (which the state controlled) 2 percent, and the private sector 63.3 percent (Xue 1981, 19). These figures, however, understate the significance of the state sector since output in heavy industry, where most of the state assets were concentrated, was down 70 percent from previous peak levels whereas output in light industry was down only 30 percent. By 1952, the share of state-owned industry had risen to 56 percent of the gross industrial output value, the share of joint state-private enterprises, which produced according to state orders, had risen to 26.9 percent, and the share of private enterprises working independently had fallen to 17.1 percent (Xue 1981, 22).

The strengthening of the state sector in industrial production was accompanied by the state assuming a dominant role in wholesale trade, accounting for 63.7 percent of the trade volume in 1952 as compared to 23.9 percent in 1950, and a rising share of retail trade, in which the state share rose from 14.9 percent in 1950 to 42.6 percent in 1952 (Xue 1981, 23). Moreover, many private retailers served as distributors or commission agents for state wholesale dealers. Thus, by the end of the recovery and reconstruction period, the state had assumed the leading role in industry and commerce, land reform had essentially been completed, and industrial and agricultural output had been restored to previous peak levels.

The period of rehabilitation and recovery was followed by the First

Table 5.2

Industrial Output Growth During the First Five-Year Plan Period

Item	Unit	1952	1957
Rolled steel	mil. met. tons	1.1	4.5
Coal	mil. met. tons	64.7	130
Electric power	bil. kwh	7.3	19.3
Cement	mil. tons	2.9	6.9

Source: Choh-ming Li (1967, 201).

Five-Year Plan, 1953–57, during which output continued to rise strongly. Table 5.2 indicates the pace of industrial expansion during this period. During the First Five-Year Plan period, moreover, China began to produce—and to produce in quantity—trucks, merchant ships, tractors, and jet airplanes (Li 1967, 201). By 1957, gross industrial output value was 2.3 times the 1952 level (Xue 1982, 972).

Also during the First Five-Year Plan period, state and joint state-private enterprises continued to grow in importance relative to private ones, which largely disappeared by the end of the period. The joint state-private enterprises began paying their former owners fixed dividends of 5 percent in 1956 (these were eliminated only in 1967, during the Cultural Revolution), and although the former owners were able to retain managerial and technical positions within the firms, control of the firms passed into the hands of state officials. Thus by 1956 the socialization of industry was essentially completed, with 67.5 percent of gross industrial output value coming from state-owned firms and 32.5 percent from joint state-private firms. In the same year, in wholesale trade, state and joint state-private firms accounted for 97.2 percent of sales and in retail trade 95.2 percent (Xue 1981, 31).

The successes in industrialization and the socialization of industry and trade, however, tended to mask a number of growing contradictions and problem areas. Industrial employment (including mining and construction) grew from 6.15 million to 10.19 million between 1952 and 1957, an increase of 4.04 million, but population grew by 71.71 million in the same period (Li 1967, 20; Xue 1982, 960). Growing at about 2.2 percent per year, the population threatened to overwhelm the employment possibilities that even a successful industrialization program would be able to create. Moreover, the relatively slow growth of agriculture, besides creating a problem for rural areas, threatened to impede the industrialization program. Whereas industrial output grew at an average annual rate of 18.0 percent between 1952 and 1957, agricultural output grew at an average rate of 4.5 percent (Xue 1982, 961). In absolute terms, the agricultural output performance must be regarded as a strong one, especially in light of the fact that collectivization was pursued vigorously during these years, but the aggregate figures tend to conceal a number of critical problem areas, with the problems intensified by the fact that the growth on a per capita basis was only 2.3 percent per year.

Between 1952 and 1957 per capita grain production rose from 288 to 306 kilograms and cotton production from 2.29 to 2.57 kilograms, but the per capita production of oil-bearing crops fell from 7.37 to 6.56 kilograms and the number of hogs per capita fell from 0.12 to 0.11 (Xue 1982, 969). Basic grain "self-sufficiency" for the Chinese peasantry can be assumed to be 275–310 kilograms per capita, and at 310 kilograms per capita, yielding 1,900–2,100 calories per day, it can be assumed that peasants will move into a surplus stage and voluntarily begin marketing grain if given the opportunity (Walker 1984, 3–4). However, even with per capita output below this level, the Chinese government had to procure large quantities of grain to sustain rapid industrialization and urbanization, as well as to supply grain-deficit rural areas. From 1953 to 1957 inclusive, the state acquired, through taxation and required sales at below-market prices, approximately 50 million tons of grain annually, amounting to 28 percent of average output (Walker 1984, 45). This high level of procurement created intense dissatisfaction in much of the countryside and made further increases in procurement difficult. Thus, although urban population rose from 71.6 million in 1952 to 92 million in 1957 and 130 million in 1960 (Hou 1968, 342), the government, after a sharp increase between 1952 and 1953, found it difficult to raise the grain procurement level further, with the average 1956–57 level actually lower than the 1953–54 level (Walker 1984, 47).

The imbalance between agricultural and industrial growth was also reflected in the inadequate supplies of raw materials agriculture provided for light industry—mainly consumer goods—in the First Five-Year Plan period. At that time, some 80–85 percent of the raw materials for light industry were supplied by the agricultural sector, and the severe underutilization of capacity in light industry reflected to a large extent the inability of the agricultural sector to provide the needed supplies. In 1957, production equipment in the cigarette industry was being used at 52 percent of capacity; the rate was 53 percent of capacity in the canned food industry, 66 percent in sugar, 75 percent in edible vegetable oils, 68 percent in flour, and 69 percent in leather (Chen 1967, 253). Only in the production of cotton textiles was a high utilization of capacity achieved—94 percent in 1956—and this depended on a high level of raw material imports and the slow growth of capacity in the industry: textile fibers averaged 8 percent of the total value of imports from 1955 through 1957 (Eckstein 1966, 106), and the number of cotton spindles installed rose from 5,610,000 in 1952 to 6,820,000 in 1956 (Chen 1967, 253). From 1952 to 1957, the average annual rate of increase in production in the textile industry was 6.5 percent (Chao 1965, 97), the slowest rate of growth for any major industry in China. It contrasts with an 11.8 percent rate for miscellaneous daily-use consumer goods (Chao 1965, 97). Cotton textiles, rationed from 1954 until the early 1980s, were the only consumer good other than foodstuffs consistently subject to rationing.

The imbalance between industrial and agricultural growth was also reflected in the emergence of problems in the international trade sphere. Of China's exports, 81.6 percent were processed or unprocessed products of agriculture and side occupations in 1953 and 71.6 percent in 1957, while over 90 percent of China's imports were producer goods or intermediate products throughout the First Five-Year Plan period (Chen 1967, 406–407). The failure of the agricultural sector to grow more rapidly meant that imports, many of which embodied technology not available at home, could not grow fast enough to meet the expanding needs of the industrial sector. Further, the inability of the agricultural sector to meet the growing food requirements of the cities made a shift in the composition of imports from producer goods to grain inevitable; this shift did indeed take place in the early 1960s.

Despite the overall successful growth performance during the First Five-Year Plan period, therefore, the development strategy it embodied could not be maintained. Rapid industrialization focusing on heavy industry and based on the extraction of surplus from the countryside through state procurement policies could not be sustained since higher levels of surplus extraction were not feasible. At the same time, the industrial sector still lacked the capacity to provide at meaningful levels the inputs like tractors and chemical fertilizers needed for agricultural modernization, so a simple shift in investment orientation in favor of agriculture, while appropriate, could have had only a limited impact. In this context, China opted for a dramatically new development strategy following the successful conclusion of the First Five-Year Plan.

From 1958 to 1960, China attempted to bring about a "Great Leap Forward" (GLF) in economic output. The heart of the GLF lay in its effort to raise dramatically the output of agriculture and of newly formed labor-intensive industries by radically reorganizing the socio-economic structure of the rural areas of the country, while maintaining and intensifying industrial development with the increased assistance anticipated from the rural areas. The establishment of the people's communes in the countryside was intended to provide a means for using off-season labor more fully through the development of rural industries and area-wide construction projects, especially in water conservancy, while increasing the availability of labor for economic construction on a year-round basis by socializing many household tasks. In the country-side, the development of local initiative and self-reliance and the estab-lishment of an institutional structure conducive to the introduction of communism, with distribution based on need, were also intended.

In the industrial sector, the GLF sought to raise output by 25 percent annually. The gap between the growth rates of heavy and light industry was to be closed not by reducing the effort to develop heavy industry but by accelerating the development of light industry, relying on labor-intensive processes wherever possible. This effort was meant to solve the urban underemployment problem as well as the sectoral imbalance. The parallel development of modern, technically advanced methods and traditional labor-intensive ones became known as "walking on two legs."

During the First Five-Year Plan, the collectivization of agriculture, described in more detail in chapter 7, had proceeded rapidly through several stages. Following the equalization of land holdings in the land reform, mutual aid teams were widely organized in which seven or eight farm households would cooperate in farming activities while retaining ownership of their land and tools. By the end of 1955 these had largely given way to elementary agricultural producers' cooper-atives (APCs), averaging about thirty households, which pooled their land for collective cultivation but retained land ownership rights and received income on the basis of both land and labor contributed. A year later these were generally amalgamated into the two-hundred-house-hold (on average) advanced APCs. The advanced APCs eliminated the return to land, and payment to members was based exclusively on their labor contributions. They were regarded by the regime as "fully socialist'' for this reason, but in the absence of a significant measure of control by their members they still failed in fact to meet one of the basic criteria for the socialist mode of production (see chapter 1).

In the winter of 1957–58, many large-scale rural construction projects were undertaken, especially in water conservancy. Each of these involved the coordinated work of many advanced APCs, which could supply labor during the agricultural off-season without any social opportunity cost (loss of alternative production). The idea emerged of using China's immense labor resources to carry out rural capital construction and develop small-scale rural industries. The key was seen as the ability to coordinate and mobilize labor on a vast scale, and thus the people's commune system was born. The first commune was established in April 1958, and by September virtually the entire countryside was organized into communes, averaging about 5,000 households or 25,000 people each.

Chapter 7 discusses the commune system in some detail, but here let us simply note that the manner in which the communes were formed, the initial lack of attention to material incentives, and the extreme mobilizational approach, with top-down directives predominant, contributed to a collapse in agricultural production. In 1958, a good harvest was already assured when the communes were formed, but in the following years output plunged. If the index of 1957 grain production is 100, the index rose to 103 in 1958 but then fell to 83 in 1959 and 67 in 1960 before stabilizing at 69 in 1961 (Ashbrook 1982, 104). Although a slow recovery began in 1962, not until 1978 did grain production per capita regain the 1957 level on a sustained basis.

Just preceding the Great Leap Forward, an extensive administrative decentralization of industrial authority was carried out, but that simply changed the level of bureaucracy at which authority was vested without turning real decision-making power over to the enterprises or direct producers themselves. During the GLF, moreover, life became completely politicized, the national statistical system was discarded, and cadres were under tremendous pressure to report sharply improved results. As a consequence, conventional standards of economic rationality were cast aside together with conventional economic practices, and the results were predictably disastrous. In much of the countryside, for example, women were mobilized for sharply increased participation in farmwork while men devoted themselves full-time to the newly formed rural industries. While farm inputs and harvested products could not be moved for lack of transport, the inadequate transport system was tied up carrying supplies for the new rural industries, such as the small-scale "backyard" steel furnaces that sprang up throughout rural China in 1958. The steel produced in these small furnaces, however, proved too brittle to withstand cold or stress and was therefore unusable. Thus labor, transport, farm inputs, and food were sacrificed on a substantial scale for nothing—although it was later claimed that the introduction to modern technology which the peasantry received was an important benefit.

During the Great Leap Forward, overall industrial production did increase sharply, with the completion of major projects begun during the First Five-Year Plan contributing an additional boost to the intense current efforts to raise output. Industrial production rose from an index of 100 in 1957 to 181 in 1960 (Ashbrook 1982, 104), but the increase was not sustainable. The disorganization associated with the GLF, the readiness to sacrifice maintenance activities for the sake of immediate output gains, the collapse of agricultural production, and the pull-out of Soviet advisers (with instructions to destroy their blueprints) in the summer of 1960 all contributed to an industrial collapse in 1961–62, when the index of industrial output fell to 105 and then stabilized at 111.

From 1961 to 1965, China returned to a more conventional, less ideological-mobilizational approach to economic development. Economic rather than political criteria were stressed, and material incentives in both industry and agriculture received renewed emphasis, with income tied more closely to work performance. The excessive accumulation rates of the GLF, which had reached 33.9 percent of gross material product in 1958 and 43.8 percent in 1959, were cut back sharply, falling to 10.4 percent in 1962; the high accumulation rates of the GLF had contributed to declining consumption, with average worker consumption falling from 205 yuan in 1957 to 195 yuan in 1958, while average peasant consumption fell from 79 yuan in 1957 to 65 yuan in 1959 and 68 yuan in 1960, years of crisis in the countryside (Dong 1982, 58).

The measures taken to restore production in the 1961–65 recovery period were successful. Industrial production increased from the index of 105 in 1961 (1957 = 100) to 199 in 1965, a new high, while agricultural production increased from an index of 69 in 1961 (1957 = 100) to 101 in 1965, just short of the 1958 peak of 103 (Ashbrook 1982, 104). The moderate economic policies that brought these favorable results, however, policies which included a sharp reduction in the accumulation rate, the restoration of material incentives, and renewed attention to living standards, were short-lived. In the mid–1960s, Mao Zedong became increasingly concerned with some of the social tendencies that were becoming manifest during this period. He was especially concerned with the emergence of a bureaucratic-technocratic elite dominating a rationalistically organized society in which ideology and solidarity would play secondary roles and the pursuit of individual benefit the primary one in motivating economic and social activity. These tendencies were certainly present. Mao, however, had lost his dominant position in the party with the collapse of the GLF and had to find some force outside the party to give expression to his concerns. He found such a force in the red guards, the millions of activist youths who, with his encouragement, launched the Great Proletarian Cultural Revolution in 1966.

The central theme of the Cultural Revolution was the need for a transformation of institutions, consciousness, and social values. Although the economic base of society had been socialized as a result of the revolution, the institutional superstructure and patterns of thought had yet to be transformed accordingly. If these were not transformed and "capitalist" ways of thinking allowed to be perpetuated, it was argued, the result could be the restoration of capitalism. The Cultural Revolution was seen by its proponents, then, as a struggle between two roads, one leading to socialism and the other to capitalism.

With the overall support of Mao, leadership in the Cultural Revolution was assumed by the so-called gang of four. Led by Jiang Qing, the wife of Mao Zedong, and including Zhang Chunqiao, Yao Wenyuan, and Wang Hongwen, all of whom were members of the Central Committee of the Communist Party, the gang of four tried to impose its own vision of socialist development on the nation. The problem was not so much their vision—they promoted the Cultural Revolution's emphasis on equality, the mass line, eliminating the three great differences (between town and country, industry and agriculture, and manual and intellectual work), making serving the people rather than personal pecuniary gain the basis for individual action, and so forth—as the means they were prepared to sanction to attain their aims, means which often contradicted the very aims themselves.

Recognizing the importance of ideas, the members of the gang of four set themselves up as a small coterie to approve the ideas that could be disseminated throughout the nation. They saw the world very much in terms of black and white, distinguishing between "socialistroaders'' (themselves) and ''capitalist-roaders,'' including all those more concerned with material comforts and incentives for the population, the preservation of individual liberties, the preservation of China's traditional culture and the nation's openness to world culture, the use of examinations in education, the borrowing of foreign technology, the use of markets and rationalistic means of economic management generally; indeed, the capitalist-roaders in practice turned out to be all those with ideas inconsistent with the gang of four's own conception of socialist propriety. The four were ideologues of a classic type.

The very terms ''capitalist road'' and ''socialist road'' reveal the pervasive lack of serious class analysis within China. By the 1960s, capitalists were no longer a meaningful social force in China and the prospects of a capitalist restoration were practically nil. The possibility of an emerging bureaucratic elite constituting itself as a new class certainly existed, but this posed issues of public policy that were far more subtle than the conflict between good and evil which the Cultural Revolution proponents projected. Indeed, it is difficult to mask the inappropriateness of the way the terms were used in China and the shallow analyses of class and of the transition to socialism underlying them. In the first part of this book and indeed throughout the entire work, the concept of class is used in a traditional way: people are grouped in terms of their ownership or other relations to the means of production, in terms of the relations with others into which their productive activity brings them, in terms of the work they do or do not do, and in terms of their access to the surplus. The ''capitalist-roaders'' in the Cultural Revolution were all those who held the ''wrong'' ideas, and who would presumably threaten the revolution itself if they had the opportunity to put them into effect. Thus the distinction between them and counter-revolutionaries becomes blurred, and indeed they were often treated as counter-revolutionaries.

The gang of four placed overwhelming emphasis on class struggle as the key issue in the transition to socialism when in fact the capitalists, landlords, and so forth had been virtually eliminated as classes. They saw the class struggle as taking place in society's ''superstructure'' of culture and ideas, rather than in its material base, and believed that an unsuccessful resolution of this struggle would lead to a capitalist restoration in China. This position is quite unpersuasive, but its validity will be explored more fully below in the chapter on the transition to socialism in China. Suffice it to say here that its consequence was an extreme politicization of Chinese society.

Opposition to the gang of four and the restrictions they imposed on people's freedom was widespread in Chinese society, but most people had no way to express their opposition. The gang was also opposed, however, by many in the Communist Party, including senior personnel who had devoted their entire lives to the revolution. When Mao Zedong died in September 1976, the gang moved to seize state power and stamp out their opponents within the party and government completely, but their opponents successfully forestalled their move, and in October 1976 all four gang members were arrested instead.

The Cultural Revolution can be divided into two principal phases, a period of active factional conflict from 1966 to 1969, when masses of young people joined the red guards and were encouraged to criticize party and government leaders following the "capitalist road," and a period of consolidation which followed until 1976 when Mao died and the gang of four were arrested. The Cultural Revolution aimed at a transformation of consciousness that would make the social good the driving force of individual behavior. People were urged to "fight self," to eschew the pursuit of personal well-being and material wealth, and to give highest priority to "serving the people." Cadres, managers, and everyone else in a position of authority in society were expected to spend about six months in a kind of rural "retreat" at a May 7th cadre school, where they would do physical work—mainly agricultural—about half time and study—mainly the socialist classics—and reflect on their social activity half time. This period was meant to reawaken their awareness of their own ties to manual work and workers, and to let them reflect on whether they had indeed been doing everything possible to serve the people.

The ethos of the Cultural Revolution was strongly antimaterialist. Since people were expected to work for the good of society rather than for material gain, wage increases and bonuses were for the most part eliminated. In agriculture, Dazhai, where everything possible was done by and for the collective (individual prosperity depended on the success of the collective), became the national model. Peasants were criticized for trying to raise cash income through activities like gathering firewood for sale or for using their private plots (a maximum 5–7 percent of commune land at the time) to produce products for sale; in some cases the private plots had to be turned over to the collective. Peasants and cadres who resisted these tendencies found themselves labelled "capitalist-roaders" and were made the object of struggle.

The impact of the Cultural Revolution on the countryside, however, was mixed. The wintertime labor-intensive capital construction projects which had characterized the Great Leap Forward received renewed emphasis, so that each year from 1970 to 1976 more than 100 million peasants participated in such rural construction activities as water conservancy, terracing, and road building. Moreover, the idealistic, egalitarian thrust of the Cultural Revolution benefited the peasants vis-à-vis their urban worker counterparts. The barefoot doctor program, traveling medical teams, and rural health care generally received great emphasis at this time. In education, examination as the basis for admission to the universities was replaced by the recommendation of one's work unit; this favored the peasants, who were at a severe disadvantage in examinations relative to urban residents.

For all the idealistic fervor that motivated many young people especially, the Cultural Revolution also had its dark side. The logic of the struggle against "capitalist" ideas and values demanded strict censorship, and Chinese people found themselves cut off from their own traditional culture as well as from foreign books and ideas. In education, the enthusiasm put into reform—including the elimination of all examinations, learning through class struggle, learning through practical activity, and so forth—and the sharp attacks on intellectuals resulted in a generation deprived of the opportunity for serious study. Further, since people were judged on the basis of their ideas and no system of protection for individual rights existed, many people were subject to vigilante action and physical abuse, after which violinists who played Western orchestral music or mathematicians who insisted on examining their students would be sent off to the countryside indefinitely to reflect on their sins and reform their thinking. Most had to vegetate in this way until the Cultural Revolution drew to a close. Many of the victims were simply on the losing side in factional struggles in which both sides wrapped themselves in the mantle of Mao, with the losers becoming "capitalist-roaders" by virtue of their defeat. It has been estimated that millions of people were unjustly victimized by the Cultural Revolution with no form of redress at the time.

In the strictly economic sphere, the lack of wage increases and frequent campaigns resulted, paradoxically, in growing material concerns and cynicism, even while the Cultural Revolution tended to discourage extra-income-oriented work effort. With all of social life highly politicized, the politically adept naturally benefitted the most, and these were not necessarily the worthiest people. Further, the wage freeze effectively froze the wage differentials that had existed ten or fifteen years earlier, and with changes in skills and duties these often no longer made sense. In industry, growth could nevertheless be sustained by a high level of investment, but this was done at the cost of improvements in workers' living standards. In agriculture, where the work is not so much machine-paced and individual initiative often plays a greater role in economic performance, labor productivity failed to grow despite massive increases in modern inputs like machinery and fertilizer (see table 5.1). Output growth was sustained on the basis of sharply rising production inputs per unit of output, limiting the net income that farm activity could provide and therefore improvements in peasant income and consumption. Although the Cultural Revolution exalted the role of the masses and made "serve the people" its central slogan, ironically, it was associated with an intensification of hierarchy on the one hand and a slighting of the masses' material needs on the other.

Following the arrest of the gang of four at the end of 1976, China passed through a phase of struggle between "reformers," led by Deng Xiaoping, and "moderates," led by Hua Guofeng. The reformers advocated a path for China that in many respects was diametrically opposed to that of the Cultural Revolution, while the moderates sought to find a mean between the two positions. At the Third Plenum of the Eleventh Party Central Committee in December 1978, the reformers won out decisively and their program was formally adopted as the national development guide. Chapter 8 details the reform program and the issues it raises; here let it suffice to note a few of its principal features.

Principal Features of the Reform Period

The reform period following 1978 marks a sharp shift away from the age of ideology that preceded it. As opposed to converting the superstructure through class struggle—a bizarre concept in the absence of any serious analysis of contemporary class structure—the emphasis of the reform era has been on the "four modernizations," that is, the basic modernization of industry, agriculture, science and technology, and national defense by the turn of the century. Deng Xiaoping's maxim that practice is the sole criterion of truth characterizes the new age and underlines its suspiciousness of dogma.

In shifting national attention from political struggle to economic construction, the reform program has been marked by a pragmatic approach. Under the system of central planning which prevailed previously, the decision-making authority of enterprises was extremely limited, and since the state absorbed the profits and losses (of the state-owned enterprises) there was little incentive to assume initiative even where it was possible. The result was the full range of problems with which students of Soviet-type economies are familiar: declining economic efficiency reflected in increasing capital requirements per unit of output, poor quality, severe underutilization of capacity due to procurement difficulties, production of "unsalable" items, a slow pace of innovation, and so forth. The reform program dealt with these by turning substantive decision-making authority over to the enterprises, by introducing a large sphere for market allocation while retaining an overall planning framework, and by providing material incentives for workers and managers who performed capably.

Enterprises under the reform regime have a say in their hiring (instead of simply having their personnel appointed by state labor bureaus), can fire workers in extreme cases (subject to review and approval by state bodies), and can use bonuses, piece rates, and other means to gear compensation to individual productivity. In most cases, they still must meet state plan requirements with part of their productive capacity but can pursue their own production plans for market sale with the remainder and are free to seek out their own suppliers for this remaining share. In the mid–1980s, all firms were scheduled to go over from a system of profit deliveries to the state to a system of tax payments. This means that the state would no longer simply cover the losses of inefficient firms, which would face closure, merger, or reorganization, and that profitable firms would be able to retain a portion of their profits for bonuses, collective welfare purposes (most workers live in enterprise-provided housing, for example), and reinvestment. For such a system to work, prices would have to reflect relative scarcities. Price reform—previously most prices were set administratively for other purposes—was therefore also a key item on the reform agenda in the mid–1980s.

The key to increasing enterprise authority lies in the extension of the use of the market. If enterprises are to act with a measure of autonomy, there must be a mechanism that replaces directives from above. If a machine breaks down, for example, the old system of planning and allocation would require seeking approval for replacement from the state organs superior to both the ordering and producing enterprises, a bureaucratic process subject to long delays. The alternative is to let the enterprise in question just go out and purchase the replacement machine, spare parts with which to repair it, or an improved machine if one is available. In any event, permitting this kind of initiative for the enterprise requires the establishment of markets in which the replacement machinery or parts can be purchased. Further, market prices must reflect relative scarcities if decision making based on price is to be economically rational. Since prices did not have to serve this function under the administrative allocation system of central planning, a major reform of the price system had to be undertaken. Thus from 1985, changing prices to reflect relative scarcities became a high-priority concern in the reform program.

The reform agenda for industry encompassed many other elements as well. Improved professional qualifications for managers, including general education and managerial and technical training, increasingly replaced political criteria for appointment. The changes included the reestablishment both of labor unions to represent the interests of workers and of congresses of workers and staff, ostensibly as a means of giving workers a major say in enterprise policies and management appointments. Throughout the country, education received renewed emphasis. The two-decade-long hiatus during which real wages failed to rise was brought to an end in the late 1970s, consistent with both the material incentive requirements of economic reform and the class interests of working people. On a macroeconomic level, this meant increasing the share of consumption relative to investment. Moreover, within the investment share, that portion allocated to directly productive spheres like manufacturing diminished while that portion allocated to "unproductive" investment like housing, schools, and hospitals increased sharply. The improved allocational efficiency associated with the introduction of the market made continued robust industrial growth possible despite the relative decline in directly productive investment.

Also in the reform period, a revival of cooperative and individual businesses took place, helping to solve employment problems and improve urban amenities for the working population as repair services, snack stands, and other urban services were restored. Finally, the reform period saw a sharp intensification of international trade and investment, a source of capital inflows, new technology, and the gains from specialization. A full analysis of these changes appears in chapter 8.

While industrial output continued to grow and material prosperity increasingly marked the urban areas during the reform period, the changes in the agricultural sector were much more dramatic still, with real per capita incomes doubling between 1978 and 1983. In agriculture, the fundamental institutional changes included introduction of the responsibility system, separation of governmental authority from the communes, de facto decollectivization, and introduction of alternative forms of economic organization on an experimental basis. The responsibility system links income much more directly with individual work effort and encourages entrepreneurial initiatives by the peasantry. It assumes many forms, but an example would be a household being assigned a plot of land on the basis of a contractual agreement to turn over to its production team a specified amount of output to cover taxes, required grain sales to the state, and its share of collective accumulation and welfare fund requirements. The output above the contracted level could be retained in its entirety (for low-value crops like grain) or in part (for high-value crops like fruits). By the early 1980s, the responsibility system was being applied throughout the Chinese countryside. Between 1978 and 1983, output in agriculture grew by an average 7.9 percent yearly. Reflecting higher purchase prices as well as the institution of the responsibility system, real peasant incomes doubled in the same period and registered a further double-digit increase in 1984.

The reform of the commune system took place more slowly, but by the end of 1984 rural townships had been reestablished everywhere but in Tibet (where they were to be introduced in 1985), effectively separating economic and political authority. The principal rationale behind this change was to limit political interference with the economic activities of the communes and to permit new forms of economic association to emerge in the countryside, forms which would be more conducive to rapid development of the productive forces. The agricultural-industrial-commercial enterprises, discussed in chapter 8, provide an example of this. The logic of the commune form had been the integration of economic, political, and social elements in a single institution. With the political and social elements split off, and with the economic elements superseded by new forms of association, the rationale for maintaining the commune as a distinct institution disappeared, and thus in 1985 the commune system was brought to an end.

Other changes that the agricultural sector experienced during the reform period include a sharp improvement in the relative terms of trade with the industrial sector, relaxation of planning directives in favor of price incentives to increase production, conscious promotion of a diversified agriculture to replace the earlier emphasis on grain production and grain self-sufficiency everywhere, revival of rural markets and private plots, and encouragement of rural industry and specialized household sideline activities.

During the reform period following Mao's death, ideology took a back seat while economic modernization, spurred by institutional reform and material incentives, came to the fore. After two decades of slow and uneven progress, living standards improved sharply in both urban and rural areas, with the gains in rural areas outpacing those in the cities. The insularity that had marked China gave way to intensified contacts with the outside world, while domestically, the intellectual conformity that marked the Maoist era was replaced by a more open intellectual and artistic life. These changes quite naturally brought their own contradictions. New inequalities, justified by the slogan, "It's all right for some people to get rich first," inevitably emerged. Material rewards were accompanied by a growing materialism, undermining the collectivist-cooperative ethos of society. The new intellectual openness had its limits tested by attacks on the Communist Party, the advocacy of multiple parties, and the libertarian defense of pornography, leading predictably to retreats. The possibility of the bureaucracy forming a new class was enhanced in some respects and diminished in others, while the new economic opportunities made conceivable for the first time the emergence of a new class based on wealth. The *Business Week* cover headline of January 14, 1985, "Capitalism in China," may not provide an adequate representation of the turn of affairs in China, but a question can legitimately be raised: What distinguishes contemporary China from capitalism? Chapter 9 will return to this question in the concluding discussion on the transition to socialism in China.

Institutionalization of the Accumulation
Process and the Pattern of Growth

Economic development takes place when accumulation and technological change are institutionalized, that is, when institutional mechanisms are established that assure the perpetuation of these processes regardless of which particular individuals hold the reigns of authority. In the advanced capitalist countries, it is the corporation that institutionalizes the accumulation process, and changes in corporate leadership rarely affect stock prices. In parallel fashion, in centrally planned economies, it is the central planning agency that fills this role, and the particular individuals heading the planning agency tend to have no more than a marginal impact on the process as a whole. Thus, for all its defects, central planning does tend to institutionalize the accumulation process by directing a significant share of the surplus into investment, and it thereby assures that economic development will take place. State ownership of enterprises, the sweeping of profits into the state budget, and routine allocation of a portion of these profits to capital replacement and expansion give the socialist state a role akin to that of the capitalist corporation in assuring perpetuation of the accumulation process.

The institution of central planning following China's socialist revolution assured that economic development would take place by transferring the economic surplus from the landowners, bureaucrats, moneylenders, and other recipients of the prerevolutionary era to the poor peasants—who used it to bring their consumption up to subsistence levels—and to the state—which used a substantial share of it for capital construction (for quantitative estimates of these changes, see Lippit 1974). Since most of the surplus accruing to private property owners in the prerevolutionary era was used unproductively, the change in surplus flows ushered in by the revolution assured that economic development would take place. The change could not assure, however, that development would proceed efficiently, that disposable incomes would rise commensurately with the expansion in national product, or that hierarchical control of production activity would diminish as the socialist intellectual heritage suggests it might. Rather, it remained for the reform era to deal with these issues.

The considerable expansion in economic output that postrevolutionary China has witnessed has been extremely uneven in two respects. First, industry has expanded much more rapidly than agriculture, and within the industrial sector, heavy industry received much greater emphasis than light industry. This meant that agricultural products and consumer goods received secondary treatment, limiting gains in consumption. Economic expansion proceeded, therefore, not on the basis of material incentives sparking individual work effort and innovation, but on the basis largely of capital deepening (increasing capital per worker). The increase in capital was so great that rapid industrial growth could be maintained (despite some decline in the rate of growth) even though the efficiency with which capital was used declined over time, so that by the late 1970s perhaps twice as much investment was required per unit of incremental output as in the mid-1950s.

Not only has economic growth in China been unbalanced sectorally, it has proceeded in uneven spurts over time. This appears to be due more to the unevenness in policy making than to internal characteristics of the economy itself. Thus, the rapid expansion of the First Five-Year Plan period was followed by the deliberate superheating of the Great Leap Forward, which led to an early collapse in agricultural production and a brief boom followed by collapse in industry. The pragmatic policies of the early-mid 1960s led to a recovery, but "putting politics in command" during the Cultural Revolution resulted in considerable disorganization and a drop in industrial output. The reimposition of central authority led to high rates of capital formation and respectable industrial growth rates in the early to mid–1970s but resulted in many imbalances as the energy, transportation, and construction materials sectors in particular lagged. This in turn led to sharp underutilization of industrial capacity and a slowdown in growth rates at the beginning of the reform period as an adjustment program had to be implemented to allow the deficient sectors, characteristically (energy and transport) with high capital-output ratios and long lead times for project completion, to regain parity with the rest of industry. By the mid–1980s, the success of this program, together with the boom in agriculture, created conditions favorable for a renewed spell of rapid economic growth.

Population Change

According to China's most thorough population census, the population reached 1.008 billion on July 1, 1982, up from 542 million in 1949. As table 5.3 indicates, the natural growth rate of the population increased to a peak of 28.5 per thousand in 1965 and began to fall sharply only after 1970, when policy makers began to take population problems seriously enough to launch a major effort to bring down the rate of population growth. Prior to that time, China experienced a population boom akin to that of other third world countries where advances in public health especially brought the death rate down sharply while the birth rate remained at high levels. (This was not the case during the GLF and its immediate aftermath, when disastrous harvests led to a sharp if temporary increase in the death rate and decrease in the birth rate.) During the time of rapid population growth prior to 1970, the predominant view was that since labor was the source of wealth, a large population was not to be feared. Ultimately, however, a more sober assessment prevailed.

It became increasingly clear over time that rapid population growth hindered economic development, slowed improvements in per capita

Table 5.3

Population Growth in China

Year	Total population (million)[a]	Per thousand population		
		Birth rate	Mortality rate	Natural growth rate
1949	541.17	36.0	20.0	16.0
1957	646.65	34.0	10.8	23.2
1965	725.38	37.9	9.5	28.4
1970	829.92	33.4	7.6	25.8
1975	924.20	23.0	7.3	15.7
1979	975.42	17.8	6.2	11.6
1981	1,000.72	20.9	6.4	14.5
1983	1,024.95	18.6	7.1	11.5

Source: State Statistical Bureau, PRC (1984) *Statistical Yearbook of China 1984*, pp. 81, 83.
a. Year-end figure.

living standards dramatically, put intense pressure on the limited arable land, contributed to the severe deficiency in urban housing, and led to problems of unemployment and underemployment in both urban and rural areas. If positive measures were not taken to control population growth, it is estimated that the population would reach 1.3 billion by the year 2000, whereas an active family-planning program could limit the total to 1.2 billion (BR, Feb. 14, 1983, 21). The population size differential of 100 million, assuming 2,200 yuan (about U.S.$700) are needed to support a child until he or she reaches sixteen (including educational and other public expenditures), represents an expenditure requirement of 220 billion yuan, equal to nearly half the total value of China's fixed assets in early 1983 (ibid.). Holding down the population size, therefore, means the freeing of substantial resources for both investment and improvement in per capita living standards.

The chief instrument for restricting population growth is the popularization of the one-child family, at one point made effectively mandatory throughout China, but in the mid–80s partially relaxed in the countryside (by increasing the circumstances under which exceptions would be allowed) due to widespread opposition and realization by the leadership of the social problems it was apt to bring. Even then, however, one-child families were encouraged and special benefits granted to them. As a consequence of the young age structure of China's population, an average of two children per family would result in the population increasing to 1.3 billion in 2000 and 1.5 billion in 2050. To hold the population size below these levels, the one-child family has been promoted through a variety of social rewards and sanctions, including material ones. In the countryside, for example, depending on the locality, peasants who agreed to have only one child could receive extra income, free child care, and so forth, while those who had two children could have 10 percent of the income to which they would otherwise be entitled withheld; the penalties for additional children became increasingly severe. The rewards and penalties have been backed up by intense personal pressure brought by local cadres. In 1985, the government eased pressures on two-child families but still tried to encourage the one-child family and retained severe penalties for having three or more children. Contraceptives and contraceptive devices are available free of charge.

As a result of China's population control program, the natural growth rate of the population dropped from 25.83 per thousand in 1970 to 11.54 per thousand in 1983; by 1984, some 124 million of the 180 million women of childbearing age were practicing contraception (BR, July 23, 1984, 4). China's plans called for bringing the natural growth rate of the population below 11 per thousand between 1985 and 1990, and below 7 per thousand between 1990 and 2000, to meet the population target of 1.2 billion in 2000 (BR, March 28, 1983, 18).

Conclusion

Although the pattern of economic expansion was not always smooth in postrevolutionary China, high rates of economic growth were attained. At the same time, the accumulation of capital became institutionalized as the profits of state-owned firms were channelled systematically into investment via the state budget. Indeed, the prime force behind the expansion was the high rate of investment in heavy industry attained through this process. Until the reform period, the concentration on heavy industry limited the resources available for light industry (consumer goods), agriculture, and such ''nonproductive'' capital expenditures as housing. The strategy of economic development this entailed limited gains in consumption. Moreover, the growing inefficiency of the administratively governed, centrally planned economy as it expanded and became more complex increased the investment levels needed to gain a given increment in output, further limiting the resources available for consumption.

The fact of economic development was assured by the institutionalization of the accumulation process, but its character must be determined, as argued in chapter 1, by the class interests objectively served. These will be examined in chapters 6 and 7, which deal with industrial and agricultural development respectively, but at this juncture some summary observations may help to clarify the overall picture.

The socialization of industry, together with land reform and collectivization in the countryside, effectively closed the door to capitalist development in China (whether that door has been reopened will be taken up in chapter 9, which deals with the transition to socialism). From the 1950s to the 1980s, the alternative development models relevant to China were the socialist and statist ones. In socialist development, as will be recalled, the interests of those who work for a living receive primary emphasis, whereas in statist development, the interests of the bureaucracy are preeminent. The analysis of these two types of development is complicated by the fact that in the postwar world they both proceed under the rubric of a statist social formation. In statist development, the rule of the bureaucracy and the statist social formation are consolidated, whereas in socialist development, the authority of the bureaucracy is progressively restricted in favor of the working classes, ultimately leading to the establishment of a socialist social formation.

During the Maoist period, two elements especially strengthened statist tendencies as opposed to socialist ones. First, accumulation became almost an end in itself; accumulation rates were high and investment was devoted primarily to the expansion of heavy industry at the sacrifice of consumption. This served the interests of the administrative-bureaucratic hierarchy at the expense of ordinary working people. Second, the bureaucratic hierarchy itself remained and was strengthened during the Maoist period, Cultural Revolution attacks on bureaucrats notwithstanding. These attacks, which were ultimately on the ideas of bureaucrats, failed to undermine the social structures that gave rise to their authority. The intensification of hierarchy and the failure to pay proper attention to popular consumption needs are both at odds with socialist development. One way to understand the reform period in China is as an effort to confront these contradictions. The remaining chapters examine in considerably greater detail the nature of the development process in China. The overriding theme is an assessment of the extent to which development has served the interests of working people, and of the extent to which a variety of contradictions have appeared to hinder this.

6. Industrial Development

Economic development in China began in earnest only after 1949 when capital accumulation became both routinized and substantial. As it unfolded in China, the development process tended to reflect the class basis of the Chinese revolution, which was carried out mainly by the mass classes of direct producers, principally workers and peasants, in alliance with revolutionary intellectuals. Nevertheless, in certain critical respects, the pattern of economic development diverged from the interests of these classes, and this is one of the important factors underlying the dramatic policy shifts the postrevolutionary era has witnessed. In this chapter, I appraise China's industrial development in particular from the standpoint of its class basis. Defining socialist economic development as development carried out by the direct producers as a class in their own interest, I propose to assess the extent to which industrial development in China adheres to the socialist model.

The concept of class interest presented here is not meant to be interpreted in a narrow sense—capital accumulation leading to long-term economic growth may be as much in the interest of the direct producers as higher current consumption, for example. Further, since the direct producers—a term meant to apply to all those doing socially useful work, not just those doing physical labor—constitute the vast majority of the population, their interest and the social good are frequently indistinguishable. In the course of the following narrative I hope to show that even while the overall thrust of China's industrial development has tended toward the socialist model, strong bureaucratic or statist elements have also been present. Public policy often wavered between the two types of development, sometimes so much so as to call into question the socialist transition. The reform movement that began in 1978 must be understood as a means of strengthening socialist elements in China's development relative to statist ones, as well as a means of enhancing economic efficiency and placing the growth process on a firmer foundation.

Economic development refers to the process of institutionalizing capital accumulation in underdeveloped countries. Depending on which classes are dominant when it is carried out, development can be capitalist, socialist, or statist (see chapter 1 for an elaboration of the corresponding development models); actual cases of course can fall in between the pure models. The statist pattern appears when a state bureaucracy with a distinct interest of its own emerges, takes control of the surplus, and directs the accumulation process along lines that give precedence to its own interest. Early development in capitalist countries tends to be associated with high levels of unemployment, poverty, inequality, and social hierarchy (World Bank 1975; Edwards 1974; Adelman 1979, 312–23). Some economists have claimed that countries that display these characteristics are not developing (see, for example, Sears 1973, 6–14), but this position misses the point because these are precisely the characteristics of early capitalist development. Socialist economic development, reflecting a different class interest, a mass class interest, displays opposite characteristics; to the extent that it deviates from this opposite character, it can legitimately be said to deviate from genuine socialist development.

Under the purely statist model of development, a state bureaucracy directs the development process in its own interest. Historically, state bureaucracies have predominated in many societies where development failed to proceed, but the international imperatives of the postcolonial era—of the modern world system as it were—mandate an attempt to institutionalize the accumulation process in most countries; it has become a condition of bureaucratic survival, a part of the legitimation process. In practice, the complex social formations in underdeveloped countries commonly result in a combination of statist and either capitalist or socialist elements. During the colonial era, the indigenous capitalist classes were suppressed in the colonies, so when independence was gained the bureaucracy took a leading role in society. Where capitalist elements are mixed with the bureaucratic, the most common course is one of privatization, a process in which public resources are turned over to the private sector.

By contrast, in revolutionary socialist societies, the communist party has typically taken a leading role in pursuing development by retaining state control over public resources and the means of production. Ostensibly state power is wielded in the interests of the mass classes in such cases, but in practice those holding party and state power may act to give precedence to their own interests, not unlike the characteristic situation in the pure statist model. Thus emerges one of the principal contradictions in the transition to socialism, a contradiction whose implications for Chinese development will be pursued in greater depth in chapter 9.

Ultimately, the character of the development process in any country is determined by which class interests predominate. It will be argued here that mass class interests have generally predominated in China, but that strong statist elements have also been present, modifying the socialist character of China's development and threatening at times to make it predominantly statist. This assessment can be evaluated most usefully by indicating first the class interests that socialist development might be expected to serve, and then assessing the Chinese experience accordingly. Since the focus here is on industrial development, I turn first to an elaboration of the specific class interests that socialist industrial development may be expected to serve.

It is possible to examine the nature of socialist industrial development under six broad headings. First, one would expect it to be characterized by essentially full employment. Associated with this, one would expect to see the development of a relatively labor-intensive technology. Second, socialist industrial development entails the minimization of hierarchies through the active participation of workers in decision making, both at the enterprise level and in other social spheres. Third, one must look for rising real wages, the elimination of inflation or protection of workers against it, and basic protection within the industrial system for the welfare and safety of workers.

The remaining three headings are concerned more with the wellbeing of society as a whole than with that of the working class in particular. Fourth, things will be produced because they are socially desirable rather than because they increase profits (of course the two are not necessarily in opposition) and products will be for mass benefit now and in the future. Thus the industrial system will be oriented toward the production of everyday necessities rather than luxury goods that only a few can afford. If goods are produced for export, imports will serve mass consumption immediately or over time in the form of capital goods; luxury goods will not have a significant place on the import menu. Fifth, the growth process will tend to incorporate the entire nation and not be at the expense of left-out regions or sectors. All regions of the country must develop and local industry must develop in the countryside; equality must characterize the development process as a whole. Sixth, and finally, socialist development implies the development of the people's capacities as producers and the avoidance of dependency; self-reliance (which should be distinguished from self-sufficiency) is a hallmark of socialist development.

In this chapter, I argue that although China has generally adhered to these broad principles of socialist economic and industrial development, giving the development process there its unique quality, several notable deviations were present, deviations so serious as to threaten the entire socialist project. Before turning to an evaluation of the social characteristics of Chinese development in the light of these principles, however, I would like briefly to review and elaborate on the macroeconomic dimensions and industrial growth rates discussed in chapter 5 and presented in table 5.1. This will provide the quantitative basis for the discussion of the institutionalization of capital accumulation that follows. That discussion in turn will be followed by an analysis of the socialist characteristics that give China's development its distinctive flavor, and of the deviations from the socialist model that underlie the reform development strategy adopted in the post-Mao era.

Industrial Growth

The period since the founding of the People's Republic in 1949 has been one of rapid industrial growth. As indicated in chapter 5, the period from 1949 to 1952 was largely one of reconstruction and rehabilitation of the nation's war-damaged capital stock. By 1952, this process had, in the main, been completed, with output in most industries restored to previous peak levels. The period since 1952, therefore, becomes the most suitable one for assessing the long-term growth of industry. Between 1952 and 1978, the growth rate of industry was 11.2 percent per year, with gross output rising from 34.30 billion yuan to 423.10 billion yuan, calculated in constant 1952 prices. The output of major industrial products was presented in table 5.1.

Although overall industrial development was rapid, the pattern of development was not smooth. The rapid development of the First Five-Year Plan period (1953–57) was continued during the Great Leap Forward (1958–60), in part because many of the large-scale projects begun during the First Five-Year Plan came on stream in 1958–59, and in part because the intensive efforts of the GLF first raised industrial production, with the extreme dislocations the GLF entailed making their full impact felt only with a lag. These problems came to a head in 1961, when industrial output dropped by 42 percent (Ashbrook 1982, 104). Growth was especially rapid in the recovery period in the early 1960s, and except for a dip early in the 1966–76 Cultural Revolution period it returned thereafter to a rate slightly under the long-term 11.2 percent average growth rate. From 1978 to 1983, industrial growth averaged 7.9 percent yearly. In 1984, industrial output rose by 14 percent (BR, March 25, 1985, 2), and in the first six months of 1985 it rose by 23.1 percent from the corresponding year-earlier figure (*New York Times*, July 15, 1985).

The decrease in the industrial growth rate during the 1978–83 reform and readjustment period reflects the remedial measures that had to be undertaken following the Cultural Revolution period, which represented a classic case of unbalanced growth. The priorities of the 1950s had been heavy industry, light industry, and agriculture, in that order, and although this ordering was formally reversed in 1960 with agriculture nominally given top priority, in fact implementation of the new ordering was not rigorously pursued until after the fall of the gang of four. From 1979 to 1985, economic policy sought to correct the imbalances associated with the earlier growth by emphasizing the energy, transport, and building materials sectors, by cutting down on the rate of capital formation (in the first few years especially), and by stepping up consumer goods production and the flow of resources into the agricultural sector. The emphasis on infrastructure with its high capital intensity in the 1978–83 period, together with the reduced accumulation rate, explains the reduced rate of industrial growth in that period, but these changes helped create the basis for much more rapid growth in the following years.

The Institutionalization of Capital Accumulation

As noted, economic development refers to the institutionalization of capital accumulation in less developed countries. The process implies that per capita income is rising on a self-sustaining basis, that it is not dependent on favorable exogenous conditions. Using 1952 prices, gross domestic capital formation in China increased from about 7 percent of gross domestic product in 1933 to 19.5 percent in 1952, 23.5

percent in 1957, and 31–32 percent in 1970 (Perkins 1975, 134). The sustained high rate of growth of industry and the high rate of accumulation are prima facie evidence that such institutionalization has occurred in China, but they are not in themselves conclusive. Thus, for example, if the high rate of growth were based on rising exports of raw materials which earn foreign exchange to purchase capital goods and technical skills abroad, the using up of the resources or their replacement with substitutes would bring the accumulation process to a halt (some of the petroleum-exporting nations could potentially find themselves in this situation).

The institutionalization of capital accumulation implies, therefore, that domestic capabilities for producing capital goods are being developed. More important still, it implies that institutional mechanisms are being formed that will channel a substantial share of the surplus into investment on a self-sustaining, semiautomatic basis, much as corporations in capitalist nations routinely channel a portion of their after-tax profits into dividend payments and a portion into reinvestment. I argued in part 2 that it is precisely the lack of such mechanisms that characterized China's economy in the period prior to 1949; the recipients of the surplus preferred on the whole not to reinvest it. In the period since the establishment of the People's Republic, by contrast, the nationalization of industry and the institution of central planning, on the one hand, and the collectivization of agriculture, on the other, have created conditions favorable to the routinization of the accumulation process.

When the People's Republic was established in 1949, the state sector accounted for 34.7 percent of the total industrial output value (Xue 1981, 19). This reflected the nationalization of enterprises owned by foreigners and bureaucratic capitalists—those who owed their industrial fortunes to positions in or ties to the government—and included nearly all of heavy industry. The so-called national capitalists were initially protected from expropriation. These were mainly smaller-scale businessmen who themselves had suffered from the inroads of imperialism and the unfair competition of the bureaucratic capitalists. Since the new government soon took control of wholesale trade, it was able to influence their activities substantially via its control over inputs and supplies, or as the sole entity capable of placing orders.

In the mid–1950s, restrictions on the remaining private businesses were tightened. The profit share of business income was divided into four parts: one part was for tax payments, one part for reinvestment, one part for worker welfare, and one part for the capitalist. These restrictions were the prelude to the formation of joint state-private corporations, which were nominally transitional entities en route to full state ownership but in effect were already state enterprises. Practically all of the remaining private enterprises in China became state-private joint enterprises by 1956–57. These enterprises were fully incorporated in the national planning process, but their former owners received a 5 percent return on their equity and were encouraged to continue working for the enterprises. In this way the state could retain their scarce managerial and technical skills even while proceeding with the socialization process.

The First Five-Year Plan in China was instituted in 1953–57, but as in the Soviet Union it is the annual plans that are the operational ones. From the standpoint of the accumulation process, what is essential here is the fact that investment decisions, including the determination of the share of national income to be devoted to investment and the sectors to receive priority, are determined by the government. Until recently, nearly all the profits and a substantial share of the depreciation funds generated by enterprises were remitted to the government, which combined them with tax receipts as the basis for financing investment; on the average, about 30 percent of China's gross domestic product was passing through the state budget, which includes the finances of local government units, prior to the reforms of the 1980s (Lardy 1978, 40). Thus state ownership of the means of production and central planning removed the investment decision from private hands and ensured that a substantial share of national income would be devoted to investment.

The embargo on China imposed by Western nations and the limited extent of Soviet aid in the 1950s—during the First Five-Year Plan Soviet aid amounted to 3 percent of gross investment (Li 1967, 199)—forced China to rely mainly on its own resources to carry out its development, a necessity reinforced by Russia's decision to withdraw all its advisers and technical assistance from China in the summer of 1960. Already in 1956 China's repayments on outstanding debts to the Soviet Union exceeded new inflows, and there was a net flow of resources from China to Russia in every year from 1956 to 1965, when China's debt was repaid. China was thus forced to be largely self-reliant in its development. Although the relative economic isolation of China, initially imposed externally and later embraced by China's leaders under the principle of self-reliance, must have slowed its growth in the short run below the potential it otherwise would have had, passing through a period of self-reliance is a highly favorable condition for institutionalizing the growth process. It implies that the technical and administrative skills needed to complement investment will be developed domestically and can therefore be reproduced and upgraded readily.

In agriculture, collectivization provided the counterpart to the socialization of industry as the basis for institutionalizing the accumulation process. The collectivization process was substantially completed with the formation of the communes in 1958. The communes contributed directly to the routinization of the accumulation process in two principal ways. First, the production teams, which prior to the reform period carried out the basic agricultural work on the communes and which were the basic unit for income distribution, were expected to set aside a certain portion of their gross receipts, usually about 7–10 percent, for investment. During the reform period, individual households—especially the specialized households—took the place of the team in sustaining accumulation at the most local level. Second, the production brigades—each of which was made up of several teams— and the communes themselves typically carried out industrial activities which although small in scale were beyond what individual farmers could undertake. Their enterprises have been operated as collectives under the township governments during the reform period but have continued to grow rapidly, systematically setting aside funds for investment. Under the reform measures to stimulate local initiative in fact, measures which gave considerable autonomy to the township industries in using their profits, reinvestment has been so vigorous as to frustrate central government efforts to reduce further the national investment level in favor of consumption (see table 6.3).

These rural enterprises serve multiple functions, providing employment, cash incomes, products needed in the countryside, and so forth, but among these, of special importance is the role they play in accumulation. They typically provide sufficient profits to finance both their own expansion and a part of the communes' or townships' investment in agriculture, including farm mechanization and capital construction. In 1980, for example, 2,260 million yuan of commune and brigade-level enterprise profits were invested directly in agriculture, "equivalent to more than 27 percent of the total amount of state aid to the people's communes plus other state spending on agriculture and related rural undertakings" (Liang 1982, 76). Thus the collectivization process has resulted in an institutional structure conducive to capital accumulation in the countryside and has provided China with a rural reinforcement for capital accumulation in industry. In both sectors of the economy, socialization played a key role in institutionalizing the accumulation process.

Socialist Characteristics of China's Industrial Development

I have argued here that the institutionalization of the capital accumulation process in China in conjunction with the rapid rate of economic growth indicates that economic development is taking place. The characteristic features of development in different countries tend to vary widely, however, and the nature of development in China remains to be established. Since the principal classes shape the development process to reflect their own concerns and interests, one would expect a country in which the direct producers are dominant—that is, a socialist country—to pursue a development path that reflects the concerns and interests of the workers, peasants, and others doing socially useful work. This gives us a standpoint from which to assess Chinese development. To the extent to which Chinese development mirrors the objective interests of the direct producers, we can properly call it an example of socialist development; to the extent to which it deviates from these interests we can say that it deviates from a socialist development path. This way of looking at the development process bears directly on the analysis of the transition to socialism in China, which is carried out more fully in chapter 9, as well as on the assessment of industrial development.

The analysis that follows suggests that industrial development in China has in the main been socialist, but that in particular instances policies have been pursued that were nonsocialist in character, sometimes so much so that the socialist project would have been endangered had remedial action not been forthcoming. The principal characteristics of socialist industrialization can be divided into two broad categories: it must on the one hand serve the interests of the workers as a class, and it must on the other serve the interests of all the direct producers, including, in addition to the workers and peasants, service, mental, and administrative workers—and indeed all those whose activity contributes to the production of socially valuable goods and services. Since almost all of society is made up of the mass classes of direct producers, the second category suggests that socialist industrial development must also serve the interests of society as a whole.

Serving the interests of workers can be broken down into three principal subcategories: (1) employment, (2) worker participation in decision making at the enterprise level and in other social spheres, and (3) worker material benefit, welfare, and safety. In taking up the question of employment, it is important to note that while industrialization per se tends to be associated with the expansion of employment under any mode of production, the insecurity of employment tends to be considerable under capitalism. It must be noted as well that the capital-intensive technologies characteristically used in contemporary capitalist third world countries have seriously limited even the secular expansion of employment there. To clarify the significance of China's employment performance, a brief digression into the employment characteristics of capitalist industrialization will be helpful.

First of all, it is well known that in the earliest stages of capitalist industrialization, the conditions of employment, including the security of employment, are typically such as to severely discourage voluntary job-seeking. Workers have no way of constraining capitalist domination of the workplace, and their jobs are dependent on competitive conditions, national and world markets, and calculations of profitability of which they have little or no knowledge, let alone control. Under these circumstances, the early labor force tends to be composed of those who have no alternative, such as the African workers forced into wage labor to pay cash taxes imposed by their colonial rulers or the small farmers or handicraftsmen elsewhere who were forced into wage labor when dispossessed of their own means of production. One might note among numerous examples of this the role of the enclosure movements in England and the squeeze on small farmers in Meiji Japan, especially around the turn of the century, which forced them to send their daughters to work in urban textile mills as contract laborers (Lippit 1978, 70).

Poor working conditions, uncertain duration of employment, low pay, and the complete dependency early industrial labor entails make the resistance to it eminently rational. Under conditions of genuinely socialist industrialization, however, where the direct producers are the dominant classes, we would expect to find a pattern of development that is far more favorable to workers. In particular, the inability to find a job or the insecurity of tenure once a position is found cannot characterize socialist development.

In the modern period, another characteristic feature of capitalist development is the relative capital intensity of production and the limited employment opportunities created. This is related in part to the significant role played by multinational corporations in the less developed countries (Muller 1973). Although limitations of empirical data and conceptual-definitional differences make precise quantification difficult, the share of the labor force either wholly unemployed or underemployed in third world nations appears to have risen from 25 percent in 1960 to 27 percent in 1970 and 29 percent in 1973 despite growing per capita output and increasing industrialization (Todaro 1977, 167). In Latin America, although the share of modern manufacturing in national product rose from 11 percent in 1925 to 25 percent in 1970, modern manufacturing's share of the work force dropped from 14.4 to 13.8 percent over the same period (Muller 1973, 133). The multinational corporations (MNCs) tend, when operating in less developed countries, to use technologies developed for conditions in their home countries, where labor is relatively expensive. Thus the jobs created for a given level of investment by multinational corporations in less developed countries are far fewer than for a comparable level of investment by domestic corporations.

In capitalist countries, considerations of profitability determine the technology used and the employment it affords (for a specific example of the way in which such considerations tend to limit employment by MNCs, see Kilby 1969, ch. 4). In socialist countries, the full and productive use of labor follows naturally from the different class structure. Under such conditions we would expect to find both institutional means of increasing and assuring employment and the consistent development of relatively labor-intensive technologies in at least some spheres of production. In China, the employment-technology experience fits the socialist model closely. And although China's labor-intensive technologies are sometimes inconsistent with capitalist profitability criteria, they have generally been consistent with broader economic efficiency criteria (American Rural Small-Scale Industry Delegation 1977).

Some urban unemployment persisted in China to the end of the First Five-Year Plan period in 1957. Kang Yonghe, director of the State Bureau of Labor, estimates the "inherited" level of unemployment at about four million in 1949 (BR, Feb. 11, 1980, 13). Although he claims that public works and other programs essentially eliminated unemployment during the First Five-Year Plan period, earlier official estimates indicated one million were unemployed in 1956, and Western observers have put the figure as high as four million, using, however, indirect estimating procedures and considerable conjecture, so that not much confidence can be placed in their figures (Howe 1971, 30–31). On the other hand, the official figures understate actual unemployment since they are based on official employment registers which under-reported unemployment systematically and which excluded unem-ployed workers in the traditional sectors and women who wanted to enter the labor force but were unable to do so (in 1949, women made up only 7.5 percent of the workers in state-owned enterprises, but the proportion increased to 21 percent in 1965 and 36 percent in 1983—BR, Feb. 4, 1985, 9).

The probable persistence of some degree of unemployment in the early years of the People's Republic may reflect the underlying condi-tions and structural features of the Chinese economy. In the First Five-Year Plan period, the private sector, especially early in the period, still accounted for a sizable share of employment. Further, most employ-ment was still in light industry, which depended heavily on agricultural raw materials. Since China was largely isolated from world markets and could not readily import replacements in those years when agricul-tural production fell, production and employment could not always be sustained (Howe 1971, 18–19). By far the most important factor in the persistence of employment difficulties, however, was the sheer magni-tude of the problems China faced.

With a miniscule industrial base to start with and a population increasing about fourteen million per year during the mid–1950s (Xue 1982, 959), China was confronted with overwhelming employment problems even while it was attempting to generate sustained economic growth and to carry out and consolidate the socialist transformation of economic institutions. Although industrial employment grew by 66 percent from 1952 to 1957, the absolute increase of about four mil-lion—from 6.15 million to 10.19 million (Li, 1967, 201)—compares to a population increase of about seventy million in the same period. Thus, although some unemployment seems likely to have persisted through the 1950s, the class basis of public policy must be assessed in light of the difficult conditions that prevailed. Any ambiguities con-cerning the 1950s, however, have been eliminated by China's subse-quent employment experience.

In 1958, as I have indicated, communes were formed throughout China's countryside, and after a two-year period of trial and error they assumed a relatively stable form until their political functions were split off with the reestablishment of township governments in the early-mid 1980s and the universal adoption of the "responsibility system" and other reforms (discussed in the following chapters) changed their essential characteristics. Since the communes were comprehensive institutions integrating industry, agriculture, capital construction, services, and local government, they were far more capable of absorbing additional workers than would be private agriculture or even small-scale producer cooperatives. By 1979, nonagricultural employment in commune enterprises at the commune and brigade level reached twenty-eight million out of a total rural labor force of some three hundred million. Since the children of commune members automatically received membership, their employment was assured whether they carried out agricultural or industrial work. Furthermore, the existence of the communes made it possible to carry out the policy in the early 1960s of sending back to the countryside those urban immigrants who had been unable to secure regular employment. It also made it possible to carry out the policy, intensified after the Cultural Revolution began in 1966, of assigning urban youths who had graduated from middle school to positions in the countryside. During the Cultural Revolution period, more than fifteen million youths were sent to the countryside, easing the pressure on urban labor markets.

In the cities, the labor bureaus took the role of assigning jobs to the new entrants into the labor market. Eligible individuals would indicate their preferences, and these together with qualifications would be matched against the new-employment requests of enterprises. The labor bureaus would also take into account other social purposes; thus if they felt, as was often the case, that enterprises in heavy industry put too much emphasis on requests for male employees, they would assign a certain proportion of female employees to them as well. Enterprises had to accept all those assigned to them and could not fire or lay off workers. In the post–1978 period this policy increasingly gave rise to complaints of the "iron rice bowl"—since workers' jobs were assured whether or not they did well, it was difficult to motivate or discipline those who did not carry out their work conscientiously—but from the standpoint of the security of employment it is of course favorable to workers, security which in one form or another is a natural accoutrement of a socialist economy.

In the area of technology China has followed a policy of "walking on two legs," using both modern and traditional, more labor-intensive technologies. Beyond this, however, China more than any other country has pioneered the use of so-called intermediate technologies, technologies which employ modern methods that are modified to reduce capital intensity and thus afford a greater level of employment per dollar of investment than "pure" modern technology would provide. Although much of the local industry, especially at the county level, was initiated not specifically to fill employment objectives but to provide agricultural inputs in short supply, compensate for the high cost of transportation, and make use of resources that could not be mobilized at reasonable cost by the urban modern sector (American Rural Small-Scale Industry Delegation 1977, 58), its impact on employment has nevertheless been favorable, and this is especially true when those employed in commune- and brigade-level enterprises are included. In the mid–1970s, a little more than half of China's chemical fertilizer and cement production was taking place in small plants dispersed throughout the country.

Thus in the 1960s and 1970s China was able to achieve essentially full employment through the reorganization of the agricultural sector, limiting the flow of people from the countryside to those few who had urban jobs waiting for them, sending to the countryside those who could not be absorbed in urban enterprises, and affording job security to all those employed while expanding industrial output and employment rapidly. This achievement, however, was not without its costs. I have already alluded to the problem of the iron rice bowl. In addition to this other serious problems existed. In the countryside, underemployment became a serious problem (see chapters 7 and 8), and this became one of the main considerations underlying the reform program. In urban areas, preventing enterprises from selecting their own workers meant they could not always secure the most qualified people. Further, the administration of employment tended to be quite rigid, and although people could request transfer of employment for personal reasons, it was quite difficult to arrange. And finally, most of those assigned to jobs in the countryside went involuntarily. After the fall of the gang of four in 1976, changes in employment policy were initiated, changes designed to rationalize the system, to make it more efficient, and at the same time to make it more responsive to the needs and desires of prospective workers.

First of all, anyone who wanted to return to the cities was permitted to do so, and the vast majority of the young people who had been sent out to the countryside did just that. This created a severely intensified employment problem in the cities in the late 1970s and early 1980s. Second, beginning in 1979, a steadily increasing number of enterprises were permitted to administer their own employment examinations, selecting from among candidates certified as qualified by the labor bureaus; this policy was popularized in 1980. The response in the late '70s-early '80s to the need to create many more jobs in a short time was shaped by a number of considerations, but underlying these was a persisting commitment to full employment.

Although the urban collective economy was regarded as socialist alongside the state-owned economy during the period of the gang of four, it held distinctly second-class status. The single most important factor in absorbing the new entrants to the labor force between 1979 and the early 1980s was the upgrading of the collective enterprises, which in fact absorbed the majority of the new entrants in 1979. Although conceptually a collective enterprise is one that is owned by its workers, with workers receiving shares of the net income remaining after the various external financial obligations have been taken care of (communes operated in this fashion), most of the urban collectives in China pay their workers regular wages (and bonuses), and the larger collective enterprises, which may employ hundreds of workers, are incorporated in the state economic plans in routine fashion. Before the late 1970s' stress on developing the urban collective mode of production, however, it was officially regarded as an "inferior" socialist form. Workers could not be paid as much as workers doing comparable work in the state sector and received fewer fringe benefits. The decision to enhance the collective sector's legitimacy reflected several considerations. With the new entrants to the labor force swelled by the young people returning from the countryside and the high birth rates of the 1960s—population planning work was not carried out effectively until the '70s—increasing employment became a pressing concern in the late 1970s. Moreover, the emphasis in industry on raising technical standards and productivity suggested that employment would remain a major concern over a relatively prolonged period of time.

There were, however, other reasons as well why the collective sector was deliberately revived from 1979. The emphasis on industrial development had relegated the commerce and service trades to a secondary role. As a result, the expansion in the urban population between the late 1950s and the late 1970s was not matched by a comparable increase in the number of workers and staff members engaged in commerce and service trades; in fact, their proportion among all workers and staff members dropped from 14.5 percent to 9.5 percent between 1957 and 1977 (BR, Aug. 3, 1979, 3). This made life in the urban areas less convenient than it might have been. To increase both employment and urban amenities, the formation and expansion of collectives and individual enterprises as well were actively encouraged in the reform period. Thus, while urban employment expanded from 95.1 million in 1978 to 117.5 million in 1983, a 23.6 percent increase, employment in urban collectives rose from 20.5 to 27.4 million, a 33.7 percent increase, and individual employment rose from 0.2 million to 2.3 million, an increase of more than tenfold (State Statistical Bureau 1984, 123; BR, May 14, 1984, xi). Whereas employment in state enterprises expanded by 13.2 million or 17.7 percent between 1978 and 1983, employment in collective and individual enterprises expanded by 9.1 million or 44.2 percent. Between 1978 and 1982, employment in the commercial and service trades expanded by 5 million; of this increase, the collective and individual sectors accounted for 2.9 million or 58 percent (State Statistical Bureau 1984, 126, 134, 137).

It should also be noted that most handicraft production takes place in collectives, and handicraft goods play an important role in providing both everyday necessities and exports. Goods produced in the second light industrial department, which is composed mainly of collective enterprises, provided the state with 5 percent of its revenues and 15 percent of its exports in 1978 (BR, Aug. 31, 1979, 11) mainly from the export of handicraft goods.

Thus a number of important considerations underlay the decision to upgrade the status of the collective sector, but among these it is clear that the concern with employment is one of the most important. Table 6.1 shows the greater employment-generating capacity of the collective sector: for each person employed in the state-owned industrial sector in 1978, 4.5 times as large an investment in fixed assets was necessary as for a person employed in the collective industrial sector.

During the late 1970s-early 1980s, urban problems were especially acute since the 1960s' baby boom generation was graduating from middle school at the same time that rusticated youths were flooding back to their home cities. At that time, employment increased rapidly, with many of the employees taking up jobs in collective enterprises, as indicated above. Even so, the increase in new positions lagged behind the increase in the labor supply. By 1980, urban unemployment reached 11 million, but the state policy of vigorous job creation, supported by the increased diversity of modes of production, reduced unemployment to 2.7 million by 1983 (Trescott 1985, 209). Thus although unemployment did appear, it was clearly neither a long-term structural problem

Table 6.1

Proportions of Collective and State Ownership in Industry, 1978

Form of ownership	Total industrial output value	Fixed assets of industrial enterprises	No. of workers & staff in industrial enterprises
Owned by the whole people	80.7%	91.8%	30,410,000 people (71.5%)
Owned by collectives	19.3%	8.2%	12,150,000 people (28.5%)

Source: Beijing Review, Feb. 11, 1980, p. 15.

nor similar to the cyclical unemployment of capitalism, but a temporary problem that met with a policy response that proved both decisive and effective.

If one considers the entire period from 1949 to the present, then it must certainly be acknowledged that China has had employment problems. Yet compared to the developed capitalist countries in their early development periods or at present, and compared to capitalist third world countries today, China's employment record must be regarded as outstanding. This conclusion can only be reinforced when the extremely low per capita income and weak industrial base at the start of the development period as well as the rapid growth in population and the labor force during it are taken into account. This is not an incidental feature of China's development. Rather, it reflects the class basis of Chinese society. In a society where the direct producers as a class are dominant, unemployment can scarcely be tolerated as an endemic feature of the economy, as a means of controlling inflation or weakening labor's claim on the national output. Essentially full employment is a distinctive characteristic of socialist economic development.

The question of participation is more complex. China has a history of "the two participations" (workers participate in management and managers in physical labor) dating back to the Great Leap Forward period (1958–60). During the Cultural Revolution period (1966–76), considerable attention was paid to the principle of the two participations, with managers quite commonly taking part in physical labor once or twice a week while "three-way committees" composed of workers, technicians, and cadres were supposed to make most of the important decisions in many enterprises. The system appeared in many respects to represent a successful attack on the hierarchical structures of authority that characterize capitalist industry, but in fact it could not overcome the extreme politicization of the workplace during the Cultural Revolution, which led the vast majority of workers to play safe by keeping their mouths shut, and which led even the most trivial issues to be passed on to the factory party secretary for a decision. Further, the role-reversal rhetoric could not gainsay the fact that the hierarchical planning system modeled on that of the Soviet Union took most of the possibilities for initiative away from the enterprise, severely circumscribing the potential for worker initiative even if workers had in fact taken a significant role in enterprise management.

In addition to these considerations, the entire institutional culture in Chinese industry has tended to militate against the independent expression of worker interests and views. As Walder (1983) argues, the workplace supplies an extremely high proportion of worker needs, from salary and bonuses to housing, medical care, ration coupons, and so on. Further, transfer between enterprises has not usually been possible, and alternative sources of need satisfaction tend to be few and inferior. In addition, workers cannot organize independently or select their own leaders to represent their independent concerns. Evaluation by superiors depends partly on work achievement, but often more on "character," including political attitudes, helpfulness, support for the initiatives of superiors, and so forth. When workers fail to display the expected behavior, they may become objects of struggle or have the offense noted in their secret records, to which they have no access but which will stay with them throughout their lives, and which will be consulted whenever promotions, raises, and so forth are at issue.

Under these circumstances, worker participation in meetings tends to be highly ritualized—a means of displaying "proper" behavior. The frequency of such meetings in China has sometimes been misinterpreted as an indication of worker control or initiative, whereas in fact the conditions that structure the meetings make them just the opposite—an exercise in subordination. Workers develop different strategies to deal with this situation. The "activists" anticipate what their superiors want and take the initiative in providing it; they tend to be upwardly mobile younger workers. Most workers, by contrast, adopt a defensive strategy, warding off potential intrusion into their personal lives by scrupulously avoiding any action that might make them conspicuous. If the activists volunteer to give up their Sundays to increase output, for example, other workers will tend to do likewise. What appears to be worker initiative based on consciousness of broader social needs, then, is more generally institutionally determined—a ritualized response to pressures inherent in the structure of work relations.

Walder's analysis suggests that extremely deep-seated institutional reforms will be necessary if a balance between worker initiative and party-state leadership (representing broader social concerns) is to be instituted at the enterprise level. The measures instituted in the post–1978 reform period, however, have barely scatched the surface. During this period, efforts have been made to revive the congresses of workers and staff at each enterprise and to elevate them to the role of principal policy-making body within the enterprise. This often conflicts, however, with the simultaneous effort to improve economic efficiency by giving managers extensive decision-making authority and concurrently making them responsible for the economic performance of their enterprises. This latter objective also limits the time managers can devote to labor participation. Since improved economic performance has been given overriding priority in the reform period, efforts to create a balance between worker initiative and the authority of the center, which in principle represents the society as a whole, have inevitably suffered. Herein lies one of the many contradictions between the development of the productive forces and the development of socialist relations of production that will have to be resolved if the transition to socialism is to proceed in China.

How then can the role of participation and the elimination of hierarchy in China's economic development be assessed? There is no absolute criterion to rely on here. It can be said that the fact that China has made efforts to implement "the two participations" and has entered successively into explorations of alternative paths of worker participation and control distinguishes the Chinese development experience from that of capitalist third world countries. It is still too early to tell whether genuinely socialist production relations will prevail in China, and it is proper to regard this as one of the decisive issues in the transition to socialism. We do know, however, that the issues are too subtle and complex to yield to Cultural Revolution-type solutions, and that the democratization and "opening" of society will play a critical role.

The issue of worker income and welfare is much less ambiguous, but in a way that at first glance may appear surprising. The gains in worker welfare that have taken place in China are clearly characteristic of socialist development, but the absence of gains in workers' real wages for two decades following the end of the First Five-Year Plan in 1957 is more consistent with the model of early capitalist economic development. Before taking up the wage issue, however, let us first note the worker welfare measures China has adopted, measures which considered in the aggregate clearly distinguish Chinese development from the characteristic pattern of capitalist development.

It should first be noted that measures to secure worker welfare have been implemented in the face of severe pressures of population and poverty on a national scale, and of great expansion of the work force. In 1949, the urban labor force was 15.33 million, consisting of 8.09 million workers and staff plus 7.24 million self-employed individuals (Zheng, 1982, 698). By 1980, the urban labor force increased to 105.25 million, of whom 80.19 million were employed in state-owned enterprises and 24.25 million in collectives; 0.81 million were self-employed (State Statistical Bureau 1983, 120). Thus those working in larger-scale enterprises increased by nearly 11.9 times in thirty-one years.

Despite the rapid increase in the work force, a comprehensive system of labor insurance was implemented and benefits improved over the years. As of 1985, ordinary workers and staff members received 60–75 percent of their regular wages at retirement; workers who joined the revolution prior to the establishment of the PRC can receive as much as 90 percent (Zheng 1982, 702). Labor insurance covers childbirth (eight-week maternity leave with full pay), old age, sickness, death, injury, and disability. Workers receive allowances for home heating and transportation, and travel subsidies to visit their families. Further, workers benefit from the heavily subsidized rent and utility charges. In 1980 in Beijing, for example, monthly rents were about 0.20 yuan per square meter of floor space, not even enough to meet maintenance costs (Zheng 1982, 702). Grain prices have also been kept low by the government, and when other food prices were raised (in 1979) to stimulate agricultural production, all workers, active and retired, received a 5-yuan monthly subsidy to cover the increased expense (BR, Nov. 9, 1979, 4).

In sharp contrast to the improvements in labor insurance and other worker benefits, real wages failed to rise for two decades following the end of the First Five-Year Plan in 1957. The increase during the First Five-Year Plan period and the subsequent stagnation are revealed in table 6.2. Not until the end of the Cultural Revolution did real wages

Table 6.2

Wages in the State Sector, 1952-1983

Year	Nominal wage (yuan) in state sector	Cost of living price index for workers & staff (1957 = 100)	Real wage (1957 yuan)	Real wage index (1957 = 100)
1952	446	91.2	489.0	77
1957	637	100.0	637.0	100
1961	537	118.2	454.3	71
1965	652	109.8	593.8	93
1970	609	108.8	559.7	88
1976	605	110.5	547.5	86
1978	644	114.3	563.4	88
1979	705	116.4	605.7	95
1980	803	125.2	641.4	101
1981	812	128.4	632.4	99
1982	836	131.0	638.2	100
1983	865	133.6	647.5	102
1984	1,006[a]	137.7	733.0	115

Sources: State Statistical Bureau (1983, 455, 490); State Statistical Bureau (1984, 425, 455); *Beijing Review* (May 14, 1984, viii, ix, xi); *Beijing Review* (March 25, 1985, viii).

a. Estimate that assumes the increase for state-sector workers over 1983 was the same as the 16.3 percent increase for all workers and staff (of whom the state sector employees accounted for 76.2 percent in 1983).

begin again to rise systematically.

China's failure to raise real wages during the ''Maoist period'' (1957–76)—during which time real wages actually fell by 14 percent on average (see table 6.2)—has been justified in terms of the need to expand employment, to prevent urban-rural differences from increasing, and to use the economic surplus for other social purposes, such as investment and public services. For the reasons I will outline below, these justifications are not adequate; they provide a sound logic for limiting wage increases but not for eliminating them altogether. Had China continued to depress worker living standards it would hardly have adhered to a socialist pattern of economic development. The gains in worker welfare have been impressive in China, ranging from the subsidized housing and utilities noted above to the provision of educational, health, and other services, but China remains a very poor country and people's cash and consumption needs cannot be neglected.

The interpretation of China's wage experience is more difficult than it may seem at first glance. Almost all enterprises have used an eight-grade wage scale since 1956, with the highest-grade workers receiving about three times the pay of those in the lowest grade. This system was scheduled to be phased out in the mid–1980s and to be replaced by a system linking wages to specific job classifications, with higher wages for more demanding, highly skilled jobs. Under the eight-grade system, apprentices worked one to three years for increasing amounts which were less than the lowest grade, and managers and technicians were capable during the Maoist period of earning above-scale wages amounting to an average of 1.6 times the highest workers' wage (Riskin 1975, 218). A general increase in the wage scale would constitute clear evidence of a rise in wages. Wages could also be increased, however, by promoting people to higher grades for given levels of competence. In parallel fashion, wages could in effect be decreased by not promoting people whose improvement in skill and experience would normally have warranted promotion in the past. Riskin (1975) shows that between 1959 and the early 1970s the wage scale remained essentially unchanged. This helps to clarify the fact that the decline in average real wages indicated in table 6.2 was caused primarily not by a change in the wage system, but by prolonged periods of wage freeze, with the newer workers, an increasing proportion of the total, frozen at the bottom end of the scale.

In the First Five-Year Plan period, money wages of workers increased rapidly, and despite moderate inflation, real wages increased as well (see table 6.2). Then, with the economic difficulties and more open inflation that attended the GLF—from 1957 to 1962 the general index of retail prices rose by 25.8 percent (Duan 1982, 671)—real wages fell sharply; as table 6.2 indicates, in 1961 they were just 71 percent of the 1957 level. Economic readjustment and price stabilization policies brought the 1965 price level down by 4.7 percent compared to 1962, but real wages in 1965 remained 7 percent below the 1957 level. During the Cultural Revolution, real wages fell again even though price stabilization was achieved, with the average real wage falling from 93 percent of the 1957 level to 86 percent between 1965 and 1976 while prices remained fairly steady. After 1976, both nominal and real wages rose strongly to 1980, after which real wages levelled off through 1983; in 1984 they again rose sharply.

Between 1978 and 1984, the average real wage increased by 30.1 percent. The increase understates the improvement in urban living standards—the real disposable income of the average urban family rose

61 percent in this period (BR, Aug. 27, 1984, statistical insert; March 25, 1985, viii)—for several reasons. First, the persons supported per wage earner, which had declined from 3.29 in 1957 to 2.06 in 1978, declined further to 1.71 in 1983 (ibid.) as the single-child household increasingly became the norm. Second, the rapid increase in employment during this period reduced the average age of employees. With many new employees entering at the bottom of the wage scale, the average wage increase would not be as great as the increase for those already employed. Third, improvements in labor insurance, welfare, and pensions are not reflected in the wages; these expenditures rose from 14.3 percent of the wage bill in 1978 to 22.4 percent in 1983 (State Statistical Bureau 1983, 491; BR, May 14, 1984, xi). And finally, there was a great housing boom that reversed the long-term decline in housing space available per urban resident, which in 1977 amounted to 3.6 square meters, a 20 percent decline from the 4.5 square meters of 1952 (Wei and Chao 1982, 55). From 1950 through 1978, 532 million square meters of apartment floor space were built in urban areas, or an average of 18.3 million square meters per year. From 1979 through 1983, an additional 395 million square meters were built, or an average of 79 million square meters per year (BR, Aug. 27, 1984, statistical insert).

Some of these same factors, of course, were at work to a lesser extent between 1957 and 1978, so the overall average decline in real wages during that period was not reflected in a decline in urban residents' real per capita income, which in fact rose by 17.6 percent over the twenty-one years (table 6.2 and ibid.). Still, when the sharp decline in per capita urban housing space is considered as well, then the lack of significant improvement in living standards over a prolonged period is immediately evident. The 61 percent increase in real per capita income of urban families from 1978 to 1984, especially when considered in conjunction with the considerable improvement in urban housing, marks a sharp break with the earlier trend.

In early capitalist development there are strong pressures limiting gains in real wages, pressures which are a natural reflection of the class basis of society. Other things being equal, the lower the wages, the higher the profits that can be realized for a given level of sales. The institutional patterns that prevail in third world countries contribute to the holding down of wages as a virtually unlimited supply of unskilled labor can often be tapped in the agricultural sector or the urban informal sector (consisting of traditional activities or modern ones that require little capital) to work at subsistence wages (Lewis 1963). Laws and regulations that restrict labor organization are also common. Where socialist development prevails, by contrast, the principal beneficiaries of the development process are properly the direct producers. The question that must by addressed, accordingly, is whether the prolonged period during which real wages in China failed to rise represents a deviation from the socialist development path.

In considering this question, it should be noted first that workers do not have a simple interest in receiving the maximum possible wages immediately. They benefit, like all members of society, from a program of investment that affords an increasing stream of real income over time. They benefit in addition from the provision of social services ranging from education and health care to social security and national defense. Thus there are legitimate claims on the economic surplus that reduce the potential cash income of workers, often in fairly direct fashion as enterprises' profit and tax remittances to the state budget are swelled in socialist countries when wages are held down. Further, there may be other legitimate reasons for limiting wage increases, such as the desire to reduce the gap in living standards between city workers and peasants, or to use the wage funds to create additional jobs. Can these alternative claims on the economic surplus and alternative socialist objectives justify China's stringent wage policy?

On a quite simple level this might appear to be the case since investment, national defense, and public services did claim a large and growing share of national income, since the wage policy did prevent the rural-urban living gap from widening significantly (Lardy 1978, 174–76), and since employment expanded rapidly. The proper question, however, is whether there existed an alternative development strategy capable of achieving these various social objectives while at the same time making rising real wages possible. The enormous policy shift in China since the 1976 fall of the gang of four and the formal adoption of the reform policy in 1978 is in effect exploring this very question.

Since real incomes in the countryside were also stagnant from 1957 to 1975, with peasant per capita consumption rising by only 22.2 percent over the eighteen years (Xue 1982, 985), the low wage policy cannot be understood as part of a deliberate effort to increase equality by reserving consumption goods for the countryside, where incomes are lower than in the cities. Rather, the development strategy pursued in China during the Maoist years relied on high rates of capital accumulation as its motor force (see table 6.3), thereby limiting the resources available for improving consumption in both urban and rural areas. Substituting ideology for material incentives and administrative directives for producer initiative, the capital-oriented development strategy pursued was coherent if flawed.

The drop in the accumulation rate and the increase in consumption standards during the reform period, with industry still performing creditably and agriculture booming, provide evidence that an alternative strategy was capable of bringing about growth while raising real wages. Table 6.3 indicates the changes in the accumulation rate. Accumulation refers in Chinese usage to net investment, including inventory increases and such "nonproductive" capital construction as housing, as well as capital construction in productive spheres like industry. The accumulation rate is accumulation as a share of national income, which is defined in socialist countries as the net material product of society, excluding most of the service sector. Although the figures in table 6.3 are not directly comparable to Western measures as a share of national income, therefore, they are nevertheless useful in revealing directions of change and orders of magnitude.

During the First Five-Year Plan, accumulation rates were modest, ranging between 22.9 and 25.5 percent of national income. Despite this, national income increased rapidly, with the average annual growth rate amounting to 8.9 percent of national income (Xue 1982, 961) or 6.1 percent of GNP according to an estimate based on Western national income accounting procedures, which include the service sector (Ashbrook 1982, 104). After the First Five-Year Plan ended, the Maoist era of high investment began. During this era, accumulation rates were high except when economic difficulties brought on a temporary reduction, as in the aftermath of the Great Leap Forward and during the early, active phase of the Cultural Revolution. Even after Mao died and the gang of four was arrested, the harmful consequences of an excessive accumulation rate were not grasped, and the rate actually rose to a 1970s high of 36.5 percent in 1978. Only with the start of the reform and readjustment program were serious efforts made to decrease the accumulation rate, which fell to 28.5 percent in 1981. The fall would have been steeper, but since the reform program permitted enterprises and localities to undertake certain investments based on their own net revenues without superior administrative approval, such investments increased rapidly even while the central government was curtailing its investments drastically. Still, the accumulation rate did fall, and since

Table 6.3

The Accumulation Rate in China, 1952-1983

Year	Accumulation rate (%)	Consumption rate (%)	Year	Accumulation rate	Consumption rate
1952	21.4	78.6	1968	21.1	78.9
1953	23.1	76.9	1969	23.2	76.8
1954	25.5	74.5	1970	32.9	67.1
1955	22.9	77.1	1971	34.1	65.9
1956	24.4	75.6	1972	31.6	68.4
1957	24.9	75.1	1973	32.9	67.1
1958	33.9	66.1	1974	32.3	67.7
1959	43.8	56.2	1975	33.9	66.1
1960	39.6	60.4	1976	30.9	69.1
1961	19.2	80.8	1977	32.3	67.7
1962	10.4	89.6	1978	36.5	63.5
1963	17.5	82.5	1979	34.6	65.4
1964	22.2	77.8	1980	31.6	68.4
1965	27.1	72.9	1981	28.5	71.5
1966	30.6	69.4	1982	29.0	71.0
1967	21.3	78.7	1983	30.0	70.0

Source: State Statistical Bureau (1984, 32).

the net material product of society is divided between accumulation and consumption, this made resources available for increased consumption. Thus between 1978 and 1983, real per capita consumption increased by 43 percent in urban areas and nearly 100 percent in the countryside (BR, Aug. 27, 1984, statistical insert). Despite the higher consumption standards, the gross output of both industry and agriculture grew by an average rate of 7.9 percent yearly during this period (BR, Aug. 27, 1984, 21). In 1984, agricultural output rose by 14.5 percent and industrial output by 14 percent (BR, March 25, 1985, i-ii), further evidence that improving consumption standards need not curtail economic growth if an appropriate development strategy is adopted.

The reform strategy implemented from the end of 1978 is discussed at some length in chapter 8, but here let us note its bearing on the low-wage policy that preceded it. The reform strategy seeks to evoke the effort and initiative of workers and enterprises by giving them greater freedom of action and rewarding them according to the success of their efforts. Since material incentives play a key role in these rewards, an increase in real wages is an essential component of the reform strategy.

Thus, under the reform, the consumption share of national income has risen at the expense of the accumulation share. Under this circumstance, more rapid technological progress acting in conjunction with the increased effort and initiative at the enterprise (or individual peasant) level substitute for pure capital formation as the primary motor force of development. The availability of this alternative development strategy and its evident success during its period of implementation indicate that the low-wage policy pursued during the Maoist era was not mandated by objective conditions. Thus, the limitation of wages from 1957 to 1976 does represent a deviation from a socialist development path, and one can properly conclude that its perpetuation in conjunction with other nonsocialist elements would have endangered the entire transition to socialism in China.

In assessing the direct impact of the Maoist development strategy on workers, then, one finds the commitment to full employment and the development of an extensive array of worker benefits to be fully consistent with the socialist development model, but the holding down of real wages and the perpetuation and intensification of hierarchy to be inconsistent with it. The characteristics of socialist industrial development, however, also include the broader social criteria specified at the beginning of this chapter. There, it will be recalled, these characteristics were divided into two groups. I have discussed thus far the way in which the pattern of industrial development has affected workers; the way in which it has affected society as a whole remains to be explored. The social characteristics of socialist industrial development indicated above were: (1) it must be oriented toward the production of necessities rather than luxury goods and toward meeting the people's needs in general, (2) it must incorporate the whole nation in the development process, avoiding the intensification of regional, urban-rural, and other forms of inequality, and (3) it must be basically self-reliant, based on building up national capacities and avoiding dependency. These social characteristics of China's development tend, with some qualification, to be strongly socialist in nature.

In discussing the nature of China's production, it might be noted first that until the early 1980s wealth differentials were modest and there was no significant class of rich people to form a market for luxury goods; such a class is a precondition for skewing industrial output toward the production of luxuries. The reform program's decentralization of initiative linked to individual material incentives has changed the income inequality picture, however, and numerous peasant-entrepreneurs have been able to pass the 10,000 yuan mark in annual earnings, with some exceeding 100,000 yuan. Such peasant households have been involved largely in specialty agricultural products, service activities, small-scale industry, and wholesale trade. Their new-found prosperity has been justified—and rural cadres warned off harassment—with the slogan, "It's all right to get rich first."

The implication of this slogan is that the initial prosperity of the few will pave the way for the ultimate prosperity of the many, and indeed there is strong social pressure for the successful to teach their techniques to others or to use some of their income philanthropically. Still, a potential contradiction to China's socialist transition exists here, and whether it will be resolved successfully will be determined only over time. Paradoxically, however, despite the emergence of some extremely prosperous peasant households, it can still be argued that the initial impact of the reform program has been to increase equality overall, since the reforms benefitted the peasants much more than urban workers, and since the peasants started with much lower incomes. Thus from 1978 to 1983 the real per capita income of urban families increased by 43 percent to 526 yuan (in 1983 prices), while the real per capita income of rural families nearly doubled to 310 yuan (BR, Aug. 27, 1984, statistical insert). The greater increase in rural incomes is reflected in the more rapid gains in the ownership of consumer durables, as table 6.4 indicates.

As basic commodities like grain, cooking oil, and cotton cloth became increasingly available during the reform era, rationing was gradually phased out or slated for elimination, but in earlier periods when they were in short supply, relatively equal distribution was assured by rationing. In this regard, China's development experience has been in marked contrast to that of capitalist countries, where the price system prevents the poor from buying. Further, housing in the cities is allocated and is typically two rooms plus (an often shared) kitchen and bathroom. There simply does not exist in China the sort of lavish luxury housing to be found in Mexico City, Rio de Janeiro, and other capitalist metropolises in the third world.

The main items of discretionary spending are typically items with a high degree of utility and capable of mass production on an increasing scale. Until recently, the most prominent among these have been bicycles—extremely important as a means of transportation in China—watches, and sewing machines. The production of these items has been expanded rapidly in the past and is still being expanded, as tables 5.1

Table 6.4

Major Durable Goods per 100 Families

Item	Urban 1978	1983	Rural 1978	1983
Sewing machines	70.4	76.2	19.8	38.1
Bicycles	135.9	159.9	30.7	63.4
Wristwatches	240.8	268.2	27.4	91.4
Radios	100.5	104.6	17.4	56.8
Television sets	57.7	83.2	—	4.0

Source: Beijing Review (Aug. 27, 1984, statistical insert).

and 6.4 indicate. Increasingly, however, radios, television sets and tape recorders are being mass produced as well. A principal characteristic of these products is that they can be extensively popularized in a few years time so that distinct classes of those who own them and those who cannot hope to own them are not created. Although differences exist in quality among goods and in purchasing power among individuals, the differences are not substantial enough to demarcate two entirely different classes of people, with the possible exception of urban-rural differences, and these, as we have seen, are diminishing rapidly. Overwhelmingly, domestic production in China is oriented toward the production of necessities, "luxury goods" which can be rapidly popularized, and capital goods.

After the fall of the gang of four, however, in the Chinese press there was considerable self-searching on the aim of socialist production, and sharp criticisms have appeared of policies favoring excessive levels of capital accumulation, policies stretching back through the Cultural Revolution to the Great Leap Forward period (see, for example, Beijing Review, Dec. 21, 1979, 9–15). These policies reflected a persistent tendency to ignore meeting the people's needs as the basic principle of socialist production, and to pursue production for its own sake. A major article in Renmin ribao (People's Daily), reprinted in Beijing Review (ibid.) explained five principal policy areas in which this tendency was manifest.

First, planners started from the desire to increase the output of the principal products, especially in heavy industry, rather than from the people's need for consumer goods. Second, as table 6.3 indicates, in the distribution of national income there was a tendency greatly to overstress accumulation at the expense of consumption. Third, in the distribution of accumulation funds, too much emphasis was put on "productive" undertakings (factories and so forth) at the expense of "nonproductive" ones (housing, schools, and so forth). During the First Five-Year Plan, nonproductive investments were 28.3 percent of the total, but this figure dropped to less than 15 percent between 1966 and 1978. Fourth, in the distribution of investment, heavy industry was emphasized at the expense of agriculture and light industry. Between 1966 and 1978, of the investment in capital construction, 55 percent went to heavy industry, 10 percent to agriculture and 5 percent to light industry. Fifth, the structure of heavy industry was oriented excessively toward meeting its own needs as opposed to those of agriculture and light industry. In 1978, 29 percent of China's steel output went into machine building, compared to 15.5 percent for agriculture and 11.7 percent for light industrial goods.

Thus, there has been a clear tendency to pursue economic growth for its own sake and to lose sight of the social purposes that legitimize socialist production. This tendency, clearly reversed since the downfall of the gang of four, is a counterpart of the low-wage policy discussed above. Although the composition of output was oriented toward necessities and capital goods, and exports were used to finance imports of the same type rather than luxury items, the excessive emphasis on capital accumulation at the expense of consumption violated the basis of socialist industrialization and required remedial action. A major element in the 1979–81 readjustment in the national economy consisted of sharply raising consumption at the expense of accumulation, a change which was based on a reconsideration of the purposes of socialist industrialization.

With respect to incorporating the entire nation into the development process, the socialist character of China's industrialization is much less ambiguous. In capitalist third world countries, the early stages of economic growth are marked characteristically by increasing regional disparities (Lardy 1978, 158–59). Capitalists, seeking to maximize profits, are drawn to the more developed regions where the required infrastructure is already in place, and government policy accommodates this. Under these conditions, intersectoral as well as interregional disparities tend to grow. Empirical tests for a broad sample of countries have confirmed this tendency (Lardy 1978, 159). China too displayed this pattern in the first half of the twentieth century, but after the socialist revolution a dramatic reversal took place. As Nicholas Lardy has shown, a consistent central government policy redistributed financial and real resources from the more developed provinces to the less developed ones, leading to a clear decline in relative inequality over time.

In the entire period from 1952 to 1974, those provinces that began with above-average per capita industrial output had slower rates of industrial growth, on average, than those provinces that began with below-average industrial output (Lardy 1978, esp. 78, 132–33, 153, 156, 161). What this means is that the development process, instead of being concentrated in those regions that had a head start at the time of liberation, has become a national one. This is true both with regard to the location of industry and with regard to the distribution of public services, especially health and education. If the economic development process is oriented toward the interest of the direct producers then it must be a national process. In this respect China has clearly pursued a socialist development course.

The last of the social indices of socialist industrial development is self-reliance. This should be distinguished carefully from autarky. Since socialist economic development is oriented toward the benefit of the people as a whole, the people must develop the abilities, including technical and other skills, to assure its continuity. This very same process provides assurance that the benefits of development will be widespread. In capitalist development, the private accumulation of capital is central. Development may or may not be self-reliant, depending on the interest of the capitalist class, which may choose to expatriate its capital, to ally itself with foreign investors, to focus primarily on borrowing and selling abroad, and so forth. Except for capital expatriation, it is not necessarily improper for socialist countries to engage in these activities, but doing so to the extent of becoming dependent on them relinquishes popular sovereignty over the development process. This was a bitter lesson brought home to the nominally socialist Poland in the summer of 1980, when its Western indebtedness passed $20 billion and it was forced to slash worker living standards to maintain the foreign credit on which it had come to depend.

China did borrow from the Soviet Union in the early to mid-1950s, but the two major economic loans, announced in 1950 and 1954, totaled only $430 million and amounted to only 3 percent of state investment during the First Five-Year Plan (Li 1967, 199). From 1956 to 1965, when the debt was fully repaid, China's exports to the Soviet Union exceeded its imports, so that in effect China was financing

Soviet development during this critical period. During the 1960s, China did not receive foreign aid but was a substantial donor of foreign aid. In the early 1970s and again after the fall of the gang of four, China accepted credit from abroad. Much of this was accounted for by the purchase of plants and equipment from overseas on extended payment terms, and by the acquisition of loans on favorable terms from international agencies. Chinese officials have maintained, however, and with evident justification, that these transactions do not violate the principle of relying in the main on the nation's own efforts (see, for example, Han Guang, vice-minister in charge of the State Capital Construction Commission, *Beijing Review*, March 23, 1979, 12–13). The large fertilizer plants ordered in the early 1970s, for example, contributed to increasing national self-sufficiency in the production of both fertilizer and grain, even while developing domestic technical and engineering skills that will accelerate the development of the domestic capacity to design and produce such plants. And when China began in the reform era to accept direct foreign investment, a source of technology and managerial expertise as well as of capital, it was typically with the proviso that full ownership would revert to China in thirty years or less.

Thus rapid industrial expansion has characterized the Chinese economy in the period since the founding of the People's Republic in 1949. The rapid expansion was sustained by a dramatic rise in the investment ratio and an institutional restructuring of the economy associated with socialization, national economic planning, and the collectivization of agriculture, which taken together put the accumulation process on a routine basis. The overall thrust of Chinese development was predominantly socialist in nature; minimization of unemployment problems, promotion of worker welfare, incorporation of the entire country into the development process, and self-reliance are all socialist characteristics of Chinese development.

There are, however, three principal qualifications that must be made to this overall assessment. First, the long period of low real wages from the late 1950s to the late 1970s was not necessitated by exogenous conditions because an alternative development strategy existed that could have raised real wages even while achieving other social objectives. Under this circumstance, the failure to increase real wages simply reflects the low priority assigned to it, and this scarcely corresponds to the class interest of the direct producers. Second, the overemphasis on accumulation at the expense of consumption, a reflection of essentially the same tendency, might also be considered an example of an "ultra-left" policy that loses sight of the ultimate purpose of socialist production. And finally, the question of participation and hierarchy has yet to be resolved.

The Cultural Revolution did attempt to deal with this question but failed badly—and inevitably. The failure was due in part to the continued administrative control of the economy, which mandated hierarchy, in part to the repressive aura of the era, which made the frank expression of ideas highly dangerous, and in part to the faulty theoretical analysis which misperceived the struggle between capitalism and socialism as central, and which failed to see the threat to socialist development posed by statist bureaucracy. The reform era addresses these shortcomings by separating, to a considerable degree, economic decision making from administrative fiat and by fostering a more open society intellectually. At the same time, however, theoretical analysis remains weak and the reform program poses new contradictions. These will be discussed in chapters 8 and 9, which deal with the reform program and the transition to socialism respectively.

7. Agricultural Development

Since economic development is class-specific in nature, patterns of sectoral development can be distinguished according to which classes are the primary beneficiaries. Chapter 6 examined industrial development in China from this perspective, assessing the extent to which it reflected the interests of workers. This chapter provides a parallel analysis of the agricultural sector, assessing the extent to which it reflects and serves the interests of the peasants.

A pattern of agricultural development that meets the self-perceived needs and objective requirements of the peasant producers, both currently and over the long term, can be referred to as socialist agricultural development. Institutions such as collective production units play a definite part in this, but their role is ultimately subordinate to the objective class interests served. Thus, for example, it would be possible for collective units to be controlled entirely by the party-state from above, and to express the interests and objectives of party-state cadres rather than those of the peasant producers. Such development would be no more socialist than it would capitalist; it would fit squarely within the statist framework outlined in chapter 1. In fact, Chinese agricultural development has been characterized by a tension between the interests and desires of the peasant producers on the one hand, and those of the party-state on the other, placing it between the socialist and statist models. Locating it precisely is the principal objective of this chapter.

According to the analysis presented below, agricultural development in China has broadly served the interests of the peasant producers, and to the extent it has done so can properly be considered socialist. Thus, for example, the "five guarantees" (food, clothing, housing, medical care, and burial expenses) assure the subsistence of the entire rural population. Whereas less than 10 percent of the peasant population received an education in the prerevolutionary era, moreover, well over 90 percent receive it right now. And medical care, virtually unavailable to the majority of peasants prior to the founding of the People's Republic, is now accessible to all.

In contrast to these benefits, it must be noted that in certain respects, agricultural development in China has been carried out in ways inimical to the interests of the peasant producers. Two areas especially stand out in this respect. First, the improvement in living standards was nominal over a prolonged period of time, most notably during the "Maoist era" which began in the mid-late 1950s with the acceleration of agricultural collectivization and the Great Leap Forward and ended with the death of Mao and the arrest of the "gang of four" in 1976. During this period, most of China's peasants (some 800 million by the late 1970s) lived at a subsistence level, obtaining little more than the bare necessities of life, and some 100 million peasants incapable of sustaining themselves had to rely on state subsidies for survival. After 1958, grain production fell, and although recovery in absolute terms took place, grain production per capita did not regain the 1957 level until 1975 (table 7.1). Although agricultural production rose in absolute terms during the Maoist period, it failed to rise appreciably in per capita terms, as table 7.1 indicates.

Since more than half of the consumer budget in China is used for food, the figures in table 7.1 also indicate the stagnation in consumption. The failure of agricultural output to grow more rapidly must be ascribed, at least in part, to a Maoist development strategy which in effect accorded a low priority to increasing peasant prosperity.

In one other important respect as well, state policies failed to mesh with the requirements of a socialist development model in agriculture. In effect, the collective institutions have been controlled not by their members but by party-state cadres appointed from above and responsible to their superiors rather than to the collective and commune members. As noted, the national interest certainly must be represented in the socialist state and not just the immediate interests of the direct producers. For the transition to socialism to proceed, however, the contradiction between the two must be resolved in a manner that gives expression to the interests of both, not just to those of the state. In institutionalizing the subordination of the peasants, Chinese policy makers were adhering more closely to the requirements of the statist development model than to those of the socialist model.

Table 7.1

Per Capita Output of Selected Agricultural Products in China, 1957-1983

Product (kg)	1957	1965	1975	1978	1983
Grain	306	272	312	319	380
Cotton	2.6	2.9	2.6	2.3	4.6
Oil-bearing crops	6.6	5.1	5.0	5.5	10.4
Pork, beef & mutton	6.3	7.7	8.7	9.0	13.8
Aquatic products	4.9	4.2	4.8	4.9	5.4

Sources: Xue (1982, 969); State Statistical Bureau (1984, 167).

In considering the situation of the peasants, we should note in addition to their subordination vis-à-vis the cadres their inferior status relative to workers and indeed to all urban residents. Chinese peasants have been second-class citizens from the founding of the People's Republic, with far more onerous travel and work restrictions than industrial or intellectual workers, considerably lower income and privileges (such as pensions on retirement), far more restricted opportunities and inferior social standing. Indeed, together with the difference between cadres and peasants, the primary social distinction recognized in the countryside is that between peasants and industrial workers or city people in general.

In the light of these considerations, on what grounds can it still be maintained that Chinese agricultural development retains many features of the socialist model? The answer to this will be explained more fully in the remainder of this chapter, but at this juncture two points especially should be raised. First, there were severe constraints on public policy. The initial conditions were extremely unfavorable, with intense population pressure limiting the arable land to about half an acre per capita. Further, if peasants had been allowed to migrate freely to the cities, for example, where enough jobs could not be provided without sacrificing the development program and where the state lacked the resources to provide sufficient food, the result would have been an economically unmanageable situation and the proliferation of such urban slums as indeed characterize those third world countries pursuing capitalist development.

Second, harsh as the experience of Chinese peasants has been, it does not match the severity characteristic of the peasant experience in capitalist countries. Thus, the enclosure movements in England literally destroyed in its entirety the yeoman class of independent peasants, while the industrial revolution and the eighteenth-century agricultural revolution leading up to it witnessed a dramatic decline in the real income of agricultural laborers (Marx 1967, 677–78). These results are not fortuitous, for rising productivity in agriculture naturally benefits most those who start in the most advantageous position and are best situated to take advantage of the newly arising possibilities.

Thus it is not surprising to find that in the 1960s' green revolution in Pakistan, the size distribution of landholdings became more skewed (Hussain 1978), the proportion of landless laborers in the rural labor force rose markedly (Ahmad 1978) while that of tenants declined, inequality increased, and poverty levels remained steady or rose (Naseem 1981). Indeed, steady or rising rural poverty rates have accompanied agricultural development in most Asian capitalist countries in the postwar period (International Labour Office 1977). This discussion cannot be pursued in detail here—suffice it to say, the Chinese peasantry has fared far better than the peasantry of, say, South Asia with regard to basic subsistence guarantees, equality, access to medical care and education, and the creation of an infrastructure capable of supporting sustained rural development in the future.

Thus from a comparative perspective, it can legitimately be argued that despite the serious shortcomings in China's agricultural development noted, development has been much more supportive of the basic interests of the peasant producers than has been the case in China's third world capitalist counterparts. This point—together with the limited policy options created by the highly unfavorable initial conditions—should be kept in mind throughout the following analysis and critique of China's agricultural development experience.

The analysis of China's agricultural development from the standpoint of its impact on the class interests of the peasantry must be based on an analysis of institutional change and economic performance since the founding of the People's Republic in 1949. Accordingly, I will turn next to a discussion of institutional change in Chinese agriculture and follow that with an analysis of economic performance. This analysis will show that up to the end of the Maoist era (1976), Chinese agriculture performed quite well from the standpoint of raising land productivity—and thereby assuring the basic subsistence needs of the population—and in basic rural capital construction, but poorly from the standpoint of raising labor productivity, which is necessary if real incomes are to rise significantly. The chapter will conclude with a brief discussion of the dramatic reforms that have taken place in the post-Mao era, which doubled peasant real incomes between 1978 and 1983, and a summary assessment of China's overall performance in agricultural development, a summary which focuses on the central contradictions the efforts at socialist agricultural development have had to confront in China.

Institutional Change

Prior to the revolution, China's rural class structure broke down as follows: poor and landless peasants, 60–70 percent; middle peasants, 20–30 percent; rich peasants, 7 percent; landlords, 3 percent. The poor and landless peasants lacked sufficient land to sustain themselves. In good times they eked out a marginal existence by supplementing the income from the tiny plots they owned (only about 10 percent of the peasants were completely landless) with income obtained as hired agricultural laborers, temporary urban work, or handicrafts and other sideline activities (see, for example, Huang 1985). When the crops failed, these peasants were subject to widespread starvation or succumbed readily to disease in their weakened state. Poor peasants in South China, where agricultural conditions are generally more favorable than in the north, considered themselves lucky if two children survived to maturity out of six or seven live births (Yang 1959, 18).

The middle peasants were generally those with enough land to sustain themselves at a modest living standard and sufficient resources to survive all but the worst natural calamities. The rich peasants were characterized by the ownership of more land than they could cultivate themselves and defined by the hiring of one or more full-time laborers. They typically did not find it economical to hire more workers than they could personally supervise or to introduce the use of machinery, and thus they never developed into a class of full-fledged rural capitalists (Huang 1985). They did, however, use the surplus they obtained to branch out into commerce, money lending, and sometimes small-scale agricultural processing activities.

The rich peasants were distinguished from landlords by virtue of the fact that they themselves engaged in physical labor. The landlords, a purely rentier class, did not typically have holdings as extensive as those to be found in other less developed countries—except for those who had accumulated enormous wealth by profiting from the opportunities for graft (discussed in part 2) that senior public office made available. Still, the landlords enjoyed a substantially higher living standard than the peasants, were free from labor, enjoyed superior status and legal privileges, and could afford to educate their children, a requisite for economic and social status.

The land reform in China, which began in the liberated areas prior to the October 1, 1949, founding of the People's Republic and spread throughout the country thereafter, was completed in 1952 with the redistribution of a reported 44 percent of the arable land area (Lippit 1974, 95). The main principle of distribution was rough equalization of landholdings on a per capita basis within each village. Since most peasants owned some land, this meant in practice that most beneficiaries received sufficient additional land to bring their holdings—adjusted for family size—up to the village average. Some 60–70 percent of the peasants benefitted from the land reform, with most poor peasants receiving sufficient additional land to become "new middle peasants." Since South China has more favorable agricultural conditions—more rainfall and a longer growing season—and higher land productivity, farm sizes there were typically smaller than in the north. Except for this qualification, landholdings were roughly equalized throughout China as a result of the land reform.

The land reform in China was significant, however, not merely in terms of its redistributive results; the manner in which it was carried out was also of great import. Ideally, a work team composed of party cadres would visit a village targeted for reform. They would stay in the homes of poor peasants and encourage them to take the initiative in organizing village meetings to carry out the reform. Although the class status of landlords and rich peasants was based ultimately on their superior landholdings and other wealth, it was reinforced (as it is in all class societies) by a variety of supportive mechanisms. These were the people who had a monopoly of education, controlled the village organizations, and so forth. By encouraging the poor peasants to take the lead in carrying out the land reform, the party meant to raise their consciousness of their own capacity for social action, and at the same time to destroy the authority and prestige of the former elite.

The nature of the process is documented in William Hinton's classic account of land reform in a North China village, *Fanshen* (1965). In much of China, however, especially in South and Central China where land reform took place relatively late, the reform did not take place in an "ideal" fashion. Perhaps under pressure to complete the process quickly, the work teams themselves assumed much of the authority for the process of redistribution. To the extent that this was so, land reform was experienced as an initiative from above. In either event, however, the social authority of the landlord class was destroyed along with the removal of its excess landholdings—landlords were entitled to equal per capita holdings after the reform but typically received worse land and were sometimes subject to mass punishment for past misbehavior when emotions were aroused in village meetings—and the former elite was never in a position even to attempt to restore its preferential position.

The land reform was followed by a series of institutional reforms intended to demonstrate to the peasants the advantages of collective farming. The Chinese leadership was aware of the disastrous consequences of forced collectivization in the Soviet Union and determined to proceed with caution. They felt that as the peasants became aware of the benefits they could gain through collective effort—Mao once indicated that at least 90 percent of the peasants should experience an improvement in income when they joined a collective (Mao 1974, 50)—and as the industrial sector of the economy increased its capacity to supply agricultural inputs, the level of collectivization could gradually be increased.

Thus when the land reform was completed, the formation of mutual aid teams was widely promoted. Based on traditional cooperative practices among the peasantry, these teams of seven or eight households were organized on either a seasonal or year-round basis. They would work on one another's land by turns, and while the individual households would retain ownership of smaller implements and tools, larger, more expensive items would often be purchased and owned in common. By 1954, 58 percent of China's farm households had joined mutual aid teams (Selden 1982, 55).

The next step up the cooperation ladder was the elementary agricultural producers' cooperative (APC). These were composed of about thirty households comprising a hamlet or natural village, with considerable variability in size. The land in the elementary APCs was pooled and worked collectively, but individual ownership titles were retained. When accounts were settled at the end of the year, funds would first be set aside for tax payments, costs of production, and other collective expenses. The remaining net income would be divided among the members on the basis of their land and labor contributions, with about half going to labor and half to the owners of land. The proportion of farm households belonging to elementary APCs increased from 14 percent in June 1955 to 59 percent in December of the same year (Selden 1982, 55).

This jump represented a dramatic shift in the approach to collectivization in China. As I have indicated, collectivization policy had been predicated on two key assumptions: the need to gain the support of the peasantry by demonstrating its financial benefits on the one hand, and the need to develop industry sufficiently to realize the potential productivity advantages of collective agriculture on the other. This approach mandated a gradual collectivization effort proceeding over many years. In the summer of 1955, however, Mao made a famous speech (Walker 1966) denouncing the gradualist approach and criticizing the cadres who followed it as tottering after the demands of the masses like old women with bound feet.

Mao argued that the masses were demanding more rapid collectivization and that tendencies toward the reemergence of class distinctions were becoming manifest. In both instances he seems to have relied on highly selective information—more broad-based national data do not bear out his contentions (Selden 1982; Friedman 1982). Perhaps of greater practical and theoretical significance is Mao's contention that changing the relations of production through more rapid collectivization could itself provide the material basis for agricultural development. The more conventional Marxist view, which had prevailed up to that point, maintained that the level of development of the forces of production would govern the appropriate organizational form for the agricultural sector. That is to say, only when industry had developed to a point at which it could provide the inputs to give a decisive productivity advantage to large-scale collective farming should such units be made the dominant form of agricultural organization.

Mao took this argument and stood it on its head. He maintained that collective organization in itself could become the motive force for agricultural development even though industrial development was still in its early stages (Mao 1974, 269). Among its other advantages, collective organization would make possible labor-intensive capital construction projects during the off-season—these subsequently indeed became a hallmark of Chinese agricultural development—and make the level of accumulation subject to greater social control. Although Mao ''won'' the argument, the issue was decided not on rational grounds but on the basis of the relative political strength of the contending advocates. When Mao swung his immense prestige as leader of the revolution in favor of accelerated collectivization, great pressure was placed on the cadres, and the force of his position among the party leaders became irresistible.

The summer of 1955 marks a turning point not only in agricultural policy but indeed in the entire character of the Chinese approach to economic development. On the one hand stood the majority of the party leaders advocating a "rationalistic," pragmatic approach to development, including the use of material incentives (mixed with moral appeals), an emphasis on the development of expertise, and a cautious approach to collectivization. On the other side stood Mao, with a stronger vision of the unique possibilities of socialist society, a belief in the almost limitless possibilities of collective mass action, confidence that moral incentives were superior to material ones in motivating action, and a commitment to egalitarianism.

The tension between these contending world views was to remain until Mao's death in September 1976, but for the most part the intervening years were marked by the ascendancy of Mao's position, which was most thorough during the Great Leap Forward period (1958-60) and the Cultural Revolution decade (1966-76). After Mao's death and especially from 1978, however, the pragmatists regained control under Deng Xiaoping, whose famous dictum "I don't care whether a cat is black or white as long as it catches mice" symbolizes the dramatic policy reversals that have marked the post-Mao era.

From 1955, however, accelerated collectivization marked the rising ascendancy of the "Maoist" approach to economic development. As I have indicated, 45 percent of the rural households joined elementary APCs between June and December 1955, bringing total membership to 59 percent by the end of the year. In the following year, however, the elementary APCs were superseded by advanced APCs, whose membership rose from 4 percent of rural households in December 1955 to 51 percent in February 1956 and 88 percent in December 1956 (Selden 1982, 55). Clearly the principle of voluntary participation had been bent as the cadres transferred to the peasantry the pressures to increase participation which they themselves experienced.

The advanced APCs were distinguished from the elementary APCS largely by their greater size and the elimination of private ownership claims to the land. Averaging about 200 households, the typical advanced APC incorporated some six or seven elementary APCs, although there was considerable variation about the mean. Further, with the elimination of private claims to the land, the entire net product of the advanced APCS—after costs of production, taxes, collective social expenditures, and funds for accumulation were set aside from gross revenues—was available for distribution to the membership on the basis of labor contributed to the collectivity. In this sense the advanced APCs are regarded as fully socialist, as compared to the "semisocialist" elementary APCs.

In the winter of 1957–58, a major effort was made to utilize agriculture's off-season surplus labor in water conservancy projects, including especially the construction of dams and irrigation works. Many of these projects were organized on a large scale, requiring the cooperation of a number of advanced APCs. Further, in the spring of 1958, the movement to construct "backyard steel furnaces" swept through rural China, with some tens of thousands of small furnaces constructed. The steel made subsequently proved too brittle for use—it snapped when subject to cold or stress—but the regime maintained that the learning experience had been a valuable one for a still largely traditional peasantry. In any event, the new activities required more extensive formal organization in the countryside. The first people's commune was set up in April 1958, and when Mao declared his approval following an inspection visit, the entire countryside was rapidly organized into communes. By August, 30 percent of rural households were members, with the proportion increasing to 98 percent the following month. This institutional reorganization took place, for the most part, after a bumper harvest for 1958 was essentially assured.

The communes initially averaged about 25,000 members or slightly more than 5,000 households; thus each incorporated an average of some 25 advanced APCs. They were organized initially at three distinct levels: production teams (usually corresponding to the earlier elementary APCs), production brigades (usually corresponding to the earlier advanced APCs), and the commune level. Subsequently, the household too became a distinct level, with each level becoming a distinct unit of account and responsible for carrying out its own specified activities.

Initially, responsibility and authority were concentrated at the commune level, reflecting the fact that the communes were, in essence, institutions imposed from above. Income distribution too—based in part on labor contribution and in part on "need"—was carried out initially at the commune level. In many cases even food was provided free in communal dining halls, and since food accounted for well over half of the typical rural family's consumption, there was little material inducement to work for the collectivity.

Further, the rapidity of the move to communization precluded an opportunity to identify and correct problem areas. Thus, for example, there was a severe shortage of people with adequate accounting or bookkeeping skills. Individuals could never be sure that they would be fairly credited with the labor contributions they made, or that villagers some distance away would not receive excessive credits. Even if the record-keeping were adequate, moreover, individuals could never be sure that there would be any net product at all available for distribution at the end of the year; it would be quite possible to work hard and conscientiously for an entire year and receive nothing in return. In short, by removing the connection between work effort and reward almost entirely, the communes in their initial form minimized material incentives to an extreme degree.

The problems this created were compounded by the unrealistic industrial production expectations for the communes. Although the backyard steel furnaces were largely abandoned by the time the communes were established, the communes were still expected to be the vehicle for the industrialization of the countryside—this indeed they have proved to be, but over a period of decades, not the few years initially anticipated. In many cases the industrial activities were not well planned out and yielded little of value. Often the men were transferred to these new activities with the women taking over an increasing proportion of the farm work, and the rural transportation system, inadequate in any event, was overloaded carrying coal and raw materials for the new small industries while agricultural supplies could not be delivered in timely fashion or at all, and while harvested food often rotted for lack of adequate transport.

Eventually, the development of rural industry became a hallmark of Chinese development and an extremely successful way of circumventing the urban-rural and intra-rural class polarizations that characterize capitalist development. In its initial stages, however, carried out without proper experimentation or understanding of the opportunity costs it imposed in lost agricultural output, rural industrialization contributed to the economic crisis that struck the Chinese countryside between 1959 and 1961. The regime blamed the precipitous decline in agricultural production during these three years (see table 7.2) on unprecedently unfavorable climatic conditions, but it is clear that the adventurism of its own policy—reorganizing the countryside on a massive scale and imposing new demands on it simultaneously without adequate experi-

Table 7.2

Fall in Agricultural Production Associated with the Great Leap Forward (million tons)

Year	Grain	Oilseeds	Cotton	Sugarcane
1957	195	4.2	1.6	10.4
1958	200	4.8	2.0	12.6
1959	170	4.1	1.7	9.0
1960	143.5	1.9	1.1	8.3
1961	147.5	1.8	0.8	4.3
1962	160	2.0	0.8	3.4
1963	170	2.5	1.2	7.8
1964	187.5	3.4	1.7	12.2
1965	194.5	3.6	2.1	13.4

Source: U.S. Department of Agriculture (1982, 36).

Note: The Great Leap Forward took place from 1958 to 1960. The collapse in agricultural output generally lagged about one year.

mentation, preparation, or analysis—was primarily to blame.

The problems with the communes proved for the most part to be organizational and administrative rather than conceptual. That is to say, the commune as an institution had a definite potential for contributing to rural development in China, a potential which was to a considerable extent realized. The government responded to the problems of the early communes by (1) increasing their number and reducing their size, (2) decentralizing the level of distribution from the commune first to the production brigade and then to the production team, (3) eliminating most free goods and services and restoring material incentives, and (4) relaxing the mobilization thrust from above and creating greater leeway for individual initiative, including the restoration of private plots which the peasants were free to use as they saw fit. The 1961–65 recovery period was by and large one in which the Maoist approach to development was temporarily eclipsed by the ascendancy the pragmatists gained after the collapse of the Great Leap Forward. Indeed, the Cultural Revolution was launched in 1966 as a response to this situation; having lost control of the party machinery, Mao turned to students and young people to return China to what he believed to be the socialist track.

In the period of relaxation, the commune emerged as a viable socio-economic institution, and by 1980 China had some 54,000 communes

(Xue 1982, 392) averaging some 15,000 members each—virtually the entire countryside was organized into communes. Accounting and bookkeeping skills were strengthened, and each level of the commune came to have fairly clearly defined responsibilities and privileges, including the household level. Formed by merging local township governments with advanced APCs, the communes had from the first a political dimension, and indeed they emerged as multifunctional economic, social, and political organizations responsible for everyday farming, rural capital construction and industrial development, education, health, cultural affairs, public security, and the full range of affairs for which local government is normally responsible.

The production team was responsible for the everyday farming and was normally the level of income distribution. Ideally, the team would use 25–30 percent of its gross receipts for costs of production, about 5 percent would be set aside for taxes (which declined over time as a proportion of output since tax increases were deliberately limited even as output grew), 2–3 percent would be set aside for welfare (to support the handicapped or elderly), and 7–10 percent for investment (Lippit 1977). This would leave about 55 percent of gross receipts to be distributed among the members on the basis of their labor contribution. Commonly, each task would be assigned a specific number of workday credits—say two workdays for plowing a field—and satisfactory completion of the task (regardless of the time actually used) would earn the peasant the prescribed number of credits. The value of each credit would be determined at the end of the year by dividing the total number of credits earned into the funds available for distribution.

The household could earn additional income through its use of the private plots, which were set at a maximum 5–7 percent of the commune's land area (this was increased to 15 percent in 1981). Ideally, the household could grow what it wanted on the private plots and sell its output or consume it itself. In practice, public policy toward the private plots fluctuated widely, and peasants were often told what to plant or even forced to turn the plots over for collective cultivation. By and large, the pragmatists advocated maximum leeway for individual use while the Maoists, regarding the private plots as a "tail of capitalism," sought to restrict peasant use of them.

The production brigade, composed of about eight teams on average (there were 710,000 brigades and 5.66 million teams at the end of 1980; Xue 1982, 392), was responsible for small-scale industrial and capital construction projects (including local roads, the construction of small dams for irrigation and power generation, and so forth). It would typically run an elementary school and operate a clinic. By 1982, about 5 percent of the brigades replaced the team as the unit of account and income distribution, down from 10 percent during the Cultural Revolution (Griffin 1984, 26). The commune level, composed of about thirteen brigades on average, carried out most of the political-administrative functions and was responsible as well for larger scale capital construction and industrial projects. The commune level was also typically responsible for operating secondary schools and hospitals. Its cadres were appointed by the state, and it was charged with carrying out national economic plans insofar as these bore on the agricultural sector. As the discussion of the reforms will indicate, however, township governments have been reestablished throughout the countryside and the political functions of the communes transferred to them. Since the commune and brigade enterprises were also split off, the communes rapidly became empty shells in the countryside, and in 1985 they were formally abolished. Understanding of the commune system, however, remains critical to an understanding of agricultural development in China, and of the new institutional structure that is emerging in the countryside.

   The Cultural Revolution, whose active phase lasted from 1966 to 1969 but whose characteristic thrust marked the Chinese economy and society for a decade, brought some important changes to the communes but by and large witnessed their continued consolidation. "In agriculture, learn from Dazhai" became a popular slogan, and indeed cadres everywhere were exhorted to apply the lessons of Dazhai. Dazhai was a poor production brigade in North China, with much of its limited land area suffering from erosion and subject to drought. Under the dynamic leadership of Chen Yonggui, who later became a member of the CCP Central Committee and then a vice-premier until Dazhai's fall from favor, the brigade members succeeded in raising their incomes dramatically. Using the winter off-season to terrace the eroded hillsides and build various water conservancy projects, and working collectively and (we are told) selflessly for the good of the community, the individual families prospered. The lesson of Dazhai was that no matter how harsh the obstacles confronted, stress on the power of the collectivity, self-reliance, and the right political attitude (working selflessly for the common good rather than selfishly for personal gain) would be able to overcome them. The peasants of Dazhai, of course, relinquished their private plots to collective cultivation.

One of the important models Dazhai provided for the commune system lay in the sphere of income distribution. The system of assigning points to specific tasks, it was argued, prompted selfish behavior and overlooked the real if not precisely quantifiable contributions of many members. Thus someone who plowed a field lightly and failed to take proper care of the animals and farm implements would be in a position to earn more work credits than someone who conscientiously took time to care for them. Or an older peasant who might no longer be strong physically but who took great pains to instruct young people in proper farm practice would not have his contribution registered. The Dazhai solution was to have the team members, through a process of mutual assessment, assign one another a certain number of points—usually ranging from six to ten—based on the team members' perception of each individual's contribution to their productive activity. The two most important criteria were typically the amount of work accomplished and political quality; the latter was expressed in conscientiousness, promptness, helping others, and so forth. The number of points assigned each individual would be multiplied by the number of days he or she worked for the collectivity to determine total workpoints for the year. Reassessment of individual ratings would take place periodically, giving members an opportunity and incentive to improve their performance. During the Cultural Revolution decade, variants of this distribution system spread widely in the Chinese countryside. Over time, however, the difference between the highest and lowest ratings tended to narrow drastically, creating a distributional pattern that has been described as an inverted pyramid, with most workers receiving the maximum number of points or just below the maximum (see, for example, Unger 1985a; Lee 1984, 137–38). In the post-Mao reform period, it was observed that this distributional system in effect offered no rewards for the most productive, thereby limiting incentives.

The unique institutional structure developed in postrevolutionary China clearly has a direct bearing on the class character of Chinese development, and in particular on the extent to which it is responsive to the needs of the peasantry and to their class authority. To analyze this character fully, however, several additional issues must first be addressed. Did the new institutional structure create conditions favorable for agricultural development in general and for socialist agricultural development in particular? Insofar as these were favorable, to what extent was the potentiality for agricultural development realized? By addressing questions such as these, I hope to show both the successes and failures of socialist economic development in China, and to clarify the factors underlying the far-ranging agricultural reforms that have taken place since 1978.

Agricultural Performance

From 1952 to 1978, grain output increased an average of 2.4 percent yearly and (gross) agricultural output as a whole by 3.2 percent yearly (State Statistical Bureau 1979, 1–2). At one level of analysis, this performance is quite creditable. Japan's agricultural development during the Meiji era (1868–1912), for example, is often cited as a model for other Asian nations, but the rate of growth in Japan's net agricultural output from the 1870s to the 1900s was only 1.7 percent (Lippit 1978, 78), compared to 2.5 percent for China from 1952 to 1973 (Ashbrook 1975, 23). Further, China's output gains came in the face of virtually no net change in agricultural land area; that is, they reflect almost in their entirety gains in land productivity.

From another perspective, however, China's agricultural performance in the 1952–78 period was less successful. During this period, population grew slightly faster than 2 percent per year, so the growth in grain output exceeded population growth by only a small margin; after 1957–58, in fact, grain output per capita declined rather precipitously (see table 7.2) and, despite subsequent recovery, did not return to the 1957 level until 1975 (see table 7.1); per capita output actually slipped below the 1957 level in 1977, and it was not until 1978 that a higher level was maintained (State Statistical Bureau 1984, 167). The poor performance in the grain sector must be assessed in the light of the fact that grain production was given such high priority in agricultural planning that even communes whose natural conditions were unsuited to grain cultivation were forced to grow grain. The emphasis on grain production in China came at the expense of a diversified agricultural development.

Overall, the limited per capita output gains in the agricultural sector must also be assessed in the light of the greatly expanded labor and material inputs the sector received, and of the institutional reforms that might have been expected to facilitate raising productivity. The collectivization of agriculture culminating in the emergence of the people's communes in 1958 systematized rural accumulation, made possible the mobilization of tens of millions of people during the off-season for work on irrigation and other capital construction projects, opened the

door to rational land-use planning, contributed to agricultural mechanization, and facilitated the spread of new technologies. The increase in
labor inputs reflects the growth of the agricultural labor force by about
100 million workers (Rawski 1979b, 125) between 1957 and 1975, and
an increase in the average number of labor days worked per year by
well over 25 percent between the early 1950s and the mid–1970s (Lippit 1982, 126–27).

Between the late 1950s and the late 1970s, moreover, a dramatic
increase in the supply of agricultural producer goods took place. Where
the 1957 supply level index is taken as 100, for example, by 1975 the
index had reached 40,672 for the total horsepower of agricultural
machinery, 13,079 for electricity consumed in rural areas (excluding
consumption by state-owned units), and 1,630 for chemical fertilizer
consumption per hectare of cultivated land (see table 7.3). While the
increases in these indices reflect the very low initial levels of agricultural inputs in China, by the 1970s the absolute levels of the inputs were
becoming quite substantial.

To provide some sense of the relative position of China's agriculture, China's chemical fertilizer consumption per hectare of arable
land, which reached 53.8 kg in 1975 and 109.2 kg in 1979, might be
compared with the 1954–55 consumption of 72.5 kg in France and
219.3 kg in Japan (Ogura 1970, 366). Despite the massive increases in
material inputs—indicated in table 7.3—and in labor, however, and
despite the institutional reforms apparently conducive to agricultural
development, the gains in output proved to be modest. According to the
estimate of Thomas Rawski (1979a, 776–77), the output per hour
worked in agriculture fell between 15 and 36 percent in the 1957–75
period even though total output grew with the increase in the labor force
and the number of hours worked.

As a counterpart to the poor labor productivity record in Chinese
agriculture, rising costs of production and pressure on peasant living
standards might be anticipated, and indeed the available empirical
materials bear out this expectation. According to a 1978 article by Yao
Lanfu in *Jingji yanjiu* (Economic Research), a survey of 2,162 production brigades showed that between 1956 and 1972 "the yield of
grains increased from 1,740 to 2,370 kilograms per hectare. Production increased by 36 percent, but production costs, excluding
labor, increased from 39.3 to 60.8 percent of the value of the grain.
This was a 54 percent increase. As a result, the net agricultural income declined, the average distribution per work day going down

Table 7.3

Agricultural Modernization

Item	Unit	1952	1957	1965	1975	1979
Total horsepower of agric. machinery	10,000 hp	25	165	1,494	10,168	18,191
Actual tractor-ploughed area	10,000 ha	14	264	1,578	3,320	4,222
as percent of total cultivated land	%	0.1	2.4	15.0	33.3	42.4
Irrigated area	10,000 ha	1,996	2,734	3,306	4,328	4,500
as percent of total cultivated land	%	18.5	24.4	31.9	43.4	45.2
Power-irrigated area	10,000 ha	32	120	809	2,289	2,532
as percent of total irrigated area	%	1.6	4.4	24.5	52.9	56.3
Consumption of chemical fertilizer	10,000 tons	8	37	194	537	1,086
per hectare of cultivated land	kg	0.7	3.3	18.7	5.8	109.2
Small-size rural hydroelec. stations generating capacity		98	544	na	68,158	83,224
	10,000 kw	0.8	2.0	na	144.4	276.3
Electricity consumed in rural areas[a]	100 mil. kwh	1.4	37.1	183.1	282.7	
per hectare of cultivated land	kwh	1.3	35.8	183.6	284.1	

Source: Xue (1982, 970).

a. Excludes electricity consumed by state-owned units in rural areas.

20 percent'' (cited in Kojima 1982, 250).

Ishikawa (1982, 115) cites the results of another survey of 1,296 production teams in twenty-two provinces carried out jointly by the State Statistical Bureau, the Bureau of Prices, and the ministries of Commerce, Food, and Agriculture in 1976. According to this survey, the average cost of grain production plus agricultural tax per 100 kilograms was 23.2 yuan and the average procurement price 21.5 yuan, leading to a loss per 100 kilograms of 1.7 yuan. The cost includes an imputed value for labor, so what the results actually reflect is a decrease in the value of the workday. In the teams surveyed, the grain yield per hectare increased between 1962 and 1976 by 1,365 kilograms and the value of output per hectare increased by 249.15 yuan, but the production cost, including the imputed value of labor, increased by 304.95 yuan.

The problem of rising production costs in Chinese agriculture prior to the reform period is clear, and the pressure it put on peasant living standards is reflected in the stagnation in peasant incomes (Lippit 1982) and the high proportion of "poor" production brigades, those with collective incomes less than 50 yuan per capita; such brigades constituted 42.8 percent of the total in 1976 (Selden and Lippit, 1982, 27). Between 1957 and 1975, real peasant per capita consumption rose by only 22.2 percent (Xue 1982, 985); this was not a very substantial increase in light of the extremely low initial levels and was heavily skewed toward suburban communes.

The economic plight of the peasants would have been harsher still were it not for the improving terms of trade with the industrial sector since the early 1950s. This improvement, however, must be qualified by recognition of the fact that the initially established terms were so highly unfavorable to agriculture that all the improvement to date has not overcome the initial disadvantage, and by the growing input requirements per unit of output (see chapter 8). It should also be noted that the basis for the official terms of trade index has not been made public, and there is reason to believe that it excludes agricultural producer goods, making its usefulness doubtful (Lardy 1983, 111). In any event, as late as the mid–1970s large parts of rural China were producing little more than their food requirements, and some 100 million people (out of an 800 million rural total), dependent on government subsidies of grain recycled from more prosperous areas, were not even doing that (*Renmin ribao*, Nov. 1, 1980).

If socialist agricultural development is characterized by its responsiveness to the class interests of those who toil in the countryside, then the limited gains in peasant living standards between the late 1950s and the late 1970s must be regarded as a deviation from the standards of socialist development. Furthermore, since favorable conditions for agricultural development and rising peasant prosperity should have been created with the advent of the commune system and the substantial increase in material and labor inputs that accompanied it, the failure of production to respond commensurately requires an explanation. This appears to be provided by two factors especially.

First, the commune as an institution had a dual nature. It was a collective organization belonging to its members, but at the same time it was an organ of state power, responsible for making local behavior accord with state and party edicts. Since the commune leaders were appointed by the party and state—although commune members or their representatives could, in principle, vote to oust them after a period of time if their behavior was unsatisfactory—they were naturally most responsive to their senior authorities in the political hierarchy. The consequence of this was that commune members tended to feel—with good reason—that the commune was not their own organization, that it was not responsive to their own needs and interests. From an efficiency standpoint, moreover, the planning proved to be quite poor, as reflected in the inattentiveness to incentives and the sacrifice of regional comparative advantage with the insistence that grain be grown everywhere.

Second, the organizational form of the commune, that is, the relations of production it established, appears in much of China to have been unsuited to the level of development of the socially productive forces. Analysis of these two points should help to clarify the reasons underlying the recent attempts at agrarian institutional reform, and they are taken up in the concluding section of this chapter. Here it should simply be noted that China's success in raising land productivity, which was certainly the priority condition for providing basic food security in the countryside, must be balanced against the failure to raise labor productivity, and that that failure can be traced in part to the violation of the conditions for socialist development in agriculture. This can be clarified by consideration of the full range of socialist development characteristics in the agricultural sector.

Socialist Agricultural Development

Socialist agricultural development, like socialist economic development in general, is characterized by its class orientation. It refers to rural development carried out by and in the interests of the peasantry. This general proposition must be made operational before it can be applied to any particular case study. To do so, I would suggest eight principal features that taken together help to distinguish socialist from capitalist and statist agricultural development. These are: (1) subsistence security, (2) income growth, (3) avoiding reliance on export markets, (4) full employment, (5) basic needs provision, including education and health, (6) rural industrialization and development, (7) equality, and (8) control by the peasantry over their lives and institutions.

Although some of these conditions are more clearly inconsistent with the dictates of capitalist development than others, the very nature of capitalist society tends to preclude the full realization of any of them. With one evident exception, these conditions are more consistent with statist development, especially because the interests of the dominant bureaucratic class will be served by a quiescent peasantry whose basic needs are met by the system. The obvious exception is point (8), since control by the peasantry over their own lives and institutions cannot under any circumstance be reconciled with bureaucratic control. One additional qualification concerning the ability of statist development to meet these conditions is in order. The bureaucratic interest in industrialization and building up the power of the state may deprive the agricultural sector of sufficient resources to meet some of these conditions fully, a problem which is likely to be intensified (by weaker economic performance) if administrative orders rather than economic forces govern resource allocation in the countryside.

In the socialist development model, all eight conditions are most likely to be fulfilled since they are consistent with the class interests of the peasants, who (by definition), together with other working people, form the dominant class. Thus, their degree of realization in any particular country can serve as a benchmark in evaluating its success in carrying out socialist agricultural development. Looking at rural development in China from this perspective, it is clear that it must be located between the socialist and statist models. As the following discussion will show, China's rural development has satisfied most of these conditions. In two of the areas, however, extreme deficiencies were clearly in evidence at the end of the Maoist era. These deficiencies, so serious as to preclude the transition to socialism had they remained uncorrected, account in part for the agricultural reform movement that has swept China in the post-Mao period. A brief examination of each of the eight areas in turn can clarify this assessment.

(1) *Subsistence security.* In very poor countries, subsistence security is usually the highest priority among the peasantry. By organizing the entire countryside into communes, the Chinese government was able to provide a safety net for everyone, expressed in the form of the famous "five guarantees": food, clothing, housing, medical care, and burial expenses. Operationally, the welfare funds set aside from gross receipts at the production team level usually serve to secure the members of those households with limited labor power, but ultimately, as when general crop failure hits a region in response to a natural disaster, the national government stands behind the guarantees. Thus in the mid-

seventies, as noted, the government was supplementing the food supplies of 100 million peasants unable to grow enough to feed themselves. In taking responsibility for assuring this most basic need of the peasants, the government was satisfying one condition for socialist rural development.

(2) Income growth. In capitalist countries, early development is often characterized by increased concentration of landholdings and its counterpart landlessness, tenants are forced off the land to become laborers or urban slum dwellers, common land is appropriated, and the mass of the rural population is deprived of access to land. In short, any gains in productivity that may take place tend to benefit the owners of land and capital primarily. Where conditions are favorable, many of the peasants may benefit as well, but such benefit is fortuitous and not the rule. Thus, the International Labour Office study of seven capitalist Asian countries cited above (1977, 9–15) found the countryside of all of them to be characterized by increasing inequality and stagnant or declining real income of the rural poor.

In socialist countries, with their different class structure, one might expect high priority to be accorded to raising peasant incomes, especially those of the poor. As noted, however, incomes in the Chinese countryside rose by only nominal amounts over a prolonged period of time. This was not inevitable—it was the outcome of a consciously chosen development strategy that placed low priority on raising disposable peasant incomes (a strategy, we may well imagine, which the peasants themselves played little part in formulating). The key elements of this strategy included minimizing material incentives, extracting the surplus from the countryside to support industrialization by maintaining unfavorable terms of trade with the industrial sector, emphasizing the production of capital goods rather than consumer goods in the industrial sector and reliance for raising agricultural output on planning directives from above, requiring the peasants to purchase increased material inputs, and requiring them to provide unpaid or low-paid labor in rural capital construction.

Radical rhetoric notwithstanding, this strategy discouraged peasant initiative. We can legitimately maintain that to the extent it was imposed on the countryside while alternatives more conducive to improving real incomes existed—as was indeed the case in China (to a certain extent, the entire reform movement and the spectacular gains in peasant real incomes it has brought about bear witness to this)—China's development strategy deviated from the socialist principle of according priority to the interests of the producing classes. In the agricultural sector, as in Chinese society generally, the party-state's monopolization of authority was characteristic more of the statist model than of the socialist one.

(3) Avoiding reliance on export markets. During the course of the twentieth century, the world economy has become increasingly integrated as a consequence of the development of capitalism on a world scale. It has become virtually impossible for any nation to develop completely outside the capitalist world system, and those countries that have attempted to do so—such as Albania and Burma—can hardly be considered exemplary development models. Nevertheless, varying degrees of involvement are possible, and any nation that becomes too deeply involved is, in effect, turning control over its own development process over to forces it is powerless to influence. As a consequence of the Great Depression, for example, silk and cocoa prices (among others) dropped precipitously, ruining the peasantries of Japan and (what is now) Ghana respectively. In the contemporary world, the advanced capitalist countries continue to import highly fluctuating quantities of agricultural products for which they pay highly fluctuating prices. Any strategy for agricultural development that relies primarily on export markets over the long run (there may be no alternatives in the short run) is violating the principles of socialist development. China, clearly, does not fall into this category and could extend its recent opening to the outside world considerably without losing control over its own development process. Self-reliance has been a hallmark of Chinese development.

(4) Full employment. Unemployment and underemployment are characteristic of capitalist third world countries and have been increasing over time (Todaro 1977). In a socialist country, where working people form the dominant class, such a situation is obviously intolerable. In China, the institution of the commune combined with restrictions on urban migration has effectively enabled the nation to avoid it. In capitalist countries, people will be hired only if capitalists or landowners find it profitable to hire them. For the commune, the situation is quite different. The members' subsistence requirements are a charge against its net earnings whether or not they work, so that as long as there is anything useful at all to be done, even though the marginal product of labor is quite low, it would be irrational to leave them idle.

In fact, not only has the rural population been fully employed (we are not maintaining here that they were efficiently employed), Chinese policy has made the nation's enormous manpower potential a key element in its development strategy. In Ragnar Nurkse's classic study, *Capital Formation in Underdeveloped Countries* (1964), the author focuses on the possibility of using what otherwise would be surplus labor—in the countryside especially—as a hidden resource for capital formation, one which would involve in the pure case no social opportunity cost at all since the workers could be newly employed on capital construction projects without sacrificing agricultural production. Doubts have been raised about whether there is such a thing as surplus labor on a year-round basis (Schultz 1964), but there is no question about its presence on a seasonal basis in prerevolutionary China (Buck 1968) or in most third world countries today. Whereas there is no mechanism in capitalist third world countries for employing such surplus labor on a substantial scale, however, China has been able to do so with great success, regularly mobilizing some tens of millions—the figure reached over one hundred million annually from 1970 to 1976— for winter work on such capital construction projects as dam construction, irrigation and drainage, road construction, afforestation, and terracing of fields.

One qualification must be made in this analysis. Maoist rhetoric notwithstanding, rural development in China relied to a considerable extent on orders and plans emanating from higher authority. This approach sacrificed the contribution that initiative on the household or small-group level might have made, and it is ultimately the main factor underlying the poor labor productivity record. It meant that much of the work accomplished was at an extremely low level of labor productivity, creating the possibility that further institutional change could uncover new sources of surplus or underutilized labor. As the discussion of the reform movement in the following chapter will show, this was indeed the case. Overall, however, China's record in handling its monumental employment problems must be evaluated highly, and it is consistent with the socialist agricultural development model.

(5) Basic needs provision, including education and health. In any country where the working classes predominate, the provision of basic needs can be expected to be accorded a high priority. This has certainly been the case in China, where in addition to the "five guarantees" there have been striking increases in school enrollments and improvements in medical care. Table 7.4 compares China to India, Pakistan, low-income countries excluding China and India, and middle-income countries. Comparisons between India and China are commonplace,

but India's lower per capita income may make the Chinese figures appear unduly favorable, so Pakistan, which has a higher per capita income, has been included as well. Table 7.4 indicates that for the significant social indicators listed there, China's figures are on a par with and typically superior to the middle-income countries as a group, countries whose per capita incomes average almost five times that of China. Since more than 80 percent of China's population is rural, moreover, China's national averages indicated in the table reflect the high level of basic needs satisfaction in the countryside.

Today elementary school attendance is almost universal in the countryside and increasing numbers of students are going on to middle and higher schools. But what is most impressive in the provision of basic needs is the extension of medical care to the countryside in a manner unprecedented among comparably low income countries.

In the 1960s and '70s, the rural medical care system started with the so-called barefoot doctors, who appeared in China at the start of the Cultural Revolution, when national attention was called to the relative neglect the peasants had suffered. The barefoot doctors were sometimes present at urban work centers as well, but they played a much more characteristic role in the countryside, where they were selected by fellow team members for an initial period of paramedical training, usually for about six months. When they returned to their production teams, they were equipped with important public health information (such as how to sanitize night soil), information on birth control, and the ability to treat simple ailments. They typically returned to production work together with other team members (hence the name "barefoot doctors") but remained available for assistance whenever emergencies arose.

When ailments were beyond their ability to treat, the barefoot doctors could direct fellow team members to a higher level in the commune health care system—the brigade clinic or commune hospital—whose personnel could in turn send patients to county or higher level hospitals when ailments were beyond their capacity to treat. In this way the peasants were integrated into a comprehensive medical care system for treatment even while great emphasis was placed on preventive medicine through vigorous public health measures. The cost of all this to individual peasants was nominal—typically about one yuan (U.S. thirty-five cents) per year, with most of the costs being shared by the various collective levels and the state.

In the mid–1980s, the growth in medical skills and in the financial

Table 7.4

Demographic and Social Indicators, China and Comparison Countries

	China	India	Pakistan	Low-income economies[a]	Middle-income economies
GNP per capita (1982 $)	310	260	380	250	1,520
Population growth rate, percent (1970-1982)	1.4	2.3	3.0	2.9	2.4
Crude birth rate per thousand (1982)	19	34	42	44	35
Crude death rate per thousand (1982)	7	13	15	16	10
Infant mortality rate per thousand (1982)	67	94	121	114	76
Life expectancy at birth, 1982 (years)	67	55	50	51	60
Daily calorie supply as percent of requirement	107	86	106	91	111
Secondary school enrollment, 1981 (percent of age group)	44	30	17	19	41

Source: World Bank (1984) "World Development Indicators."

a. Excluding China and India.

resources of Chinese society brought the barefoot doctor era to a close. It was replaced by a system that stressed greater professionalism, including more extensive formal training and full-time status for the health care workers who received it. Still, the health care system maintained deep roots in the countryside. Thus, highlighted by the medical care system, the extension of education, and the five guarantees, Chinese peasants have enjoyed guarantees of basic needs that are consistent with the socialist development model and far exceed what is provided their counterparts in countries with comparable per capita incomes that are pursuing capitalist economic development.

(6) Rural industrialization and development. The characteristic pattern of development in capitalist countries emphasizes urban development at the expense of the countryside. In cases where the latter "develops" as well, moreover, it is usually on the basis of increasingly capital-intensive "modern" farming, which displaces peasants from their usual activities and often bars them from the land altogether. Thus in countries as diverse as Mexico and Pakistan, the "green revolution" has concentrated the gains from increased productivity in a few hands,

leaving the mass of the peasantry in a state of continued or even worsening impoverishment. In capitalist countries, whether stagnation or modernization characterizes the countryside, development is commonly marked by massive migrations from rural to urban areas, swelling urban slums, or to foreign countries in search of employment.

A development pattern consistent with the interests of the peasant producers, to the contrary, requires what might be thought of as an "urbanization" of the countryside—the development of rural industries and the full gamut of urban amenities and employment opportunities. In this respect too, China's development experience stands as a model for socialist countries. The early disastrous experience with backyard steel furnaces and the small-scale enterprises of the Great Leap Forward notwithstanding, the development of relatively small-scale enterprises in the countryside ultimately proved to be highly successful. Steel could not be made successfully in the very small furnaces built in 1958, but it can be made in rural areas in plants much smaller than those currently used in the West. Such plants, which complement rather than displace larger ones, are now present in many of China's 2,300 counties, as are small-scale chemical fertilizer, cement, and agricultural machinery factories. In the mid–1970s, rural plants supplied more than half of China's chemical fertilizer and cement output, while small-scale hydroelectric power-generating stations contributed substantially to the widespread electrification of the countryside (see table 7.3). Enterprises that process agricultural products to provide consumer goods and others that serve as subcontractors for large state-owned firms have also flourished. The general principle of rural industrialization mandates making use of rural labor power without competing with urban industrial centers for resources; local resources are used that would be uneconomical for large-scale exploitation or whose transport costs would be too high for urban use.

The materials produced in the rural basic industries are earmarked for the most part for rural industrial development to serve the needs of the peasants. The farm tool and machinery industry as well as a variety of consumer goods industries have been actively developed in the countryside. Moreover, many suburban communes have developed thriving light industrial enterprises. Overall, in the early 1980s brigade- and commune-level rural industries employed some 31 million people—over 9 percent of the rural labor force—and accounted for about 13 percent of China's industrial output (BR, April 16, 1984, 7) and one-third of the collective income generated in the countryside

(Griffin 1984, 211). While precise data are lacking, long-term growth rates appear to be in the 10–15 percent range, accelerating to more than 20 percent in the early 1980s (Griffin 1984, 39, 211), and with their very high average profit rates, rural industries appear to account for the major portion of rural accumulation. By 1986, almost one peasant in five was not employed in agriculture, compared to the one in ten ratio that prevailed in 1980 (BR, July 14, 1986, 28).

William Hinton (1982), in his account of the current situation in Longbow Village, the poverty-stricken village whose land reform process he detailed in Fanshen, dramatizes the catalytic role of rural industrialization in transforming village life. Although the state had appropriated one-third of village land for (state-owned) industrial enterprises, the village received the (standard) value of three years' crops. It was able to benefit from this capital infusion as well as from the additional nightsoil provided by the large numbers of workers and their families, and the demand for fresh vegetables they provided (which made possible shifting some land from lower value grain crops to higher value vegetables).

> In the last few years Longbow has been remarkably successful both in farming and in industrial sidelines. Whereas in 1948 grain yields averaged less than 10 bushels to the acre, they now average 100. . . . With the capital derived in part from the transfer of the land . . . four thriving local industries have been built: a cement plant producing 15 to 20 tons of cement a day, a sawmill that saws 10,000 board feet a day, a woodworking shop that makes handles for saws, and a polishing shop that finishes steel blades for the Taihang Sawblade Works. These industries employ only 12 percent of the labor power of the village but bring in about 70 percent of the income.
>
> The returns from all enterprises, both agricultural and industrial, have underwritten not only a rising standard of living in terms of housing, clothing and food, but greatly expanded social services as well. Every child in Longbow now goes to the eight year school. Every family receives medical care under a cooperative plan that costs $.50 per person per year for doctors' services and provides drugs at one-half the market price. Everyone is entitled to a free bath every week and a haircut every month. Grain is ground for all at a central location at reasonable fees, and there is a library, a political night school, a drama group, and a large contingent of stiltwalkers—to mention but a few of the extracurricular activities. . . . What all this adds up to is a Longbow Village that is no longer rural. It is suburban, a community in transition from agriculture to industry where the way of life is undergoing not only socialization but

urbanization and industrialization all at the same time. This may not be a typical situation in the Chinese countryside, but it is something that is happening everywhere that industry is taking hold, and the process here may be taken as a symbol of the future of the nation. (pp. 100–101)

Thus the development of rural, small-scale industries has played a central role in China's integrated rural development strategy, and changes in the reform period appear to be accelerating that role. The contrast with capitalist-style development could not be more striking.

(7) Equality. With regard to equality as well, the Chinese record of rural development is clearly in accord with the requirements of socialist development. This is not to suggest that perfect equality was sought or attained—this is certainly not the case. However, beginning with the land reform, which eliminated the main source of class differentiation in rural China, and continuing through the various stages of collectivization which assured roughly equal access to material inputs as well as land, and which prevented the reemergence of a differentiated class structure based on unequal ownership of land and capital, the egalitarian thrust of Chinese policy has been unmistakable.

Differences have appeared among communes and regions based on locational advantages and differential growing conditions, but it is hard to see how public policy could have eliminated these without taking such thoroughly irrational measures as prohibiting suburban communes from industrial activity or from growing fruits and vegetables. Rather, public policy has sought to mitigate differentials by spreading development to smaller cities and subsidizing the development of less industrialized provinces (Lardy 1978). Further, the post-Mao reforms have been accompanied by the intensification of measures already in use to aid the lowest income production teams. Griffin (1984, 46–48) lists some of these measures, which include exemption in whole or part from the compulsory grain quota; negotiated prices—usually about twice the quota price—for grain delivered; interest-free or very low interest loans; preferential technical assistance and training; and prefectural and county grants for a variety of projects including (some) water projects, public utilities, schools, agricultural inputs, and directly productive activities. Based on a summer 1982 field study in rural China by seven people, Griffin reports that contrary to suggestions that the reform movement would intensify inequality, the limited findings of the research group found no tendency in that direction and some indication that differentials were narrowing.

What will happen over a period of time is of course subject to conjecture, but it is important to keep in mind that the transformation of the Chinese countryside during the reform period as earlier is by no means an uncontrolled process subject to "blind" market forces. To the contrary, while cadres have now been withdrawn from direct interference in production activities, they continue to be responsible for creating the institutional framework within which production activity proceeds (throughout rural China there are countless variations in the implementation of the reform program), and to be evaluated according to the extent to which their areas are successful both in economic terms and in meeting the other policy goals of the party, including equality.

During the Maoist era, policies to maintain equality by aiding the disadvantaged were supplemented by placing a lid on allowable peasant earnings. Removing that lid has indeed been a source of increased inequality in the reform period as a few entrepreneurially oriented peasants have proven enormously successful, raising their incomes in a few cases to well over 10,000 yuan per year. Against this, however, must be set the sharp decrease in the income gap between peasants and workers.

Among the most significant forms of inequality persisting in contemporary China is that between peasants and workers, who are perceived by the peasants as having a preferred class status. During the reform period, from 1978 to 1983, however, the per capita income of rural families nearly doubled in real terms to 310 yuan (in 1983 prices) while the per capita income of urban families rose 43 percent in real terms to 526 yuan (in 1983 prices; BR, Aug. 27, 1984). Thus per capita rural incomes rose from 42.4 percent of urban incomes in 1978 to 58.9 percent in 1983, marking a substantial improvement in equality between households in the two sectors.

Inequality is intrinsic to the capitalist accumulation process in its early stages, with profits growing faster than wages. Relative equality, by contrast, is in the class interest of those who work for a living, and as such must be one of the central social goals of socialist economic development. Looking at the Chinese development performance as a whole, including both the Maoist and post-Maoist periods, we can hardly fault the government for its commitment to the socialist standard of equality. Further, even during the reform period when the concepts of the "iron rice bowl" (having an assured income regardless of work effort and effectiveness) and "everyone eating from the same big pot" (everyone receiving the same income regardless of work effort and effectiveness) have come under attack, the basic commitment to relative equality in income and consumption has clearly remained undiminished.

(8) Peasant control over their lives and institutions. In capitalist societies, peasants are ultimately victims (occasionally, quite fortuitously, beneficiaries) of forces over which they have little or no control. The most fundamental characteristic of socialist society, by contrast, is the opportunity it affords the direct producers to determine the contours of their own productive activity, living conditions, and ultimately society itself. It is evident that this cannot always be done directly—chaos would result. Class representatives, therefore, must assume a certain degree of authority and initiative in leadership.

At the same time, however, it is always possible for such representatives to arrogate to themselves an excess of authority and to represent ideas or interests, including class interests, quite distinct from those of the peasantry. In the extreme case, as when a bureaucratic class uses its access to the power and resources of the state to pursue its own interests, the ''representatives'' may come to be a dominating force over the peasantry, in clear contradiction to the requirements of socialist development. In any state where the prerequisite for socialism has been established by instituting public ownership of the means of production as the primary ownership form, therefore, the ensuing period of socialist transition is marked by a tension between the need for representation and leadership on the one hand, and the possibility on the other that such representation and leadership may be turned into a force inimical to the interest of the peasants. This indeed, as I have argued earlier, is one of the principal contradictions to be resolved if the transition to socialism is to continue.

In China, the organization of the countryside has been extremely hierarchical. When planning has been wise and cadres dedicated, the peasants have often benefitted. To be the passive beneficiary of leaders locked in ideological struggle or pursuing their own visions of social change, however, does not meet the condition for socialist development. Moreover, when cadres are inadequate, abuse their authority, or err, the peasants have had little recourse. Similarly, when national leaders decide on a development strategy—as during the Maoist era—that effectively assigns low priority to increasing peasant consumption or decide to mobilize the peasants to attack agricultural production like the enemy in a military campaign, peasant input is effectively nil.

Besides contradicting the requirements of socialist economic development in and of itself, the hierarchical organization of the countryside discourages the peasant initiative that is essential if the full productivity potential of the rural forces of production is to be realized. That is to say, the poor labor productivity record of Chinese agriculture must be ascribed in large measure to its hierarchical organization. This is reflected in the decline in labor productivity during the Maoist era and the sharp rise in the reform era, when production decisions were largely turned over to the individual households.

Yet even during the reform period, peasant ability to resist cadre demands, no matter how inimical these may be to their interests, is almost totally lacking. In this respect, China's rural development continues to display a statist character and has clearly failed to fulfill the socialist development requirements. This is not to maintain that national interests and leadership have no role to play in the countryside; quite the contrary is the case. But in resolving the contradiction between the immediate interests of the peasant producers and the national interest in finding a source of accumulation, providing urban residents with low-cost grain, and so forth, a balance must be struck that accords a significantly greater role to peasant self-determination. Probably greater democratization in the selection of rural officials, now typically appointed from above, would be a necessary part of any effort to create such a balance, together with clearer legal specification of the duties and authority of such officials. In the mid–1980s, rapid institutional change continued to mark the countryside (see chapter 8), offering an opportunity to enhance markedly the participation of peasants in shaping their own communities, but there was scant evidence that the authorities were seizing this opportunity.

In one sense, the reform movement in the agricultural sector has made public policy more responsive to peasant demands by decentralizing much of production management to the household level, thereby freeing peasant initiative, by according high priority to peasant incomes (which, as noted, nearly doubled in real terms between 1978 and 1983), and by restricting political interference with economic production. From another perspective, however, this is one more instance in which the benefit of the peasants derives from the beneficence of a public policy that they are powerless to influence. To the extent that this is so, the conditions for socialist rural development have yet to be established.

Peasant disadvantage exists, moreover, not only vis-à-vis the authority of the rural cadres, but vis-à-vis urban workers as well. Every

Chinese inherits at birth the mother's classification as urban or rural, and this classification can be changed only under exceptional circumstances (Potter 1983, 465). Peasants have not even been allowed to be present in cities without letters of reference from their brigades justifying the trip, and marriage between peasants and workers is extremely rare. Peasants view their own status as quite inferior to that of workers, whose salaries are not dependent on the production risks of their enterprises, who receive pensions and other benefits not generally available to the peasants, and who enjoy greater mobility, higher incomes, and so forth.

The circumstances under which this class stratification emerged are not difficult to ascertain. Faced with the impossibility of providing employment, housing, food, and social services for the peasants who would flock to urban areas if given the chance, the Chinese regime had to take strong measures to restrict mobility. Whatever the logic of this decision, however, in combination with other disadvantages peasants experience, their subordinate role in their own communities (vis-à-vis cadres) and the rarity of urban-rural intermarriage, the peasantry emerges as a distinctly subordinate class or social stratum in contemporary China—and perceives itself as such. As William Hinton (1982, 114) writes: "In the real order that determines priorities in China, peasants occupy the lowest rung, just as they always have historically. Any official at any level takes precedence over a peasant when there is an opportunity to travel, to study, or to receive an honor. Anything created by a peasant who lives in the administrative sphere of a higher official, if it will enhance the latter's career, can be moved, removed, manipulated, or expropriated by that official just as if he were the lord of a feudal fief."

If we assess China's rural development from the perspective of the socialist development model, we find strong consistency in six of the eight areas covered: subsistence security, avoiding reliance on export markets, full employment, basic needs provision including education and health, rural industrialization and development, and equality. In two of the areas, however, income growth and peasant control over their own lives and institutions, economic policy and social reality in the Maoist era were inconsistent with the socialist development model.

In the post-Mao period, economic reform—combined with sharply higher purchase prices—has addressed the income issue directly. By widely decentralizing production management to the household level, moreover, the reform has increased peasant control. However, the reform remains a process that is carefully controlled by lower-level cadres responding to the authority of their superiors. Both cadre leadership and such authority will continue to be essential elements in the development of the Chinese countryside, but such development will be genuinely socialist only when these elements are balanced by a far greater measure of peasant control over rural life and institutions.

The Reform Period

The period following Mao's death in September 1976 was marked by a struggle between centrists (led by Hua Guofeng, who briefly became party chairman and premier) and reformers (led by Vice-Premier Deng Xiaoping, who declined higher title after the reformers won out). In this struggle, the reformers sought a sweeping change in the economic system and indeed in the very assumptions on which it is based, while the centrists sought merely to remedy some of the more glaring deficiencies in the economy. At the December 1978 Third Plenary Session of the Communist Party's Eleventh Central Committee, the reformers decisively won control of the party and thus of national policy. The sweeping changes ushered in during the following years, however, had been anticipated by experimental changes in various parts of the country. These were carried out most extensively in Sichuan under provincial Party Secretary Zhao Ziyang, who subsequently became premier.

A more comprehensive treatment of the agricultural reforms ushered in on a national scale from 1979 appears in chapter 8. Here, however, some discussion is in order both to complete the picture of agricultural development in China and to clarify the manner in which the reforms must be understood as a response, in large part, to the deficiencies in socialist development discussed above. In particular, the reforms address the two principal contradictions noted above: the failure of peasant incomes to rise appreciably during the Maoist era and the perpetuation of hierarchy in the countryside, in which the peasantry was by and large reduced to dependency on the benevolence of cadres. As the discussions below and in the reform chapter will make clear, the reforms have contributed to the spectacular gains in peasant incomes noted above and to some reduction in the rural hierarchy. To a considerable extent, however, that hierarchy remains intact, and the reform period has spawned new contradictions which will have to be resolved in their turn if the transition to socialism is to proceed in China.

There are two central aspects to the economic reform in the countryside. First, economic management has, in the main, been moved from what was the third tier in the commune structure, the production team, to what was the fourth tier, the household. Initially, this was largely done by means of the contract or "production responsibility" system, which left intact the rural planning apparatus. In this system the household would sign a contract with the team to deliver a certain level of output and was free to keep a specified portion of the output—which could be as high as 100 percent—above this level. The household also paid a penalty in case of a shortfall. The planning mechanism was maintained via the contract, which could specify the crop, input requirements, and so forth. In the most extreme form of this system (*bao gan dao hu*)—which was also the most common—the household contracted to turn over to the team the relatively modest quantity of output needed to cover its share of the taxes, of the delivery quota, and of the accumulation and welfare funds. It could use whatever method of cultivation it wished and keep all of the above-quota output. As Griffin (1984, 28–29) observes, "The arrangement is equivalent to a fixed rental tenancy system in which the length of tenure is one year, renewable by the landowner (in this case the team) and the rent is specified in volume rather than value terms. Over 64 percent of the 617,000 teams in Sichuan (as of 1982) practise this form of the production responsibility system." By the mid–1980s, a variant of this system became prevalent throughout rural China.

The second central aspect of the reform involves the dissolution of the commune as a multifunction economic, political, and social unit. Basically, township governments have been reestablished throughout the countryside to assume responsibility for traditional local governmental activities, ranging from vital statistics record-keeping and tax collection to public security. At the same time, the local party committees have been directed to withdraw from direct participation in economic activity, limiting their role to a supervisory one and making sure that party policies are being adhered to. These changes initially left the communes as multilevel economic units, but with expanded rights against arbitrary political interference. By 1985, however, the commune system was abolished, and experimentation continued with new forms of corporate and cooperative enterprise.

In one case, for example, in Guanghan county, Sichuan, an experiment was begun in September 1981 to dissolve all the communes, reestablish township governments, and transform all 2,459 production teams into independent cooperatives (Griffin 1984, 34–35). The commune-level industries were transformed into industrial corporations, with the cooperatives receiving shares in both these and the former brigade industries. The former teams or coops can enter into joint ventures with other coops, or with an industrial corporation or village-level (former brigade) industry. Although cooperative members may form joint ventures too, as in the case of a four- or five-person bicycle repair shop, most focus on farming, signing contracts with the cooperative on a group or individual household basis.

In principle, arrangements like this are meant to relate organizational scale to economies of scale (avoiding the loss in efficiency that occurs when the size of the organization exceeds the size necessary for maximum economies of scale), enhance incentives by relating incomes more closely to the net value of output of each producer or producing unit, avoid political interference with economic decision-making, and release the initiative and entrepreneurial potential of the rural population. Although the initial changes were quite successful in raising output and incomes, the reform process gained a momentum of its own leading toward the full-scale privatization of farm management. And although the land is not privately owned, long-term lease arrangements have become increasingly the norm.

In terms of real output gains, the 7.9 percent average annual increase in gross agricultural output from 1978 to 1983 must be considered quite spectacular. If the question of attributing these gains to the reforms themselves is raised, however, caution would be advisable on two counts especially. First, the favorable initial conditions into which the reforms were introduced (see table 7.3)—extensive irrigation (45 percent of the land area), extensive electrification and mechanization, a considerable chemical fertilizer capacity (109.2 kg/hectare of cultivated land in 1979), and so forth—were the result of the "labor accumulation" and rapid industrialization of the Maoist era. Thus, to a considerable extent the reform results could not have been produced earlier, and what tends to appear as the outcome of replacing administrative bureaucracy with a system tied more to individual incentives may in part be the outcome of replacing the bureaucratic, *dirigiste* development with a more decentralized system when the former had already served its purpose. In short, the new production relations rather than standing as a preferential alternative in some absolute sense may simply be the sequentially logical shift once the forces of production (capital, technology, skills, etc.) had reached a certain level.

The other point to be stressed is that the impact of the new production relations per se cannot be fully distinguished from that of the concurrent changes. The sharply higher purchase prices for agricultural products, for example, or the shift in planning to permit greater specialization (and away from requiring all communes to be substantially self-sufficient in grain) could presumably in themselves have had a marked impact on incentives and efficiency quite distinct from that of the production responsibility system or the emerging institutional reorganization of the countryside. Thus one must be wary of attributing the entire gain in agricultural production and productivity to the reforms.

These caveats can help us to put the reform movement in the agricultural sector into proper perspective. Rather than focus on the reforms per se, it may be more appropriate to examine them within the context of the entire development strategy and approach, of which they constituted an essential part. To the extent to which development is planned, it is possible to distinguish between two broad approaches, which were identified in the Soviet industrialization debates as early as the 1920s. One seeks to base economic growth on the restriction of current consumption, freeing the maximum level of resources for investment, especially in heavy industry. The high level of accumulation can promote rapid industrialization, especially if more productive technologies are embodied in the newly installed capital equipment.

The other approach seeks a more balanced growth pattern through the simultaneous stimulation of investment and consumption. The availability of consumption goods is presumed to stimulate efforts to work more diligently and, if the opportunities are present, to innovate and take the initiative in production activities. Whereas the first strategy relies on the power of the planning hierarchy to curtail consumption in the interest of attaining extremely high investment levels, and thus basically on the productive power of capital per se, the second seeks to compensate for lower investment (higher consumption) by greater incentives, initiative, innovation, and efficiency at the micro level. The second strategy then, if successful, will lower the incremental capital-output ratio and permit a given level of growth to proceed with a lower investment and thus higher consumption rate.

The Soviet Union and Maoist China followed the first approach to development. In principle, however—and this is a great irony—it is the second approach that is much more compatible with socialist development requirements because it reflects the immediate consumption aspirations of the direct producers and allows them far greater initiative in production activities generally. Can one then reject the Soviet and

Maoist development strategy in toto?

I believe the answer is no, because the problem of "primitive accumulation" under socialism must be recognized. That is to say, in the earliest stages of development, consumer-goods production capacity will inevitably be limited, in an agriculture deprived of modern inputs as well as in industry. Thus it is inevitable that to a certain extent, industrialization must be pursued on the basis of the extraction of purchasing power from the direct producers, whether it be through taxation, limited wages, or control over the terms of trade between the agricultural and industrial sectors. However, this approach must be pursued only to the extent that the alternative approach outlined is not feasible. Both the Soviet and Maoist approaches to development failed to recognize this. They are both characterized by an excessive centralization of authority, but whereas such centralization was to a certain extent inevitable initially, its very success increasingly opened new possibilities for the devolution of authority and the gradual emergence of a strategy marked simultaneously by increasing producer initiative and responsiveness to mass consumption demands. In short, the initial conditions in China mandated a large measure of primitive accumulation, but such accumulation in itself gradually created conditions for the parallel emergence and ultimately increasing dominance of the second strategy. In the last analysis, the major shortcoming of the Soviet-Maoist strategy lay in the rigidity and dogmatism that prevented the emergence of an alternative more responsive to the needs of the producers as development proceeded, as the forces of production increasingly developed to a point where new relations of production were possible.

Viewed from this perspective, the rapid gains in production and productivity of the reform era in China reflect in part a "catch-up" phenomenon as new production relations are introduced in an overprepared environment. The new strategy, it is clear, reflects the interests of the peasant producers much more than its antecedent. Nevertheless, in assessing the Maoist strategy, its achievements in increasing land productivity, providing subsistence security, and fostering high rates of capital formation—both urban and rural—should be kept in mind. And in both the Maoist and reform strategies, in a nation avowedly committed to socialist development, the powerlessness of the peasants to shape the institutions governing their own lives has remained a constant.

8. Economic Reform and Development Strategy

Both the system of economic planning in China and the development strategy adopted were based initially on the Soviet model. Not surprisingly, both the successes attained and the problems encountered proved to be similar in many respects. The Soviet-type approach of highly concentrating economic authority to mobilize resources for a limited sector of the economy proved, in both countries, to be much more successful in the early stages of development than subsequently, when the economic system, responding to the early successes, became much larger and more complex. This was reflected in the Soviet Union in a marked slowing of the economic growth rate, from 6 percent per year in the 1950s to less than 4 percent in the 1970s and about 3 percent at the end of the decade (Gregory and Stuart 1981, 400). It was reflected there as well in the unsuccessful attempt at administrative decentralization, which saw the authority of the economic ministries over enterprises replaced by the authority of the regions where they were located in 1957, followed by a full-scale return to the ministerial system in 1965.

In China too, changes in the locus of administrative control were attempted; between 1958 and 1978 there were two major decentralizations and recentralizations. The stage was set by the socialist transformation of the economy during the First Five-Year Plan period (1953–57). In the early years following the founding of the People's Republic, China was divided into greater administrative regions, with each region having basic control over the enterprises located within it. These regions were abolished in 1954 and a centralized, Soviet-type system of economic administration gradually formed to direct the national economy; by 1957, the number of enterprises under central management increased to 9,300 from 2,800 in 1953 (Wang 1982, 72).

The nationalization of industry was by and large completed by 1956, and this was accompanied by a tightening of state administrative control over the enterprises. Plans for state-owned enterprises were dictated by the central government, and little autonomy was left to the enterprises themselves. They had to turn over their profits and even their depreciation allowances to the central authorities, which distributed the important means of production to them. In practically every significant area of enterprise management—including employment, use of financial and material resources, procurement of means of production, and marketing—the enterprises had to seek the approval of state administrative organs.

The problems such systems create are well known to students of the Soviet economy. They can be divided into two broad categories. On the one hand there is the bureaucratization of economic management and on the other the problem of incentives. To take up the issue of bureaucratization first, suppose, for example, that a machine breaks down. The enterprise cannot simply go out and order spare parts or a replacement. It must seek the approval of its administrative superior, which then must deal with the agency that is superior to the producer of replacement machinery or spare parts. Since enterprises are evaluated above all in terms of quota fulfillment or gross output, they naturally resist special orders or give them low priority; the problem is compounded because the potential producer of replacement parts will already have its output for the year allocated according to plan. The replacement is apt to take months to arrive, and if it is defective in any respect, the bureaucratic nightmare will be prolonged.

Defective or low-quality products are endemic in the system; since the prime measure of success is in meeting or surpassing the quota in quantitative terms, low quality is hard to measure, and often quality must be sacrificed to meet the quantitative targets. Among the many additional problems, the measures taken to avoid the bureaucracy stand out. Enterprises tend to hoard materials to avoid being caught short, and they try to develop the capacity to produce replacement parts themselves, leading to duplication of uneconomically small-scale facilities. As the economy becomes increasingly complex and interdependent, however, the relative inflexibility of the system in adjusting to unexpected events, and the fact that those in authority are removed from the production facilities themselves, begins to weigh more and more heavily on economic performance. Thus pressures to introduce some type of economic reform have appeared in every Soviet-type economy.

The second category of problems has to do with incentives. Workers hired by state enterprises in China could not be fired—they had an "iron rice bowl." Further, for most of the Cultural Revolution period wages were effectively frozen and bonuses frowned upon, so material incentives for improved performance were lacking. Between 1957 and 1976, in fact, there was a 14 percent decline in average real wages (see table 6.2), although household incomes rose during this period as their labor force participation rates increased. As far as enterprise management in the Soviet-type economy is concerned, the state receives all profits and absorbs all losses, limiting incentives in this area as well. Further, since managers are given their production plans and have their supplies, suppliers, and product recipients designated, they have very little room for initiative or innovation. In short, with enterprises and their personnel lacking autonomy and subordinate in every respect to party-state administration, the Soviet-type economy is more statist than socialist.

A possible solution to the problems of the Soviet-type economy, perhaps the only solution, is the introduction of market relationships among enterprises within the overall planning framework. However, a combination of left-wing dogmatism and a failure to understand the essential features of socialism precluded this solution in the Soviet Union until the time of this writing (1986) and in China until 1978. In both countries, the dominant element within the leadership believed that the introduction of market elements would restore capitalism or at the least capitalist behavior and identified socialism exclusively with the administratively planned economy. As I have argued, however, the essence of socialism lies not in the particular tools used to pursue national economic goals, but in which class interests objectively are served. And the system that effectively diminished real wages while rendering workers as well as managers incapable of taking the initiative in directing their own productive activity can hardly be called socialist.

The solutions attempted in China, as well as in the Soviet Union, failed to grasp this fundamental point and thus were limited, initially, to experiments in administrative decentralization and recentralization. The first major decentralization in China came in 1958, when over 8,000 enterprises or 87 percent of those administered by the central authorities were turned over to local—including provincial—authorities for administration, with the central government ministries retaining control only over those deemed especially important or experimental in nature (Wang 1982, 73). Financing and revenues were shared between the local and central governments, and centrally allocated supplies were reduced to 130 in 1958, some 75 percent less than in 1957. At the same time, the local authorities were given the power to hire temporary workers, raise production targets, and approve some capital construction projects. Enterprises, which had previously been permitted to retain a very small share of their profits for bonuses, were now permitted to retain somewhat more to cover certain costs and collective welfare expenses as well. Planning was carried out both regionally and centrally, with the State Planning Commission and State Economic Commission basing national plans in part on the local ones.

Although this reform stimulated the initiative of the local authorities and brought the superior agencies somewhat closer to the enterprises they were supervising, it could not begin to deal with the fundamental problems we have noted. Business decisions still could not be made by the enterprises themselves, which for the most part continued to be deprived of the authority to take the initiative, a means that would make it possible (even if firms had the authority to purchase their own supplies, for example, there were no markets), and the incentive to do so. At the same time, the decentralization gave rise to new problems, often reflecting the ambitions of the local authorities. These typically raised production quotas, increased employment and payrolls, and initiated numerous capital construction projects. Accumulation (investment) as a share of national income, which had ranged from 22.9 to 25.5 percent during the First Five-Year Plan period and was 24.9 percent in 1957, rose to 33.9 percent in 1958 and 43.8 percent in 1959 while the consumption share dropped accordingly (see table 6.3). As a consequence of the administrative decentralization, central planning was greatly weakened, shortages of consumer goods led to inflationary pressures, and shortages of raw materials forced many enterprises and construction projects to suspend operations for longer or shorter periods. All of these problems were exacerbated by the Great Leap Forward (1958–60), which placed tremendous pressure on local authorities to show spectacular increases in output. The result of parallel pressures in agriculture was a sharp drop in output beginning in 1959, with the collapse in industrial production taking place two years later.

The response to this was a period of economic readjustment and recentralization beginning in 1961. State enterprises were no longer permitted to retain a portion of their profits, and most were reassigned administratively to the central government. By 1963, central ministries were responsible for over 10,000 enterprises, and centrally allocated supplies increased to more than 500. In effect, the decentralization of 1958 was almost completely undone. The problems to which it had given rise were overcome, but the problems that had generated the decentralization naturally reemerged.

From 1964, some administrative authority was transferred back to the localities, and in 1970 decentralization on a substantial scale was attempted once again. Most of the enterprises under central ministries were handed back to the supervision of local authorities, including the Anshan Iron and Steel Complex and the Taqing Oilfield, both giant enterprises. From 1966 to 1972, the list of centrally allocated materials was cut by 61 percent. For twelve key products, each province or region would try to be as self-sufficient as possible but would arrange ahead of time with the national government to cover shortages or provide surpluses. Local governments were permitted to keep a substantial share of their revenues and, once again, to assume considerable responsibility for capital construction in their areas.

Once again, the reform shifted authority from one administrative level to another but left the enterprises subordinate to the bureaucracy and without significant decision-making authority. The bureaucratization of production even with administrative control at the city level is expressed clearly in the experience of the Beijing Television Picture Tube Plant, which was forced to halt production for a total of three years and ten months during the seven-year span from 1973 to 1979 inclusive owing to its inability to rectify the quality deficiencies of its glass casing suppliers. Refused permission by the economic bureaucracy to manufacture the casings itself, the plant was forced to rely on outside suppliers, which were repeatedly redesignated, and it was never able to deal with these suppliers directly. The procedures to be followed when quality control issues arose capture the flavor of just how bureaucratic the whole process was.

> The Beijing Picture Tube Plant is subordinate to the Beijing Broadcasting and Television Company, which is under the leadership of the Beijing Electronic Instruments Bureau. As for the glass casing plant, it is subordinate to the Beijing Glass Manufacturing General Plant, which is under the leadership of the Beijing Municipal Light Industry Bureau. For this reason, in the event of quality disputes arising between the glass casing manufacture and picture tube manufacture, the procedure involves a

whole series of contacts from the workshop to the picture tube plant, then
to the broadcasting and Television Company, the Instruments Bureau, the
municipality, the Light Industry Bureau, the glass manufacturing general
plant, the glass screen manufacturing plant and finally the relevant workshop or team. . . . Hence, whenever a problem of quality arises, it results
in the plant stopping production for several months. (*Jingji guanli* [Eco-
nomic Management] 8 [Aug. 15, 1980], 15–17. Translated in FBIS, *Daily
Report*, Oct. 3, 1980, L13.)

The decentralization, moreover, like its earlier counterparts, was
marked by an excessive accumulation rate (which averaged 33 percent
of national income between 1970 and 1978; Wei and Chao 1982, 54)
and the initiation of an excessive number of capital construction projects, with inadequate supplies causing the projects to be stretched out
over many years. It appears that at least part of the criticism directed at
the gang of four for the economic "chaos" of the Cultural Revolution
years is in fact a reaction to the problems that administrative decentralization efforts raised once again. The policy response was still another
recentralization, more limited this time but with almost 1,000 enterprises retransferred to central government control in 1978 alone.

Above all, what the cycles of decentralization and recentralization
demonstrated, was the inability of shifting the level of administrative
authority to deal with the fundamental problems of the Chinese economy. These problems were expressed especially in the growing incremental capital-output ratio (ICOR) and its ramifications. The implication of the rising ICOR is that to maintain a high rate of industrial
growth in China, the share of accumulation in national income had to
be raised sharply while gains in consumption were suppressed. I have
already referred to the failure of real wages to rise between 1957 and
1976, and the nominal gain in peasant real incomes over the same
interval. As table 8.1 shows, one can also point to the rise in the
accumulation rate from 24.2 percent of national income during the
First Five-Year Plan period, 1953–57, to 33.0 percent of national
income during the Fourth Five-Year Plan period, 1971–75. Between
these five-year plan periods, moreover, the proportion of accumulation
funds going into housing, schools, hospitals, and other structures with a
direct bearing on people's welfare fell sharply from 40.2 percent to
22.5 percent of total accumulation, while the proportion devoted to
investment in plant and equipment (to serve material production) rose
accordingly.

The higher accumulation rate during the Fourth Five-Year Plan

Table 8.1

Accumulation and Economic Growth During First, Third, and Fourth Five-Year Plan Periods

	1st 5-Year Plan, 1953-57	3rd 5-Year Plan, 1966-70	4th 5-Year Plan, 1971-75
Annual growth rate of national income	8.9%	8.4%	5.6%
Annual growth rate of gross value of industrial products	18.0%	11.7%	9.1%
Accumulation as percentage of national income	24.2%	26.3%	33.0%
Increase in national income per 100 yuan accumulation	35 yuan	26 yuan	16 yuan
Accumulation for material production (% of total)	59.8%	74.5%	77.5%
Accumulation for nonmaterial production[a] (% of total)	40.2%	25.5%	22.5%

Source: Dong (1982, 60-61).

a. Accumulation for nonmaterial production refers to investment in housing, schools, hospitals and other structures that do not serve material production directly.

period helped to sustain the growth of the national economy at a respectable if reduced rate, but the sharply rising ICOR is reflected in the fact that each hundred yuan of accumulation gave rise to a thirty-five yuan increase in national income in the former period but only a sixteen yuan increase in national income in the latter; the growing share of national output devoted to directly productive investment limited improvement in living standards. At the same time, the concentration of economic, political and social authority in a single hierarchy became, as the development of the economy made alternative arrangements more feasible, increasingly incompatible with the socialist principle of producer authority.

When the reformers, led by Deng Xiaoping, gained control of the party machinery, they steered China down a path of reform that went far beyond the administrative decentralizations that had previously been attempted. Deng's famous maxim, ''Seek truth from facts,'' symbolizes the reformers' freedom from dogma, and starting with the historic Third Plenary Session of the Chinese Communist Party's Eleventh Central Committee in December 1978, they turned China down the only path capable of limiting the power of the hierarchy, creating the conditions for producer authority and increasing mass consumption on a substantial scale. They committed themselves to a program of market socialism within the overall framework of national economic planning, a program which only a few years earlier would have been regarded as heretical. The program of economic reform that they introduced, however, can be understood properly only within the context of the new development strategy that accompanied it, so before examining the reforms in industry and agriculture, consideration of the new development strategy as a whole is in order.

The New Development Strategy

The Maoist economic strategy, as noted, was marked by administrative control over economic activity. This meant the concentration of economic authority in a few hands, and since these were the same hands that wielded political and social power, it meant a unified hierarchy within the country. Such a hierarchy facilitates the implementation of crash programs based on mobilizing resources to pursue certain objectives. Increasing the national accumulation rate to develop heavy (producer goods) industry was its most notable economic achievement. Thus the machine tool, iron and steel, petroleum, and other heavy industries developed with great rapidity during the Maoist era.

The same strategy that concentrates decision-making power, however, is also prone to internal contradictions that limit its effectiveness. Producing units, which know their own needs and possibilities best, are deprived of the authority to act independently. The problems are magnified whenever something unanticipated occurs, such as raw materials failing to arrive or machinery breaking down; under such circumstances, the inflexibility of the system becomes increasingly onerous.

As the economy grows in size and complexity, moreover, the interactions within the economy grow and the efficiency problems multiply. As this happens, increasing levels of investment become necessary to yield a given increment in output (that is, the ICOR rises). Since all of national income is divided between consumption and investment, a given level of economic growth can be maintained only by restricting consumption. Thus the Maoist strategy requires restricting consumption and the production of a rising proportion of capital goods as a condition for maintaining rapid economic growth. The rising investment requirements associated with this strategy and the decreasing contribution to output of the newly formed (incremental) capital are both reflected in table 8.1. The Maoist strategy, accordingly, is incompatible with reliance on material incentives to stimulate producer initiative; physical capital equipment and the technology embodied in it must play the overwhelmingly dominant role in sustaining economic growth. In effect, the rhetoric of the era denouncing material incentives was making a virtue of necessity.

Since workers find the system unresponsive to their needs for greater income and for control over their productive activity, they are apt to become increasingly alienated over time, and indeed just this happened during the Maoist era as workers became decreasingly responsive to exhortations and production campaigns, more inclined to cynicism, and increasingly concerned with their material status (Walder 1982). The growing disaffection of workers means the system had to become more repressive to maintain labor discipline or compensate for lack of worker motivation by still higher levels of investment.

The reform movement appeared in this context. The key element in the reform is turning economic decision-making over to the direct producers, workers, and managers in both industry and agriculture. This becomes possible only when markets are established, since in the absence of markets producers can be guided only by administrative authorities. National economic planning is maintained under the reform system, but wherever possible bureaucratic orders are limited and indirect means of control are used.

To turn authority over to enterprises, it is necessary to institute a system of rewards for success and penalties for failure. Under the old system, profits were simply turned over to the state (with limited exceptions) and losses absorbed by the state. Under the new system, taxes on enterprises replace profit remittances, and enterprises are permitted to retain a substantial share of their profits for replacement of equipment, net investment, collective welfare (such as the construction of worker housing), and bonuses. If the bonuses exceed a certain level, the enterprise must pay a substantial tax on them. Other features of the reforms will be discussed more fully below, but here should be noted the implications for development strategy. Rewarding the producers with higher pay for higher productivity requires a corresponding increase in the production of consumer goods, including agricultural products, which still enter into the majority of consumer goods either directly or in processed form (some 70 percent of the raw materials for light industry come from the agricultural sector). Thus the strategy requires a significant rise in agricultural output, a diminution in the share of national income going into investment, and a corresponding increase in the share going into consumption. Table 8.2 shows the changes in agricultural output and the consumption and investment shares between 1978 and 1983. The first year of the reform program is 1979; during the reform period, the accumulation rate did not fall as rapidly as the national authorities intended since local authorities and enterprises increased their investment.

With a lower investment rate, economic growth must rely less on physical capital formation, more on technical change, innovation, producer initiative, and efficient use of resources. All of these call for measures to strengthen the decision-making powers of the enterprises, while the technical change requirement in particular points toward upgrading educational standards and expanding economic contacts with the more developed countries. Thus economic reform must be understood as more than an alternative approach to resource allocation. In fact, it forms the central element in an alternative development strategy.

By transferring decision-making authority from political and administrative organs to producing units, the reform seeks to substitute their initiative for pure physical capital formation as the key motive force in economic growth. To do so, the reform must make the producing units and individuals responsible for their own economic performance, rewarding success and penalizing failure. This in turn requires both systemic change, including especially the increased use of markets throughout the economy, and a change in the structure of production favoring agriculture and consumer goods industries relative to producer goods industries. The point is not to downgrade producer goods but merely to establish balance among the three sectors. To stimulate agriculture, parallel changes are necessary to replace the authoritarian pattern of economic orders emanating from above. In agriculture, incentives are especially important since more of the work is person-paced rather than machine-paced, and thus a reform of the price structure was also necessary.

Agricultural prices were set in the early 1950s at extremely low levels relative to industrial prices, and although agriculture was favored in subsequent changes, these never were sufficient to compensate for the initial disadvantage. Moreover, official price indices appear to omit agricultural producer goods (Lardy 1983). Since these were priced quite high relative to farm products, their rapidly increasing use in the 1960s and 1970s actually put downward pressure on peasant incomes (Lardy 1983). Thus, to stimulate increased production in

Table 8.2

Consumption Rate, Investment Rate, and Growth Rates of Agriculture and Light Industry During the Reform Period

	1978	1979	1980	1981	1982	1983
Consumption rate (% of national income)	63.5	65.4	68.4	71.5	71.0	70.0
Investment rate (% of national income)	36.5	34.6	31.6	28.5	29.0	30.0
Increase in gross value of agricultural output (%)	9.0	8.6	3.9	6.6	11.0	9.5
Increase in gross value of light industrial output[a] (%)	10.8	9.6	18.4	14.1	5.7	8.7

Source: State Statistical Bureau (1984, 26, 32).

a. Includes primarily consumer goods.

agriculture, sharp increases in the prices paid to producers were necessary, and these were increased accordingly; the overall purchase price index for farm and sideline products rose by 22.1 percent in 1979 and an additional 7.1 percent in 1980 (Xue 1982, 322). The substantial rise in peasant incomes to which these price increases contributed required further increases in the output of consumer goods. At the same time, the state did not wish to shift the price increases to urban consumers, and in fact it could not if it wished to stimulate production incentives in the industrial sector as well. Thus it absorbed much of the producer price rise itself, subsidizing urban consumers by leaving their prices unchanged, and when it ultimately did raise the price of food to consumers, it accompanied the increase with a five-yuan monthly subsidy to all urban workers and retired employees, in effect shifting the form of the subsidy but not its substance. These changes entailed a sharp increase in state subsidies, which rose from 14.3 percent of state revenue in 1978 to 42.7 percent in 1981 (BR, Feb. 21, 1983, 17), further restricting the capacity of the central government to finance capital formation through the budget.

Thus, economic reform is embodied in structural changes in the Chinese economy that go far beyond the mechanism for resource allocation. It implies the development of consumption relative to investment and thus of agriculture relative to industry, and of light industry relative to heavy industry. It requires the widespread introduction of the market as a condition for producer autonomy and the corresponding weakening of political and bureaucratic controls over the producing units. It means that planning must be carried out increasingly through indirect means, like changing relative prices, and decreasingly through administrative orders. Perhaps most significantly, it implies a strategy of development that maximizes the autonomy of producing units and individuals and uses their initiative to replace centrally directed physical capital formation as the prime motive force of development. This in turn has many ramifications, especially the increased importance of technological change in bringing about development, and thus of education and international economic relations as well.

Planning versus the Market

The essence of the reform in industry is the transfer of decision-making authority from supervisory-administrative organs to producing enterprises. Whereas in the past the enterprises were essentially appendages of state administrative organs, whether central or local, the reform program aims to make them autonomous units to a far greater extent, with an internal dynamic of their own. In addition to the extended authority given to the enterprises, all firms were slated by the end of 1984 to be changed from a system of profit deliveries to the state to a system of tax payments. This decision followed a period of experimentation in which enterprises following the tax system showed improved economic performance. The significance of the changeover lies in the fact that under a system of profit remittances, the state captures all profits and absorbs all losses, sharply reducing incentives for superior performance at the enterprise level, while under a tax system such incentives can be expanded by allowing firms to retain a share of their profits for expansion or distribution (as bonuses).

Although experimentation preceded the widespread implementation of reforms in both industry and agriculture, the industrial reforms had to be phased in much more slowly than the agricultural ones since the inherited price structure did not reflect social opportunity costs. Relatively high prices for such consumer durables as bicycles and sewing machines, for example, were meant to limit consumer buying power and provide budgetary funds, while low energy prices were essentially an accounting matter within the state sector. Since the market system assumes firms will respond to price signals, a thoroughgoing price reform is a prerequisite for its implementation; otherwise there would be a stampede to produce bicycles and sewing machines, firms would be encouraged to waste energy, and so forth. As of the mid–1980s, therefore, the focus of reform was on the price structure.

The direction of the reform was to free decision-making at the level of the producing unit as far as possible, while reserving for state planning the central role in determining such macroeconomic parameters as the level and direction of investment, sectoral balance, economic growth and structure, and the overall direction of the economy. In short, as of the mid–1980s, China was moving toward a mixture of planning and market guidance for enterprises, with planning taking precedence. The priority of planning is reflected in the fact that in key areas enterprises must first satisfy plan requirements with a certain proportion of their output before they can seek out their own suppliers, markets, and so forth with their remaining capacity. Further, an example from the agricultural sector indicates that to the extent that the controlled market does not yield the social and economic objectives sought, direct intervention will replace it.

In the first few reform years, the elimination of grain acreage requirements led to a decline in grain acreage (in favor of other crops) that threatened to get out of hand; between 1978 and 1981, the total sown area under grain fell from 120.6 to 113.9 million hectares (U.S. Department of Agriculture 1982, 19). The state simply stepped back in and reimposed certain acreage requirements to check the decline. Planning, as this example makes clear, is not being abandoned in favor of the market. Rather, the market is being used as a more effective tool than administrative orders to pursue social objectives within an overall planning framework, and where the market fails to fulfill its function, it is simply superseded by direct administrative action.

As I have indicated, the economic reforms are set in the broader framework of a new economic strategy, one which seeks to replace the overwhelming role played by capital accumulation during the Maoist era with greater balance of the productive forces. To the extent possible, human initiative and effectiveness in productive activity, together with accelerated technological progress, are being substituted for capital as the motive force of economic growth and development. This in turn implies a need to develop material incentives and rewards for the human actors, a diminution of the share of accumulation in national income in favor of consumption, sharp improvement in the relative performance of the agricultural sector, substantive improvements in education and technical training, and an increase in investment and trade in the international sphere. The focus of planning in the reform period is not on issuing production orders to individual enterprises but on assuring that these macroeconomic objectives are met.

To these points may be added overall economic balance among the sectors as an important objective of public policy. Thus, the early reform period was also a period of adjustment in which those industrial sectors creating bottlenecks in the rest of the economy, especially energy and transportation, received priority. These are high capital-output industries, so channeling investment resources to them, especially in the case of multiyear projects, implies a temporary slowing in the growth rate of national income (which indeed fell from 12.4 percent in 1978 to 7.0 percent in 1980; Wei and Chao 1982, 240), but such slowing indicates in this instance strengthened control over the long-term direction of the economy rather than a failure in the reform program. Precisely because these have been bottleneck sectors—as late as 1984 some 20 percent of industrial capacity remained unutilized as a consequence of energy shortages (BR, Sept. 24, 1984, 7)—the emphasis accorded them should ultimately contribute to a spurt in economic growth followed by a settling back to a sustainable balanced growth path. The increase in the industrial (gross value of output) growth rate to 10.5 percent in 1983 (Zhao 1984, i), 14 percent in 1984 (BR, March 25, 1985, ii), and 23.1 percent in the first half of 1985 (BR, July 29, 1985, 4) may reflect this.

Finally, it is important to keep in mind the fact that as direct administrative control over the economy is being phased out, it is being replaced by indirect economic measures to assure that enterprise behavior will be consistent with national economic purposes. This includes use of the price system, the tax system, the banking system, and so forth. In some cases it is possible to readjust relative prices, for example, to encourage additional output of those products whose prices are raised or input costs reduced. Low-cost loans dispensed through the banking system may have the same effect. Relative price changes and subsidized loans are especially widely used in agriculture, where they have contributed to the spectacular overall output gains and more balanced product mix in that sector. Importantly, such tools can also be used selectively in pursuing equality. Thus, the poorest production teams were often exempted from grain production quotas altogether, with the quota price being replaced by a negotiated price (Griffin 1984, 47). This is significant because in effect there was a three-tier price system for grain—the quota price, the 50 percent higher above-quota price, and a free-market price about twice the quota price—and the negotiated prices for the poorest teams were set at levels comparable to the free-market price. Thus, the transformation begun at the end of the 1970s from a purely administered economy to one marked by a delegation of authority to the enterprise level marked not an abrogation of planning but a reform in the method of its implementation from direct to indirect means; the extended use of the market in China must be understood in this context.

The Reform in Industry

The basic thrust of the reform is to make individual decision-making units responsible for their economic performance by according them substantive decision-making authority on the one hand, and by tying their incomes as closely as possible to their economic performance on the other. The systemic villain is perceived as "everyone eating from the same big pot," which means the failure to distinguish between enterpises that perform well and those that do not, and between individuals who are more productive and those who are less so, and to reward the high performers accordingly.

In changing the relations between the enterprises and the state, key roles have been assumed by the substantial delegation of decision-making authority to the enterprise level, the extension of the market system which was a necessary condition for making this possible, the replacement of profit remittances with tax payments, and the reform of the enterprise management system. In changing the relations between the worker and the enterprise, a key role was played by gearing remuneration, including base pay and bonuses, to productivity. The extension of worker authority within the enterprise to the selection of managers up to and including, on a limited experimental basis, factory directors was also emphasized early in the reform period, and the newly restored congresses of workers and staff were to have been elevated in principle to the role of chief policy-making body within each enterprise. This objective, however, was deemphasized when it came increasingly into clear conflict with the professionalization of management and efforts to extend the "responsibility system" to managers (gearing their pay and promotions to enterprise performance). The conflict between these two objectives is another evident case of the contradiction between developing socialist relations of production (by democratizing the workplace) and developing the forces of production (improving economic efficiency and growth by professionalizing enterprise management). This contradiction, one of the critical issues in the transition to socialism, warrants further consideration, but I will first take up the relations between the enterprise and the state.

As China's industrial system took shape in the 1950s, the Soviet system provided the basic model, which included the concentration of authority in the hands of the enterprise director. Subsequently, authority was shifted to the factory party committee and in practice was wielded by the party secretary. This led to a confused situation in which political and economic criteria for enterprise and individual performance could not be clearly differentiated. Should the employee who faithfully follows party directives be promoted, for example, or the one who is more productive?

To deal with such problems and to provide more clear-cut guidelines for evaluating management performance, party committees have been ordered to refrain from involving themselves in management, and to restrict their role to assuring compliance with party and state directives. Responsibility for the economic performance of the enterprise has been restored to the director, working together with the chief engineer and accountant. With the director assuming responsibility for the overall economic performance of the enterprise, appointment and reappointment to all managerial positions have been made dependent on professional qualifications and performance. With a system of taxes replacing profit remittances, moreover, successful enterprise performance permits the enterprises considerable discretion over the use of their profits for expansion, equipment renovation, development of new and improved products, bonuses, and such collective welfare expenditures as employee housing.

The development of the market plays a key role in shifting responsibility for its economic actions to the enterprise, for as long as the enterprise is an appendage of an administrative organ its autonomy is too severely curtailed to enable it to assume full responsibility. This is reflected, for example, in the "success criterion" problem which systematically afflicts Soviet-type economies. A variety of criteria are commonly used in such economies, but output inevitably outweighs all others. Given the stress on maximizing output, quality, variety, and suitability for users naturally tend to suffer. Under this system, "production for the warehouse"—producing goods not in demand but which will nevertheless be reflected in plant output and national product statistics—became one characteristic of the Chinese economy. By contrast, under the discipline of the market, goods that cannot be sold will prove a pure loss for the enterprise. This effect will be heightened as the state moves away from the simple allocation of capital goods to enterprises to a variety of payment requirements for such goods, including outright sale, interest charges on borrowed funds, leasing, or the levying of an asset tax.

In evaluating the increasing role of the market in China, it is important to keep in mind the distinction between the market system and capitalism. Although the market assumes a central role in the capitalist mode of production, it is analytically distinguishable from the capitalist mode, and in fact its existence predates capitalism. Under socialism, the market has a necessary role to play in limiting hierarchy and allowing the development of the forces of production to reach their full potential. This is by no means meant to deny, however, that the presence of the market will raise certain contradictions for socialist societies. In fact, it will inevitably do so, just as it does for capitalist ones, although the nature of the contradictions characteristically varies between the two systems. Market forces under capitalism, for example, may lead to equilibrium at less than full-employment levels, requiring government intervention to restore the economy to its full productive potential, while under socialism, an excessive role for the market may spark an individualistic materialism that contradicts the collective and cooperative ethos of the system, besides giving rise to marked increases in inequality. I will return to the contradictions raised by the reform movement in the conclusion to the chapter and in chapter 9. Let it suffice to observe at this point that ultimately socialism and capitalism are distinguished essentially not by the use of the market, but by the class interests objectively served. In socialist countries, freeing the direct producers from the heavy weight of hierarchy and improving their material well-being markedly, in both of which the market plays a critical role, most assuredly serves their interests.

Before leaving the impact of the reform movement on industrial organization, it may be appropriate to take note of three additional aspects of the reform. The first involves the manner in which the institutional implementation of the reform varies by industry, the second involves the varied ownership forms now permitted, and the third involves the opening to the outside world through various forms of trade, investment, and international financial flows. Let us take up first the varied forms of the reform by industry.

In the construction industry, state enterprises used to be assigned specific capital construction tasks and allocated their equipment and raw materials by the state. As in other industries, the state would cover the losses and receive the surpluses generated. A particular problem this entailed was the stretching out of construction times, in many cases to extreme lengths. Under the reform, a system of competitive bids is being instituted to promote low-cost production. Some materials, at least at first, will continue to be allocated, but a parallel system of markets is being developed to give construction enterprises an incentive to obtain their own materials from the lowest-cost producers and without bureaucratic delays. Firms will borrow much of their working capital and pay interest and taxes on the capital equipment alloted to them. These costs will rise the longer the production period drags on. On the other hand, the price specified in the construction contract includes such costs involved in the normative time to completion, so that early completion will save costs and raise profits for the construction enterprise.

In the field of commerce, too, with most products allocated through the state commercial network, the bureaucratization of the economy discouraged performance. Under the reform, multiple channels of commodity circulation have appeared. Enterprises can make contracts directly with their suppliers or the purchasers of their output, and in many cities, wholesale markets and trade fairs are being developed to enable enterprises to display their products and take orders from purchasers directly. In ways like this, the entire economic system is becoming much more flexible.

Another aspect of the reform is the reemergence of urban collectives and individually run enterprises. These had been discouraged on the grounds that state enterprise represented a ''higher'' ownership form and that the petty commodity production of individual producers was a precursor of capitalism and the capitalist mentality. However, just as capitalist or statist social formations can encompass a variety of modes of production, so too can a socialist one. Moreover, the dogmatic rejection of multiple modes of production failed to take account of the fact that the state simply lacked the resources to employ fully the urban population, and to avoid unemployment it had to resort to such draconian measures as sending involuntarily some fifteen to eighteen million urban high school graduates out to settle in the countryside. The capital requirements per worker in collective and individual enterprises, by contrast, are far smaller, so that a given amount of capital can provide a far higher level of employment. Thus, as table 6.1 indicates, the capital requirements per worker were 4.5 times as great in the state sector as in the cooperative sector.

Besides its inability to provide full employment in state-owned enterprises, the state lacked the organizational resources to provide many of the urban amenities that could be provided most efficiently through the collective or individual form. Snack stands, laundries, bicycle repair shops, barber shops, and other enterprises traditionally run by individuals had largely disappeared from urban China by the mid-1970s, making urban life just that much more difficult to cope with. Restaurants and other service activities together with handicrafts and small-scale production generally were far too limited to serve the needs of the urban population and provide full employment, which became a pressing problem in the late 1970s; at that time, the 1960s' baby boom generation (before China's population policies were successfully implemented from about 1970) finished middle school and the forcibly rusticated youths, permitted to return home, flooded back to the cities. By allowing a diversity of production relations, the authorities were able simultaneously to cope with the bulge in the urban labor supply, improve the amenities of urban life, and raise incomes and output.

Once again, it is clear that the ideologically inspired criticism of the collective and individual forms is wide of the mark. Clearly urban workers benefit from being able to have their laundry done or have lunch at a corner noodle stand instead of having to walk five blocks to a restaurant (which is apt to have worse food at higher prices). Clearly the working population as a whole benefits from higher levels of employment and income. And just as clearly the collective enterprises and extremely marginal individual ones offer no threat to the socialist transition.

Finally with regard to the relations between the enterprise and the state, the continuing and accelerating opening of China to international economic contacts should be noted. Between 1979 and June 1984, China received U.S.$12.5 billion in foreign loans and $3.3 billion in foreign investment. In the same span, more than 2,900 contracts valued at nearly $8 billion were signed with foreign firms, including 31 offshore oil exploration contracts (*Wall Street Journal*, Sept. 25, 1984, 33). The commitment to the opening to the outside world was emphasized by the opening up of fourteen new coastal cities as special economic zones for foreign investors in May 1984, and the initialing with Great Britain of the agreement for the return of Hong Kong to Chinese sovereignty under terms that will permit its economic autonomy—including its free-trade-oriented capitalist system—for at least fifty years.

The object of the opening to the outside world is to accelerate the modernization of the economy through the infusion of capital and advanced technology from abroad, thereby raising as well the skill level of Chinese workers and technicians and the managerial level of enterprises. The question of course arises as to whether China's involvement in the capitalist world economy will compromise the national policy of self-reliance and create a situation of dependency. This might indeed happen if the process were allowed to proceed out of control and foreign debts allowed to grow excessively in relation to China's export capacity. The Chinese government is clearly aware of this problem, however, and when the early euphoria of signing contracts with foreign companies began to get out of hand in 1978–79, it sharply cut back the scale of its foreign commitments so as not to overextend itself, and it has proceeded prudently since then. Further, foreign equity investments cannot involve the alienation of land and provide typically for the ultimate transfer of equity to China. In principle, the opening to the outside world can, if controlled carefully by a strong government conscious of the potential pitfalls, contribute strongly to China's modernization without leading to dependency.

Consider, for example, the contracts signed in 1972 for the import of complete sets of equipment for thirteen large-capacity chemical fertilizer plants, turnkey projects which involved the training of Chinese personnel to operate them. The import of these plants, completed in the late 1970s, enabled China to reduce its reliance on the import of chemical fertilizers and ultimately of grain as well. At the same time strengthening the technical capacity of the domestic industry, it hastened the day when China could itself supply complete sets of equipment for the domestic industry; in 1979, the first large-scale chemical fertilizer plant using Chinese-designed and manufactured equipment exclusively began operation in Shanghai. The net result of the plant imports has clearly been a gain for Chinese autonomy, as well as the benefit gained from accelerated growth and modernization. Similarly, the offshore oil exploration contracts signed in the early 1980s can be expected to sustain China's energy independence, speed the modernization of the domestic industry, and assure exports into the twenty-first century, thereby hastening the overall pace of modernization. This is not to deny the contradictions to which any such policies will inevitably give rise, but the real issue is how such contradictions will be handled. Ultimately, since all policy choices and indeed all human activities give rise to contradictions, any effort to avoid contradictions altogether can lead only to complete immobilization.

Finally, in considering China's industrial reforms, one must be cognizant of their impact on relations within the workplace. I have noted that the relations between the enterprise and the state will be less hierarchical, but that in itself does not necessarily imply that the relations within the enterprise will be less so. Although greater autonomy for enterprises is a necessary condition for enhancing worker authority within the enterprises, it is by no means a sufficient condition for doing so. From the standpoint of the workers, the reforms within the enterprises have been marked by two basic changes. First, the responsibility system is being applied increasingly within the enterprises, gearing worker income more closely to both individual productivity and the success of the enterprise as a whole. Second, the congress of workers and staff has in principle been elevated to the role of chief policy-making organ within the enterprise, and the workers have begun electing factory officials, including even the plant director in some enterprises, subject to the approval of higher authorities.

The development of the responsibility system within the enterprises is basically an effort to do away with the phenomenon of "everyone eating from the same big pot," to reward greater productivity with higher pay and bonuses, and to penalize lower productivity with lower pay and bonuses. There is no single formula by which this is done. Depending on the industry, wages may be supplemented by bonuses, piece rates may be used, and so forth. Promotions are to be made more readily, and to depend on qualifications and performance. It is important to keep in mind that these changes are taking place in an environment of rising real incomes, with real wages rising by some 30 percent between 1978 and 1984 (see table 6.2), following two decades of stagnation (urban household income rose even faster—by 43 percent just between 1978 and 1983—as the labor force participation rate increased). In practice, therefore, the implementation of the responsibility system in industry means not that some are gaining at the expense of others, but that the most productive now have the opportunity to raise their incomes faster than others.

Further, it is important to keep in mind as well the point that the funds available for bonus payments depend on the enterprise's meeting basic state planning norms for output, economizing inputs, quality, and so forth, and on its profitability. Thus the workers' self-interest is tied to the overall successful performance of the enterprise as well as to their individual productivity, and workers who perform well are contributing not only to their personal success but to that of their coworkers as well. It has already been observed that the prolonged failure of real wages to rise during the Maoist period can scarcely be reconciled with the principle that the socialist state exists to serve the interests of the working classes. The introduction of the responsibility system in industry relies on material inducements to increase worker productivity and initiative, and to the extent it is successful increases the real output on which such inducements ultimately depend. To date it has been an effective tool in raising output and incomes, as the data on industrial output and real wages indicate. The principle of distribution according to labor, which the responsibility system entails, appears to be a suitable one for developing the productive forces at this stage in Chinese history while responding to the workers' desire for improved living standards. Once again, this assessment is made with full cognizance of the potential contradictions inherent in such a remuneration policy, but I will take up this issue in the concluding section of this chapter and in chapter 9.

The congress of workers and staff, directly elected by the workers and staff, is to be

> the organ of power for the enterprise and has the right to make decisions on: the orientation and policy of production and management, long-term and annual plans, measures for major technical renovation, important rewards and punishments for workers and staff members and the setting up, revision or abolition of regulations for the whole factory. It elects a director and discusses the list of deputy directors recommended by the director, and then submits the names to the higher leading body for appointment . . . the director assumes full responsibility for the management of the enterprise. He submits major programmes to the congress for examination and is responsible for their implementation. (BR, Nov. 17, 1980, 3)

There are two principal elements in the movement to elevate the authority of the congresses. One is the socialist principle that the enterprise should indeed embody the authority of the workers, modified by the recognition that the broader social interest must also be represented. The other is the concern to elevate workers' involvement in enterprise performance, to stimulate their initiative and effort by making the institutional form reflect their authority. It must be recognized at the same time, however, that other factors in the reform movement are tending to check this extension of worker authority. The professionalization of management, the increasing emphasis on formal educational qualifications and even examinations, and the reintroduction of one-man responsibility under the director, while not in themselves precluding the establishment of the congress as a policy-making organ with broad supervisory powers, render it more difficult. Further, the Chinese cultural tradition of hierarchy, reinforced by the experience if not the rhetoric of the Maoist years, discourages the workers from being outspoken even while it encourages state and party authorities to focus on the managerial reform and state-enterprise relations rather than intraenterprise reform. Finally, it is important to bear in mind that while the reform in industry, like that in agriculture, enjoys widespread popular support, both are essentially top-down programs implemented by those wielding authority within the party-state. In time, the congresses may indeed assume the role intended for them, but the path will not be a smooth one.

The Reform in Agriculture

As the discussion of agricultural development indicates, the Maoist era was marked by declining labor productivity in agriculture, stagnation in peasant real incomes, and a hierarchical structure of authority in the countryside. In part the situation in agriculture was a consequence of policy choices, in part a consequence of systemic deficiencies. Although the terms of trade between industry and agriculture improved for agriculture over the period, the initial terms had favored industry so extremely that agriculture remained a source of substantial net surplus to finance industrialization throughout the period. Also, the policy requiring all communes to approach self-sufficiency in grain production, discouraging specialization and exchange, inhibited the development of a more productive agricultural sector. Thus, between 1957 and 1977, the real value of the labor day declined by a third (Watson 1983, 77), and this may be expected to have had a substantial impact both on the peasants' incentive to work and on their support for the system of collective agriculture as it evolved in China.

The role of policy choice in transferring surplus from the agricultural sector to the state is shown clearly by the price differential between industrial and agricultural products, for only a small part of the surplus transfer took the form of rural taxes. Most of it by far came from the "underpricing" of agricultural products and the "overpricing" of industrial products sold to the peasants (yielding high profits to state-owned enterprises). As an indicator of the significance of underpricing, it might be noted that in the summer of 1982, even after grain procurement prices had been raised sharply, free-market prices were about twice the quota price for grain and about one-third higher than the above-quota price (Lardy 1985, 50). Paying peasants less than the market value of their produce, then, remains an important source of surplus transfer in China. As the higher purchase prices and increased freedom to sell on the open market indicate, however, the surplus transfer during the reform period is far less onerous than it was during the Maoist period and has been accompanied during the reform period by striking gains in peasant incomes and consumption.

The failure of labor productivity and peasant incomes to rise appreciably during the Maoist era can also be linked to the incentive systems used at the time. Under the system of collective assessment of individual workpoint ratings (multiplied by the number of days worked for the collective), which came into widespread use during the Cultural Revolution, some two-thirds of the peasants received the maximum rating, making the income distribution in effect an inverted pyramid and discouraging special effort (Lee 1984, 138). Even more than in industry, the income distribution system in agriculture discouraged extra effort, since tasks in agriculture depend much more on individual initiative than in industry, where much of the work is machine-paced. Moreover, the collective system of production as it developed in China depended critically on the quality of local leadership, which was often poor.

In theoretical terms, the inability of the agricultural sector to reach its full production potential may also be understood to be a consequence of excessive haste in transforming the production relations to a more collective, egalitarian mode before the forces of production had developed sufficiently to permit this. The thrust of the reforms in this context is to tie incomes as closely as possible to individual effort and productive accomplishment, to make individuals responsible for their own performance. In this context, the "responsibility system" emerged as the dominant compensation system in Chinese agriculture. Assuming a variety of forms, it spread rapidly throughout the agricultural sector from 1979 to 1984, with nearly 100 percent of the production units adopting it in some form. Its rapid spread was accompanied by striking gains in agricultural performance and peasant incomes. Whereas the gross value of agricultural output grew at an average rate of 3.2 percent per year from 1952 to 1978, between 1978 and 1983 the average annual growth rate rose to 7.9 percent (BR, Aug. 13, 1984, 16–17); in the same span, aided by a sharp rise in prices paid for agricultural produce, real peasant incomes nearly doubled.

The most common form the responsibility system assumed, *bao gan dao hu*, involved full-scale transfer of production responsibility from the team to the household. The household, which was responsible for supplying the inputs, agreed to pay its share of the taxes and mandatory grain-sale quota to the team, plus an additional amount to cover its share of the collective accumulation, services, and welfare funds. Any surplus above the total amount agreed upon was retained by the household. While the household was still responsible for the payments in the case of a shortfall, the individual quotas were usually set low enough so that any household exercising normal diligence would be able to produce a surplus; the emphasis was on positive inducements rather than punitive measures. In effect, this most extreme form of the responsibility system is akin to tenant farming, with the peasants paying the taxes and a fixed rent to the team as landowner. With the dissolution of the communes, it became the basic remuneration system throughout rural China.

The other forms of the responsibility system, which tended to be concentrated among the higher-income teams, were characterized by retention of the workpoint system even while production responsibility was delegated to individuals, households, and work groups. A household would be assigned responsibility for a certain piece of land, for example, or a work group for maintaining and harvesting an orchard, with the specified quota (the contract may also specify input requirements) being turned over to the team in exchange for an agreed number of workpoints. If output exceeded the quota, the household or team members would retain a specified share of it (or its monetary equivalent if it is turned over to the team and sold), a share which varied depending on the nature of the crop and the amount of (team-provided) capital that went into its production. Thus at the Donggucheng Production Brigade of the Taoyuan People's Commune near Shijiachuang in Hebei province, the apple orchard and greenhouse teams received 15 percent of the over-quota output (but lost 5 percent of their workday credits if they fell short of the quota), those growing Chinese cabbages received 50 percent, and those growing grain 100 percent, all in addition to their basic workpoint allotments (Lippit 1982).

The responsibility system was applied in ingenious fashion to practically every productive activity in the Chinese countryside. Also in the Donggucheng Brigade, the collective pig-raising, to which individuals used to be assigned on a rotating basis, became the responsibility of two people on a year-round basis. They were placed in charge of one hundred pigs, received a certain amount of food from the brigade, and were expected to increase the weight of the pigs by a specified amount. There were also breeding quotas; within a year's time each sow was expected to provide two litters averaging seven piglets each, and each piglet was expected to grow fifteen jin (1 jin = 1.1 lb.) within forty-five days. If those in charge met the quota they would receive 350 workday credits. If they exceeded the quota they would get 15 percent of the extra income. If they fulfilled only 90 percent of the plan, they would lose 10 percent of the 350 workday credits. If the litters averaged more than seven, they would receive one yuan for each extra pig.

Far to the east of Shijiachuang, in Yentai prefecture, Shandong province, a coastal team owns several fishing boats. Previously, different people would man the boats on a daily basis in exchange for workpoints. Under the responsibility system, the arrangements changed drastically. The boats were leased out on an annual basis to four-man groups, which were responsible for maintenance, repairs, and operating expenses. Cadres and experienced fishermen decided after discussions to set a minimum contract price of 4,000 yuan per boat in 1982, but at that price there were more groups of fishermen than boats. The price was then raised until at 5,000 yuan per boat the number of bidders equaled the number of boats. All of the groups exceeded by far the previous record catch and earnings, and by the end of April all had earned the 5,000 yuan contract price. After deducting expenses, all income earned during the remainder of the year was to go to the crew members.

The responsibility system clearly contributed to an intensification of work effort and the rising productivity of the agricultural sector. It also brought in its wake a variety of problems. Theft of individually farmed crops ready for harvest is one. As a consequence, some peasants began to sleep on "their land" to guard their crops as harvest time drew near; their behavior harkens back to the private farming of the prerevolutionary era. Another problem was the premium the responsibility system placed on family labor power. In some cases this led to children being kept out of school and in others it intensified resistance to the national family-planning policy of limiting the number of children. This is very difficult to resist effectively, however, and the press has reported instances of parents resorting to female infanticide as an alternative.

At the time of this writing (1985), the responsibility system is being replaced increasingly by forms of privatization that are at once simpler and more extreme. For the most part, the workpoint system is disappearing and peasants discharge their obligations through financial payments to the team, after which they may engage in farm or nonfarm activities of their choice. At the same time, the former commune- and brigade-owned industries have been converted into cooperatives owned collectively by the peasants. The institutional changes brought with them many new problems. Among the problems of private farming that have tended to reappear under the new system is that of negative externalities; just as in a private economy, each peasant trying to maximize his own income does not take into account the harmful consequences his actions may have for his neighbors or for the nation as a whole. In Inner Mongolia, for example, where the economy is primarily pastoral, the collectively owned sheep and cattle have been divided up and contracted out to individual households, which must return animals of comparable worth after three years but which can keep all the meat, milk, and wool they can produce in the interim. As a consequence, the herdsmen have been trying to increase their herds as rapidly as possible, resulting in severe overgrazing (Schell 1984). Denuded of its grass cover, much of the region's topsoil has been blown off by its fierce winds. The policy response to this problem has been to "privatize" grazing lands. These are now rented out to individual families on a long-term basis for a few cents per acre. Presumably the families will now have an interest in preventing overgrazing.

The responsibility system and privatization have been introduced into an environment in which substantial capital construction had been accomplished by collective effort over thirty years. Although the reforms tended to free the peasants from the heavy hand of bureaucratic authority and a pressured mobilization approach to economic affairs, they also benefited from the legacy of that approach. With the strength of the collective severely diminished, the question arises as to what force will be responsible for the maintenance and further development of rural capital construction. For some period of time, the legacy of the past will sustain current activities, but it will not do so indefinitely. It is not yet clear what the solution to this problem will be (Hinton 1983; Schell 1984).

Perhaps the issue of greatest concern is the potential effect on Chinese income distribution and social structure of the widespread introduction of the responsibility system and private economic activity. Lin Zili (1983), among others, defended the responsibility system at least in theoretical terms as preserving the cooperative economy. Lin pointed out that the cooperative continued to own the land, allocate it and determine contract terms. Further, although in most cases peasants provide their own inputs, this is well within the means of the average household, and the team can provide low-interest loans or other forms of subsidy for the few who cannot. Griffin (1984), reporting on his 1982 field survey of teams in Sichuan and Yunnan provinces, provides supporting evidence for this, showing that intrateam inequality had actually declined slightly during the reform period. Further, as already indicated, the substantial growth of peasant incomes relative to urban incomes has sharply diminished peasant-worker inequality, widely perceived in China to be a prime source of inequity.

Even granting the validity of these observations and arguments, however, the fact remains that even the responsibility system had the potential to create substantial increases in inequality and a transformation of the social order to accompany it; this potential is magnified many times by the more extreme forms of privatization that are replacing the responsibility system. The slogan of the reform period has been to "let some get rich first," and like the peasant in Dali Commune near Guangzhou who earned 17,000 yuan in a recent year raising ducks for export to Hong Kong, some have been doing it with a vengeance. The question to be raised, however, is why expect the initial inequality to be overcome at some indefinite future date as the remainder of the population outperforms the initially successful entrepreneurs? Would not the reverse expectation be more probable, with the initially successful, bolstered by the capital and business experience they have accumulated, continuing to outperform the rest of the population and widen the income gap? Not only does this seem more likely in the light of experience elsewhere, the absence of a developed institutional structure to limit the growth of inequality must also be taken into consideration. With a rudimentary progressive income tax and no taxes on personal wealth and inheritance, institutional means of limiting the growth in inequality remain deficient. While this can be remedied in time, it remains to be seen how vigorously corrective measures will be pursued, especially since they contradict the material-incentive thrust that stands at the core of the reform movement.

In connection with the rise of considerable inequalities in rural income and wealth lies the issue of emerging changes in social structure that might normally be expected to accompany it. In a society placing a premium on the individual pursuit and acquisition of wealth, social standing and prestige will naturally accrue to the financially successful. We can imagine that they will be called on to patronize village activities, and that they would quite naturally tend to develop close ties with local officials. At the very least we are talking about the emergence of a distinct stratum among the peasantry with a social influence that extends beyond the wealth on which it is based. To some extent this can be controlled if the party keeps a firm grip on its cadres and its cadres on rural society. But to the extent this is true, the hierarchical structure of Chinese rural society will be perpetuated.

Although the emerging contradictions of the new course admit no easy solutions, there is no reason to assume a priori that they cannot be contained or resolved, or that their emergence in itself invalidates the reform effort; any policy course will give rise to contradictions, and success in implementation depends in large measure on the skill with which these are handled. Although the viability of the reform effort and its consistency with the transition to socialism can be determined only over time, it may be possible now to assess the reasons for which the commune system of collective agriculture was abandoned. The real problem, if we look at the history of agricultural collectivization in China since the mid–1950s, appears to be the unsatisfactory relationship that had emerged between the party-state and the peasants. This was a consequence of the party-state imposing its vision and goals on the direct producers before they had developed the consciousness to accept it or the material conditions existed to justify it. In the process, the peasant producers' material aspirations, desire for autonomy, and perhaps ultimately their support for the collective vision were sacrificed. The consequence was a slowing of agricultural development well below the possible level. If this is correct, an alternative might have been found in a policy decision to interfere less and adopt measures supportive of local initiative and the legitimate material interests of the peasants. Indeed, that is just what has happened since 1979 with the adoption of the responsibility system, the reopening of markets, and so forth, policies which led to a great surge in agricultural output and incomes even before the general dismantling of the communes. Viewed from this perspective, the demise of the commune system represents only in part the efficiency logic of new forms of economic association in the countryside, for it represents as well the loss of peasant confidence in the system brought on by the imposition of the collective form from above without due regard for peasant interests and local control.

Economic Reform and Socialist Transition

Socialist economic development depends in the final analysis on the adoption of policies that reflect the interest of the working classes, in rural as well as in urban areas, and on the growing authority of those classes to shape the social reality at every level and thus their own existence as well. Viewed from this perspective, the economic experience of the Maoist years posed two central contradictions for the transition to socialism in China. First, the failure of real wages to increase and the nominal gains in peasant incomes over two decades were inconsistent with the interest and needs of the working classes. Second, the perpetuation and intensification of a bureaucratic-administrative hierarchy that completely controlled the lives of ordinary working people contradicted one of the most fundamental premises of socialist society.

These contradictions were not fortuitous. They emerged as a natural consequence of the Maoist approach to economic development, a mobilizational, military-campaign type of approach in which the vision and will of the central leaders became the dynamic motive force underlying social change, and centrally directed capital accumulation the principal route to economic growth and development. To the extent that the leadership is indeed in tune with the mass of the population, this approach can yield dramatic results for a limited period of time. Stretched over the better part of two decades, however, its internal contradictions were bound to intensify. Making economic activity an extension of state administration, and depriving of decision-making authority thereby the individuals and enterprises directly involved in production, inevitably leads to decreasing dynamic efficiency in an increasingly complex economy. Under such circumstances, economic growth can be sustained only by increasing the investment share of national income at the expense of consumption. And as people see the realization of their aspirations for improved living standards postponed indefinitely, as they experience the arbitrary exercise of authority over them increasingly as an institutionalized fact, they become less responsive to exhortational rhetoric and more alienated from the leadership and its goals. As a consequence, the authority of the hierarchical structure must be strengthened. Further, since the Maoist approach makes a fetish of central planning to the exclusion of almost all market elements, erroneously confusing the existence of markets per se with capitalism, it bars the only institutional mechanism capable of transferring economic authority from the bureaucracy to the productive units and ultimately their workers.

Above all, the reform period, ushered in by the Third Plenum of the party's Eleventh Central Committee in December 1978, is characterized by its alternative development strategy, one which seeks to eliminate the excessive authority of the center by restoring a balance between it and the producing units. To do so, incentives must be offered for hard work, innovation, and the assumption of initiative. This requires reducing the investment share of national income in favor of consumption and increasing nonproductive investment—that is, investment in housing, schools, museums, hospitals, and so forth—as a share of total investment. This strategy seeks to compensate for the decrease in productive investment by an increase in work effort, innovation, initiative, and efficiency in the productive units in every sector of the economy.

This in turn requires the use of markets; there is simply no alternative if real decision-making authority is to be turned over to the producing units. It should be emphasized in this regard that the major decisions for the economy can remain centrally determined, and indeed in a socialist economy they must be. Thus, during the very period in which the use of the market economy was spreading throughout China, the main parameters of the economy remained firmly under central direction; indeed, during this period, the initiatives of the center were in many respects unprecedented. Thus, the center undertook to reduce the national savings-investment rate sharply in favor of consumption—the rate dropped from 36.5 percent in 1978 to 28.5 percent in 1981 (table 6.3) even while the share of nonproductive investment in the total rose sharply (BR, Feb. 21. 1983, 13)—to restore a balance between light and heavy industry by sharply limiting the latter to release resources for the former, to raise consumption sharply, to emphasize within the industrial sector the development of the energy and transport sectors, to strengthen greatly education, and to open the economy to international trade and investment on a substantial scale yet in a carefully controlled manner. If anything, the experience of the reform period shows that freeing the center from detailed concern with microeconomic affairs can create an environment in which it can address more directly the macroeconomic issues that form the core concerns of economic planning.

The reform period can be understood, then, as one in which the shortcomings of the Maoist period with regard to mass consumption and hierarchical social organization were addressed through the adoption of a new economic strategy that incorporated extensive use of market allocation and material incentives within an overall planning framework. The reform of hierarchy has been attenuated, however. The separation of political and economic authority, in conjunction with the professionalization of management, has indeed made the party-state less intrusive in everyday life. Nevertheless, the rural cooperatives are dominated by cadres who dispose of a sizable portion of the surplus generated as they see fit, and the democratization of the workplace remains a distant goal. At the same time, new contradictions have inevitably emerged from the reform process. These are discussed in chapter 9, on the transition to socialism and the outlook for the Chinese economy.

9. The Transition to Socialism

According to the theoretical framework developed in chapter 1, economic development throughout the third world has been marked in the postwar era by the central role of the state. With the state taking the lead in all of the less developed countries in defining intersectoral economic relations and economic relations with the capitalist world economy, in defining the parameters within which economic activities are conducted, and often in carrying out production directly via the medium of parastatal corporations, a "statist" social formation has everywhere been the rule. Within the statist social formation, however, three distinct models of development can be distinguished: capitalist, statist, and socialist.

Under capitalist development, the system of private ownership of the means of production is gradually strengthened, the transfer of public resources to the private sector proceeds apace, public officials gain an increasing stake in the private sector, and ultimately the state becomes subordinate to the newly emerging capitalist class. Under statist development, by contrast, the authority of the state as an independent actor is preserved and strengthened, and the bureaucracy emerges as an independent class, one whose interest cannot be reduced or subordinated to that of other classes in the society. Finally, under socialist development, the class interest of people who work for a living becomes predominant. As under statist development, public ownership of the means production remains the norm, but under socialist development this is supplemented by the extended authority of working people to shape their own lives at every level of social activity, and the ultimate subordination of the bureaucracy to their authority.

The transition to socialism refers to the assumption of control by working people over their own lives and of social activity at every level, and to the emergence of their class interest as the predominant one in society. The history of the twentieth century suggests that the transition process is most likely to appear after a "socialist" revolution, but only if such a revolution is followed by a process of socialist development. Although the revolutionary transformation of ownership relations appears to be a necessary condition for socialist development, it by no means provides assurance that development will in fact assume a socialist form. Of particular relevance in this regard is the tendency for the revolutionary leadership to retain control in its own hands, consolidating its own power ostensibly as the agent of the working classes but ultimately emerging with a distinct class interest of its own. In terms of the analytical framework presented here, this would mean the consolidation of a statist social formation rather than the emergence of a socialist one.

In part III, I have attempted to lay out the criteria for socialist development and to evaluate the development process in China accordingly. This can help "locate" the Chinese experience, but it cannot adequately explain its dynamics—the forces at work propelling Chinese society down one path or another. This chapter focuses on the dynamics through an examination of the principal contradictions confronted by Chinese society in the postrevolutionary era. As spelled out in chapter 1, these include (1) the contradiction between the immediate producers and society, (2) the contradiction between advanced consciousness and popular control of social institutions, (3) the contradiction between the leaders and the masses, and (4) the contradiction between the forces and relations of production. The transition to socialism depends on satisfactory resolutions to each of these contradictions, resolutions which give expression to the opposite poles of each contradiction. Since the contradictions are continually being recreated in new form, each resolution is provisional, and we can speak of progress in the transition to socialism as emerging from a succession of successful resolutions. The extent to which economic development in China adheres to the socialist model depends on the resolutions to the contradictions that emerge from social practice in China.

Three Contradictions

The essence of the contradiction between the immediate producers and society lies in the potential for conflict between the interests of individuals or of people at particular workplaces and the class interests of working people taken collectively. A surplus will have to be extracted from industry and agriculture, for example, to finance investment or improvements in social services. Pressures to raise productivity or hold down wages may be part of this process. From the perspective of those at particular workplaces, such pressures may well be viewed with hostility.

Socialist development requires a resolution to this contradiction that gives expression to both its poles. Indeed, as the following discussion suggests, a similar synthesis of opposites is required for each of the principal contradictions. Much of the discussion in part 3 has emphasized the decline in real wages during the Maoist era (1957–76) and the failure of peasant incomes to rise appreciably. This, together with the maintenance of a strict hierarchy which is at once social, political, and economic, was seen as inconsistent with the socialist development model. Restated in terms of the contradiction between the interests of the immediate producers and society, we can say that the broad social interest in industrialization via high rates of capital formation was pursued vigorously, while working people's interest in higher income and living standards received scant attention. The one-sided resolution of the contradiction between the two was possible because of the continuing hierarchy in Chinese social structure.

The transition to socialism requires a resolution that gives expression to both poles of the contradiction, not just one. In the reform period beginning in 1978, a new development strategy was adopted that does give expression to the material needs and interests of working people—not instead of a high rate of capital formation but alongside it. Thus consumption grew from 63.5 percent to 71.0 percent of net material expenditures between 1978 and 1982, while personal consumption grew from 56.2 percent to 63.1 percent (Yeh 1984, 704). Since this rising proportion was buttressed by a growing national income, the absolute increases in consumption were substantial.

The reform policies, moreover, are a response in large measure to pressures generated at the grassroots level. Several times in the past, local cadres had found that allocating land to individual households for cultivation under a contract system was highly popular and an effective means of raising productivity. In 1956–57, this practice spread from Zhejiang to several other provinces, in 1959 it was implemented in Henan, and in the early 1960s it was put into effect in Anhui (Zhang 1985, 12–13). In each case it was seen as a means of overcoming the contradiction between the individual and collective (that is, state) interests, and in each case the practice was criticized as "rightist" by the center and crushed. Only in 1979, under the reform leadership, was the experiment allowed to continue. It appeared then in Anhui province, where it spread to over 10 percent of the households by the end of the year; with central support it was then extended over the entire country. Although the spread of the individual management system represents the response of the center to grassroots pressures, it should also be noted that once the center had decided on decollectivization, even those peasants who would have preferred to retain the collective in stronger form were given no choice in the matter (Unger 1985b).

The persistence of hierarchy has been a greater problem, however, in the resolution of the second and third of the major contradictions. The second, it will be recalled, arises from the fact that while a heightened consciousness and leadership based on it are required for a socialist transition, the opportunity for working people to shape their own institutions and future is equally essential. The mass line during the Maoist era represented a clear awareness of the need to resolve this contradiction, but one which failed because the absolute concentration of authority in the hands of the leadership was retained; under these circumstances the leadership heard only what it wanted to hear as the expression of popular opinion, or only those who were prepared to voice what they knew the leadership wanted to hear dared to do so. During the Cultural Revolution, efforts to portray the masses as the ultimate authority were belied by the gang of four's control of the media to define correct thought and its readiness to subject all "deviant" thinkers to a form of social excommunication. Despite the rhetoric of the era, therefore, the contradiction was resolved in a fashion that perpetuated hierarchy, and did so in an especially oppressive form since ideologues were ensconced at the top of the hierarchy.

The muting of rhetoric during the succeeding reform era, and the unmistakably more open, responsive, and popular policies that have characterized it, however, should not be allowed to obscure the fact that the Chinese hierarchy remains intact, and that the resolution of the contradiction between party leadership and mass participation in the shaping of society remains overwhelmingly skewed toward the former. This appears both in the realm of ideas and leadership (the second of the contradictions specified), and in the realm of class interest (the third of the contradictions).

As the discussion in chapter 1 indicates, societies that have carried out socialist revolutions, including the nationalization of private property and the implementation of central planning, have merely created necessary preconditions for a transition to socialism. In postrevolutionary society, party cadres serve nominally as representatives of the working classes. Since they gain privileged access to the power and resources of the state, however, and the state assumes the leading role in the economy, there is a strong possibility for them to develop distinct interests of their own. Under such circumstances, the bureaucrats may come to constitute a distinct class, while the statist social formation that marks the transition period becomes consolidated.

The critical considerations in the potential emergence of the bureaucracy as a distinct class include the development of mechanisms to transmit class status to subsequent generations (to secure privileged status for the offspring of the cadres), the emergence of a material interest that is quite distinct from that of ordinary people as the cadres use their position to channel a significant share of the surplus into exorbitant expense accounts or their own pockets, and the disappearance (or absence) of institutional mechanisms to assure some measure of control over their activities by the working population whose interests they nominally represent.

If the bureaucracy emerges as a distinct class, the transition to socialism cannot proceed. In the case of China, it is far too early to make a definitive assessment concerning the constitution of the bureaucracy as a distinct class. One can, however, analyze the impact of the change in investment strategy from the Maoist to the reformist era and observe certain tendencies that have arisen. The observations that follow are not meant to be definitive; they are meant rather to indicate the manner in which the framework presented can be applied to the analysis of class structure and social formation in contemporary China, and to provide a basis for evaluating the ongoing changes that are taking place.

The Question of Cadre Class Formation in the Reform Era

In certain respects, the social forces unleashed during the reform era have tended to diminish the prospects for the bureaucracy emerging as a distinct class, but in other respects they have tended to strengthen them. The resulting picture, as a consequence, remains quite ambiguous. Here I would like first to look briefly at some of the forces weakening the prospects for independent class status, and then to look at some of the forces strengthening them.

The commitment to economic growth and modernization that emerged to take priority status in the reform era has tended to separate economic and political authority—at least to a modest extent—in Chinese society. The elimination of the communes, for example, transferred their political powers to the reconstituted township governments, while the peasant households have assumed control, in large measure, over their own economic activity. Thus, whereas in the past, social, political, and economic authority was concentrated in a single hierarchy with senior cadres in control, that hierarchy has now been partially fragmented.

Parallel changes can be found throughout Chinese society. Whereas the party-branch secretary was the ultimate economic authority within state enterprises during the Maoist period, the party has been ordered to restrict its enterprise activities to assuring compliance with party and government policies and explicitly to refrain from interference with management decisions. The purposes of this change are to increase the professionalism of enterprise management and to establish clear economic criteria for evaluating management performance. In general, the reforms have tended to strengthen the autonomy of professionals in all spheres. As a consequence of these changes, there has been some separation of economic and political authority.

Within the political sphere, reforms have been initiated that aim at the professionalization of the party-state administrative apparatus, thereby limiting the possibilities for the personal abuse of authority. Senior cadres, who previously had no retirement requirement, have generally been forced to retire, and professional qualifications have become an important factor in the selection of their replacements. Counterbalancing the reforms in the cadre system, however, are a number of factors that leave open the possibility of cadre class formation.

First, there is still a lack of accountability for the cadres and a lack of control over their activities by working people. The commune and brigade industries, for example, are now formally collectives owned by all the former commune and brigade members. They have been turned over to the newly reconstituted township governments, which are supposed to administer them on behalf of their members, the peasants in each township. In fact, however, the peasants have no way to control these collectives, or to control the disposition of the net proceeds they generate. The cadres tend to have a much stronger interest than the peasants in reinvesting these proceeds, for example, and in some cases in building extravagant office facilities and purchasing cars for administrative use. Thus one of the major problems faced by the reform government has been local investment racing out of control despite efforts to limit aggregate investment; this has resulted in a higher than planned investment ratio, inflationary pressures, delays in the completion of investment projects, and misallocation of investment resources between the center and the localities. And it has come about in large measure because the interest of the peasant "owners" of the collectives is not receiving adequate representation.

The lack of accountability that characterizes the cadre system as a whole is buttressed by the retention of the system of having senior cadres appoint junior ones; this tends to make the cadre system extremely hierarchical and self-contained, insulating it from outside influence of any kind, including popular influence. Beginning in 1984, a reform in the cadre system was adopted in principle and gradually implemented; the reform attempts to apply the "responsibility system" to cadres in government agencies and enterprises. If managers and other cadres are to be responsible for the performance of their units, they must have control over the selection of the personnel who work with them. Thus, a plant director has the right to assemble his own (senior) management team and to appoint workshop heads, and the workshop heads can appoint the work team leaders under them. In similar fashion, at the Chinese Academy of Social Sciences, the leading center for social science research in China, the president of the Academy appoints the head of each institute, the institute head appoints the chairs of the various departments within the institute, and the chairs appoint their members.

This type of pyramid, based on personal or committee authority to make appointments, remains characteristic of the Chinese bureaucratic system. It is ameliorated in certain respects by the frequent use of consultations with a unit's members when a head is to be appointed, or polls which may be used for guidance, but ultimate authority remains firmly in the hands of the senior officials empowered to make appointments.

Finally, as the possibilities for personal enrichment have expanded during the reform era, especially in the countryside where private entrepreneurship is now actively encouraged, cadres and their family members appear often to have been able to use their political position and greater education to seize the most attractive opportunities (see, for example, Diamond 1985, 791). Moreover, as material prosperity has become increasingly "acceptable," cadres are able to channel state or collective funds into the creation of a more luxurious working environment for themselves. In general, the growing prosperity of the reform era has raised the surplus, increasing the possibilities for the cadres to channel an increasing share of it to themselves in office or to family members or former cadres in the private sector.

These changes all have a bearing on the question of cadre class formation, but, as noted, the net impact remains ambiguous. On the one hand, the increased professionalization of the cadre system, including the growing concern with formal qualifications, performance, and merit, enhances the administrative character of the bureaucracy as a vehicle for carrying out the purposes of society. On the other hand, the lack of external accountability, the retention of strict hierarchy within the cadre system, and the growing possibilities for material benefit enhance the possibility that the bureaucracy will emerge as a distinct class with an interest of its own. Although the net effect of these opposing forces is unlikely to become clear for a prolonged period, the rapid rise of many children of senior cadres to responsible posts in recent years (see, for example, *Wall Street Journal*, Oct. 29, 1985, 1) suggests that the possibility of the bureaucracy emerging as a distinct class most definitely remains.

The Fourth Contradiction: Relations versus Forces of Production

Mao Zedong placed primary emphasis on developing socialist relations of production as the key to economic development and socialist transition. He believed that social institutions should give maximum scope to people's more selfless instincts and their cooperative spirit. These socialist virtues would ultimately emerge as a material force as well, motivating people to work harder, limiting the demand for consumption goods and thus making higher levels of investment possible, and creating investment possibilities in capital construction—like labor-intensive projects to develop irrigation—which were beyond the scope of individual initiative. In short, Mao believed in maintaining a kind of purity of spirit, in emphasizing egalitarianism, selflessness, and cooperation, as the basis for socialist development. The egalitarian, cooperative relations of production for which this vision calls are clearly consistent with the ultimate goals of socialist development.

Emphasizing what appear to be socialist relations of production, however, may not be conducive to the most rapid development of the forces of production, and in various respects it may slow the development of these forces significantly. People may not after all be motivated to work intensively without tangible rewards; even though the internalization of such behavior patterns may emerge naturally as a result of socialist development, it can hardly be presumed as a condition for it. Furthermore, efficient development of the forces of production requires a considerable decentralization of decision making to the enterprises or other units actually carrying out production activities. Such decentralization requires coordination through the market, and the market functions in conjunction with material incentives and income differentiation.

The contradiction between the relations and forces of production has been intensified by the presence of the other contradictions that have been noted. It is certainly clear that under the appropriate circumstances, people can be highly motivated by nonmaterial objectives, and this has been manifest in activities as diverse as athletic contests and warfare. What has not been established—and what appears quite suspect—is that third parties can induce such motivation where it is lacking initially. Moreover, any attempt to induce such motivation may ultimately prove counterproductive if people come to see themselves as objects of manipulation. Such a response may well account for much of the widespread cynicism that the repeated ''socialist'' campaigns eventually induced in the Chinese people during the Maoist era.

In the countryside, the problems of the people's communes displayed with special clarity the contradiction between the forces and relations of production, and its interplay with the other contradictions noted. The collectivization of agriculture was meant in part to lay the basis for socialist production relations in the countryside, but the vastly stepped up pace of labor productivity growth in agriculture from the inception of the reform period suggests that collectivization held back the development of the forces of production. Ironically, that in turn undermined support for the collective form—the people's commune—since it did not allow adequate improvement in people's living standards. Perhaps an even greater irony exists in the fact that although the communes were collective in form, they clearly were established from above and were not sufficiently responsive to the wishes and needs of their members to provide the basis for a truly collectivist ethos. To some extent central control was necessary to serve broader social purposes like assuring adequate investment funds and urban grain supplies. By sacrificing local interests to national interests in a one-sided fashion, however, and by controlling local affairs almost completely from the center, the administration undermined the possibility for evoking greater initiative and commitment from the peasants, a force which might well have improved economic performance. Thus the one-sided resolution of one contradiction may well have precluded the balanced resolution of another.

At one level of analysis, it is possible to argue that the contradiction between the forces and relations of production was resolved one-sidedly in favor of the relations of production during the Maoist era, and that the pendulum has swung in the opposite direction during the reform period. This assessment must be qualified, however, by the recognition that such institutions as the communes, firmly controlled from above, cannot really be classified as having socialist production relations, despite the egalitarian image they project. Moreover, account must also be taken of the rapid rate of capital construction during the Maoist era, the enhanced scope for worker-peasant initiative during the reform era, and the steps taken to limit polarization in income and wealth during the reform era, all of which qualify the assessment further. Nevertheless, in the sense that the Maoist strategy failed to develop the productive forces sufficiently to permit significant improvements in living standards to accompany capital construction, thereby undermining popular support for the socialist project, and in the sense that the reform strategy encourages self-seeking behavior and paves the way for growing differentials in income and wealth, the image of movement between opposite extremes in the resolution of this contradiction captures an important element of truth.

The Role of the Market

In the policy reversals that have marked the transition from Maoism to reform, the new-found acceptability of a central role for the market holds a critical place. Marx (1967) saw the market as playing a major role in the extraction and realization of value produced by the direct producers, and consistent with this perspective the Soviet Union and those states following its lead have emphasized central planning, with centrally directed allocation of goods and services, as the core of their economic construction effort. Since the market as an institution long

predates capitalism, however, the two concepts are clearly not cotermi-
nous. Further, central planning as it has evolved in practice has proven
inconsistent with socialist economic relations in certain critical respects.

Alec Nove (1979, 122), in an important essay, highlights the para-
doxical contradiction between central planning and socialist economic
relations. If there is no market to provide guidelines to producing units
concerning product mix and production methods, production directives must come from above. Central planning, in short, mandates
hierarchy, depriving those involved in productive activity of the opportunity for intiative and control of the workplace. Since producer control
is an important component of socialist economic relations, the mandated hierarchy of traditional central planning is inconsistent with the
development of such relations.

To avoid this hierarchy, the market must play some role. Under
capitalism, hierarchy within the enterprise tends to deprive workers of
authority. Under central planning, this aspect of hierarchy is typically
retained in modified form and reinforced by the imposition of an
external hierarchy that subordinates the entire enterprise to the administrative apparatus of the party-state. Reducing the power of the administrative hierarchy creates a condition that is necessary to enhance
producer authority, but which by no means in itself can assure it; in the
extreme case, the managerial elite within each enterprise will simply
replace the state bureaucracy as the ultimate authority, recreating conditions akin to capitalism.

As indicated, beginning in 1984 the practice of making managers
fully responsible for the performance of their enterprises was generally
implemented throughout China, with enterprise heads given the rights
to appoint their own senior management teams and to establish their
own systems of rewards and punishments for workers according to
worker productivity. Whether it is true or not, the belief that productivity and performance depend on concentrating enterprise authority in
the hands of management precludes the democratization of the workplace.

Early in the reform period, especially in the late 1970s and early
1980s, China's reform leadership indicated its awareness of the importance of spurring democratization within the enterprise. Efforts to
enhance the role of the congress of workers and staff, and to promote
the election of plant managers by workers, reflect this. These efforts,
however, posed the threat of interference with the modernization drive

insofar as they conflicted with the professionalization of management and efforts to introduce a system of rewards and promotions based on managerial performance. Thus after a flurry of announcements about the importance of extending worker authority in the workplace and the initiation of concrete measures to put this into effect, largely by re-establishing and upgrading the role of the congress of workers and staff, and by having workers elect managers, the Chinese leadership has fallen silent; the professionalization of management and the sup-posed benefits this affords for the development of the forces of produc-tion has clearly been given precedence over the development of more socialist relations of production.

Identifying the market with capitalism, the Maoist leadership made every effort to deny it a role in the economy. In doing so, they made resource allocation an administrative matter, imposing a bureaucratic hierarchy over the direct producers and reducing economic efficiency and incentives. A high level of investment and growth could neverthe-less be maintained, but only at the cost of improving popular living standards. The reform leaders, by expanding the role of the market greatly, reduced the impact of the administrative hierarchy and set the stage for a remarkable improvement in living standards. Did they at the same time create the conditions for a transition to capitalism?

This question must be considered at two levels. In the first place, as was argued in chapter 1, the character of a social formation depends on which classes are dominant, that is, on which classes have authority and receive the surplus. The extension of the market in China has benefitted working people primarily, and the capitalist class remains miniscule and powerless. In this sense it can hardly be equated with the revival of capitalism. At another level, however, it must be recognized that the expanded role of the market does pose several powerful contradictions for the socialist transition. Whether or not this transition can remain a viable project—in the sense of deepening the authority of working people over their own lives and over the entire society at every level, as well as of increasing the effectiveness with which their class interests are expressed in public policy—depends on the success with which the market-posed contradictions are resolved.

At this point, only the most preliminary observations are possible concerning this point. First, in terms of the development models pre-sented in chapter 1, the strengthening of the statist social formation must be considered together with transitions to socialism or capitalism. The emergence of a privileged managerial elite within the state-owned sector, for example, would strengthen statist forces. The failure to pursue vigorously the earlier efforts at enterprise democratization (which may however be resumed at a later date) and the tendency to go to an extreme, especially in the countryside, in tying income to individual productive performance, suggest that the contradiction between the forces and relations of production is being resolved one-sidedly in favor of the former. To the extent that this is so, the enhanced role of the market, despite its initial contribution to the socialist transition by improving people's material welfare and diminishing bureaucratic authority, may ultimately pose new obstacles to the socialist transition. Whether or not it does so will depend on the success with which the contradictions posed or intensified by the development of the market system are resolved.

The Social Formation under Reform

In many respects, China's social formation during the reform era reflects socialist elements, especially since the class interests of working people are reflected extensively in public policy. Nevertheless, in the last analysis China's social formation remains largely statist in character. Even though a more rationalistic social engineering has replaced ideological belief as the basis for public policy, economic initiative remains for the most part in the hands of the party-state, and the statist mode of production continues to prevail. New institutional forms have appeared or reappeared, however, and the social formation has changed markedly since the Maoist era. This change has definite implications for the transition to socialism, since it thrusts to the fore new contradictions or new forms of old ones.

To specify the new social formation, it is appropriate to start with the specific mix of modes of production that characterizes it. First, the state-owned enterprise remains the characteristic form in industry; all large-scale industrial enterprises remain under state ownership. These are, however, given much more autonomy in their operations than before, and they have been freed in many respects from direct subordination to administrative authorities (although they must still give priority to plan fulfillment with a specified portion of their output). The extension of the market system has made their enhanced autonomy possible, and this has been supplemented by the replacement of the profit-remittance system with a tax system and permission, within specified limits, to determine their own use of retained earnings. Accompanying these changes have been the withdrawal of the party from direct intervention in business decisions, the professionalization of management, and the reinstitution of management responsibility for enterprise performance, a system initially modeled on that of the Soviet Union which was introduced in the early 1950s and subsequently abandoned. Within the enterprise, then, political interference with management decision-making has been curtailed, but the managers must now take full responsibility for their success or failure.

In earlier chapters it was emphasized that the introduction of the market system is an essential precondition for the extension of worker authority in the workplace, but it was noted as well that it is not a sufficient condition. The industrial system reform makes this crystal clear, for the subordination of workers within the workplace has been maintained under the new arrangements. This has not come about due to a lack of awareness on the part of the authorities, but it appears to be due to a conscious decision to give priority to the professionalization of management at the expense of the democratization of the workplace, which was to have been pursued through worker election of managers and the enhanced status of the congresses of workers and staff. One can reasonably assert that workers are better off under the new arrangements with higher incomes and improved housing and other benefits. Nevertheless, the mode of production of the large enterprises remains firmly statist in character.

Also in the urban industrial sector, the cooperative mode of production has been strengthened and expanded markedly, and the individual petty-commodity mode of production has been revived, especially in the service sector (including restaurants, repair services, and so forth). As of the end of 1983, there were 87.7 million staff and workers in state-owned enterprises, 27.4 million in urban collective enterprises, and 2.3 million self-employed urban workers (State Statistical Bureau 1984, 108). Finally, although it is not officially recognized as such, the capitalist mode of production has reappeared in urban and rural areas, and "there are many private enterprises whose properties are worth more than one million yuan, have an annual gross income more than several hundred thousand yuan, and total employment over one hundred people" (Zhang 1985, 25). These still account for a very small proportion of industrial activity and employment, and the party allows their development because it feels they contribute to the modernization drive and believes it can ultimately control them completely.

In the countryside, the decollectivization of agriculture has been accompanied by the emergence of several new modes of production. It is important to keep in mind, when considering these, that the people's communes they have replaced were clearly statist in character despite a superficially socialist form; as indicated, they were firmly controlled from above and reflected the goals of the national leadership above all. The split-up of the communes has brought the development of small-scale individual production in the rural sector—essentially the petty-commodity production of peasant households—on the one hand, and new patterns of cooperative development on the other.

The vast majority of peasants now make fixed payments to cover the use of land, tax obligations, welfare payments, and so forth and are free to use the balance of their output for consumption or sale on the market. Most provide most of their own food, but there are varying degrees of commodity production, and an increasing number of households—the most prosperous in the countryside—are specializing completely in one of the many "sideline" activities and producing almost exclusively for the market. This production involves, among other activities, construction, service activities (transport, repair services, and so forth), and a wide range of specialized crop production and processing activities. In some cases the newly formed enterprises have become quite extensive in scale and can most properly be classified as part of the capitalist mode of production. Also, some individuals have become extremely prosperous through extensive trading activity and can most properly be considered as new merchant capitalists. The regime is actively promoting peasant entrepreneurship and the development of sideline activities, in part to absorb the displaced agricultural labor appearing as a consequence of the rapid increase in agricultural productivity, and in part because growing rural productivity creates necessary conditions for the success of the overall modernization drive.

Together with the emergence of petty commodity production and some capitalist production and trading activity in the countryside, the former brigade and commune enterprises, now in the form of cooperatives run under township leadership, have demonstrated explosive growth. This is due in part to the fact that they are free now to dispose of the surplus as they wish and to enter new activities freely, in part to the fact that cadres rather than the membership control the surplus— and have more of a vested interest in reinvestment than the peasants who would most certainly prefer greater distribution of profits—and in part to the boom conditions that have emerged in the countryside and the national economy as a whole, creating particularly auspicious conditions for small business. As in the past when the center has loosened the reins, local investment has boomed, pushing national investment levels well above target, depriving higher-priority investment activities of needed resources, and creating inflationary pressures. Nevertheless, the stimulus to an all-round development in the countryside has been considerable.

In describing China's new social formation, the dramatic institutional changes taking place in the various activities that tie production activities together should also be noted. These include, to enumerate just some of them, the emergence of commercial law and the use of contracts, a wide variety of sales and distribution mechanisms, new commercial financing arrangements including commercial loans, leasing, stock sales, and so forth, and many new financial institutions; a stock market is under consideration.

Certainly China's social formation today is markedly different from what it was in the Maoist years; there is a much richer mix of various modes of production, and an environment has been created in which vast opportunities for initiative and innovation have been opened up and seized at the individual and enterprise level. Moreover, it is appropriate to point out that socialist elements in the social formation have been enhanced in the sense that public policies represent much more fully the objective class interests of working people. Nevertheless, the social formation remains predominantly statist in the sense that the statist mode of production continues to characterize large-scale industry, that the levers of economic activity remain firmly in the hands of the state, and above all because working people remain powerless to shape their own environment, even at the workplace let alone the other levels of society.

The Prospects for China

The pragmatic, market-oriented activity that has spread through China like wildfire raises the question of whether China is in the process of a transition to capitalism. Unquestionably the policies currently being pursued would, if left unchecked, lead in that direction. And precisely because economic policy has been so competent in the reform era— focusing initially on agriculture as the weak link in the economy, holding down investment and increasing consumption, focusing on energy and transport as the weak links in the industrial sector, and so forth—conditions for an economic boom were created by the mid-

1980s which would give all the greater impetus to the private pursuit of prosperity. Yet one factor stands in the way of any simple transition to capitalism: the Communist Party and the vision its leading members have of a socialist future.

The party is committed to modernizing the country and to raising sharply living standards, and it is prepared to implement a wide range of practical policies toward that end. At the same time, it remains committed to the vision of an egalitarian society in which the basic needs of the entire population are provided for at much higher than minimum levels. It also remains committed to public ownership of the main means of production and to centrally planning the main macro-economic variables, providing direction for the economy as a whole, and assuring full employment. If these commitments or the party's control should weaken, then a transition to capitalism based on the forces unleashed in China's economic reform would become quite possible; neither eventuality, however, seems probable at this time.

It should also be kept in mind that the party is in a position to institute policies and create pressures that soften some of the contradictions to which its pursuit of modernization has given rise. Some of these were discussed in chapter 6, for example, which described various types of subsidy being provided to the poorest production teams. The pressures are reflected in the behavior of rural entrepreneurs donating money for village schools and other public purposes, and in the frequent willingness of specialized households in the 10,000-yuan class to teach their production techniques to others. The party is now spurring rural entrepreneurship as a means of speeding development and promoting employment, but it retains the option of curtailing it if the contradictions to which it gives rise prove unmanageable.

In analyzing the possibilities for transition from one form of social formation to another, the critical issues revolve around class formation and the rise of a predominant mode of production. Capitalism is a system in which the capitalist class is pre-eminent and the capitalist mode of production predominant. The capitalist class and capitalist mode of production are still miniscule in China, and while their further development in the rural sector especially appears likely, such development is completely at the sufferance of the party, which appears most unlikely to allow it to assume significant proportions. Ironically, however, the very same retention of firm central control directing the entire society is an obstacle to the transition to socialism as much as it is to the transition to capitalism.

I have argued that the essence of socialism lies in the class dominance of working people, in their ability to shape the society at every
level and their own lives with it, and that socialism is reflected objectively in institutional arrangements and policies that give expression to
their class interest. Nominally, the Communist Party reflects that interest, but since it exists in fact as a hierarchy that is beyond the authority
of ordinary working people, the critical element of working class control which alone can assure representation is lacking. The existence,
therefore, of an autonomous, self-perpetuating hierarchy within Chinese society is an obstacle equally to the emergence of capitalism and to
the emergence of socialism.

How stable is this situation? It can legitimately be maintained that
the situation is still quite fluid. On the one hand, the interests of the
working classes are much more satisfactorily represented during the
reform era than during the Maoist one, as reflected in the much higher
degree of prosperity, the rapidly expanding opportunities for personal
development, and the sharply improved environment for a more open
expression of ideas. Moreover, the objective of quadrupling national
income between 1980 and 2000 appears well within reach. If anything,
an unprecedented economic boom appears to be in store for the end of
the twentieth century, allowing the economic targets to be reached early
and permitting per capita national income to approach U.S. $1,000, at
which point the basic needs of the entire population at a minimum level
of comfort can be assured. Thus, the reform policies are clearly serving
the interests of working people.

At the same time, it is not objectively possible for the bureaucracy to
congeal as a new class at this time. During the Maoist era, those who
held higher administrative positions within the party-state enjoyed elite
status. Under the reform, a new group of professional managers, and
indeed of other professionals as well, has also begun to emerge. It is far
too early for this new group, whose outlook and interest is apt to be
quite different from that of the administrators in certain key respects, to
be integrated with the latter. Thus, for example, the managers prefer
extension of the market and enterprise authority, while the administrators see their own authority undermined by these developments. During the reform era of extraordinarily rapid social, economic, and institutional change, an era in which the composition of the elite is changing
as well, it appears that the conditions are not favorable for the congeal-
ing of the bureaucracy as a new class.

The outlook for China into the beginning of the twenty-first century, then, is for the continuation of a statist social formation, but one that has not yet assumed stable form. Capitalism could emerge only as a consequence of cynicism and corruption, with the extensive privatization of public resources accompanied by a complete loosening of control by the state over private economic activity; it appears most improbable. Statism could become consolidated if the new managers and other professionals merge with the present cadres to form a new class that controls society, appropriates a sizable share of the surplus, and reproduces itself. Socialism will emerge if the party, having guided China to a new age of prosperity and established the institutional framework for the new society, proves willing to dismantle the hierarchy it has created and to share authority with working people. It would require the democratization of Chinese society, from the workplace to the state. At present, China's development path lies somewhere between the statist and socialist models.

References

Adelman, Irma (1979) "Growth, Income Distribution and Equity-Oriented Development Strategies," in Charles Wilber, ed., *The Political Economy of Development and Underdevelopment*, 2d ed. New York: Random House.

Ahmad, Nigar (1978) "Peasant Struggle in a Feudal Setting." International Labour Office World Employment Program Research Working Paper.

American Rural Small-Scale Industry Delegation (1977) *Rural Small-Scale Industry in the People's Republic of China*. Berkeley: University of California Press.

Andors, Stephen (1980) "The Political and Organizational Implications of China's New Economic Policies," *Bulletin of Concerned Asian Scholars* 12, 2 (April-June).

Ashbrook, Arthur, Jr. (1982) "China: Economic Modernization and Long Term Performance," in U.S. Congress, Joint Economic Committee, *China Under the Four Modernizations*, part 1. Washington, D.C.: GPO.

————. (1975) "China: Economic Overview, 1975," in U.S. Congress, Joint Economic Committee, *China: A Reassessment of the Economy*. Washington, D.C.: GPO.

Balazs, Etienne (1972) *Chinese Civilization and Bureaucracy*. New Haven: Yale University Press.

Banaji, Jairus (1977) "Modes of Production in a Materialist Conception of History," *Capital and Class* 3 (Autumn).

Banister, Judith (1977) "China's Demographic Transition in the Asian Context," paper presented at the Conference on the Modern Chinese Economy in a Comparative Context, Stanford University, January 1977.

Baran, Paul (1968) *The Political Economy of Growth*. New York: Monthly Review Press.

Baran, Paul, and E. J. Hobsbawm (1973) "The Stages of Economic Growth: A Review," in C. K. Wilber, ed., *The Political Economy of Development and Underdevelopment*. New York: Random House.

Barnett, Robert (1941) *Economic Shanghai*. New York: Institute of Pacific Relations.

Beijing Review (BR): issues indicated by dates in text.

Buck, John Lossing (1968) *Land Utilization in China*. New York: Paragon Book Reprint Corporation.

Chang, Chung-li (1974) *The Chinese Gentry*. Seattle: University of Washington Press.

————. (1962) *The Income of the Chinese Gentry*. Seattle: University of Washington Press.

Chang, John K. (1969) *Industrial Development in Pre-Communist China*. Chicago: Aldine.

Chao, Kang (1965) *The Rate and Pattern of Industrial Growth in Communist China*. Ann Arbor: University of Michigan Press.

Chen, Han-seng (1973) *Landlord and Peasant in China*. Westport, Ct.: Hyperion.

Chen, Nai-Ruenn (1967) *Chinese Economic Statistics*. Chicago: Aldine.

Chesneaux, Jean, Marianne Bastid, and Marie-Claire Bergére (1976) *China from the Opium Wars to the 1911 Revolution*. New York: Pantheon.

China Handbook Series (1984) *Economy*. Beijing: Foreign Languages Press.

Dennerline, Jerry (1975) "Fiscal Reform and Local Control: The Gentry-Bureaucratic Alliance Survives the Conquest," in Frederic Wakeman, ed., *Conflict and Control in Late Imperial China*. Berkeley: University of California Press.

Dernberger, Robert (1975) "The Role of the Foreigner in China's Economic Development, 1840–1949," in Dwight Perkins, ed., *China's Modern Economy in Historical Perspective*. Stanford: Stanford University Press.

Diamond, Norma (1985) "Rural Collectivization and Decollectivization in China—A Review Article," *Journal of Asian Studies* 44, 4 (August).

————. (1983) "Model Villages and Village Realities," *Modern China* 9, 2 (April).

Dobb, Maurice (1975) *Studies in the Development of Capitalism*. New York: International Publishers.

Dong Furen (1982) "The Relationship Between Accumulation and Consumption in China's Economic Development," in George C. Wang, ed., *Economic Reform in the PRC*. Boulder: Westview.

Duan Jianke (1982) "Prices in China," in Xue Muqiao, ed., *Almanac of China's Economy 1981*. Hong Kong: Modern Cultural Co.

Eberhard, Wolfram (1971) *A History of China*. Berkeley: University of California Press.

————. (1962) *Social Mobility in Traditional China*. Leiden: E. J. Brill.

Eckstein, Alexander (1966) *Communist China's Economic Growth and Foreign Trade*. New York: McGraw-Hill.

Eckstein, Alexander, John K. Fairbank, and L. S. Yang (1975) "Economic Change in Early Modern China," in Alexander Eckstein, *China's Economic Development*. Ann Arbor: University of Michigan Press.

Edwards, Edgar O. (1974) *Employment in Developing Nations*. New York: Columbia University Press.

Elvin, Mark (1973) *The Pattern of the Chinese Past*. Stanford: Stanford University Press.

Esherick, Joseph (1972) "Harvard on China: The Apologetics of Imperialism," *Bulletin of Concerned Asian Scholars* 4, 4 (December).

Fairbank, John K. (1971) *The United States and China*. Cambridge: Harvard University Press.

Fairbank, John K., and Edwin O. Reischauer (1960) *East Asia: The Great Tradition*. Boston: Houghton Mifflin.

Fei, Hsiao-tung (1968) *China's Gentry*. Chicago: University of Chicago Press.

Feuerwerker, Albert (1976a) *The Foreign Establishment in China in the Early Twentieth Century*. Ann Arbor: University of Michigan Center for Chinese Studies.

————. (1976b) *State and Society in Eighteenth-Century China: The Ch'ing Empire in Its Glory*. Ann Arbor: University of Michigan Center for Chinese Studies.

————. (1975) *Rebellion in Nineteenth-Century China*. Ann Arbor: University of Michigan Center for Chinese Studies.

————. (1969) *The Chinese Economy, ca. 1870–1911*. Ann Arbor: University of Michigan Center for Chinese Studies.

————. (1968) *The Chinese Economy, 1912–1949*. Ann Arbor: University of Michigan Center for Chinese Studies.

Foreign Broadcast Information Service (FBIS) (1980) *Daily Report*, October 3, pp. L10-L15.

Foster-Carter, Aiden (1978) "The Modes of Production Controversy," *New Left*

Review 107.

Frank, André Gunder (1973) "The Development of Underdevelopment," in C. K. Wilber, ed., *The Political Economy of Development and Underdevelopment*. New York: Random House.

―――. (1972) "The Development of Underdevelopment," in James D. Cockcroft, André Gunder Frank, and Dale L. Johnson, eds., *Dependence and Underdevelopment*. Garden City, N.Y.: Anchor Books.

―――. (1967) *Capitalism and Underdevelopment in Latin America*. New York: Monthly Review Press.

Franke, Wolfgang (1967a) *China and the West: The Cultural Encounter, 13th to 20th Centuries*. New York: Harper Torchbooks.

―――. (1967b) "The Taiping Rebellion," in F. Schurmann and O. Schell, eds., *Imperial China*. New York: Vintage Books.

Friedman, Edward (1982) "Maoism, Titoism, Stalinism: Some Origins and Consequences of the Maoist Theory of the Socialist Transition," in Mark Selden and Victor D. Lippit, eds., *The Transition to Socialism in China*. Armonk, N.Y.: M. E. Sharpe.

Furtado, Celso (1973) "The Concept of External Dependence in the Study of Underdevelopment," in C. K. Wilber, ed., *The Political Economy of Development and Underdevelopment*. New York: Random House.

Gernet, Jacques (1970) *Daily Life in China on the Eve of the Mongol Invasion, 1250–1276*. Stanford: Stanford University Press.

Gregory, Paul R., and Robert C. Stuart (1981) *Soviet Economic Structure and Performance*. New York: Harper and Row.

Griffin, Keith (1973) "Underdevelopment in History," in C. K. Wilber, ed., *The Political Economy of Development and Underdevelopment*. New York: Random House.

Griffin, Keith, ed. (1984) *Institutional Reform and Economic Development in the Chinese Countryside*. Armonk, N.Y.: M. E. Sharpe.

Griffin, Keith, and A. Ghose (1979) "Growth and Impoverishment in the Rural Areas of Asia," *World Development* 7, 4/5 (April/May).

Haeger, John W. (1975) "Introduction," in J. W. Haeger, ed., *Crisis and Prosperity in Sung China*. Tucson: University of Arizona Press.

Hinton, William (1983) "China's New Family Contract System," *Monthly Review* (November).

―――. (1982) "Village in Transition," in Mark Selden and Victor D. Lippit, eds., *The Transition to Socialism in China*. Armonk, N.Y.: M. E. Sharpe.

―――. (1965) *Fanshen*. New York: Monthly Review Press.

Ho, Ping-ti (1962) *The Ladder of Success in Imperial China*. New York: Columbia University Press.

―――. (1959) *Studies on the Population of China, 1368–1953*. Cambridge: Harvard University Press.

Hou, Chi-ming (1965) *Foreign Investment and Economic Development in China*. Cambridge: Harvard University Press.

Howe, Christopher (1973) *Wage Patterns and Wage Policy in Modern China 1919–1972*. Cambridge: Cambridge University Press.

―――. (1971) *Employment and Economic Growth in Urban China 1949–1957*. Cambridge: Cambridge University Press.

Huang, Philip (1985) *The Peasant Economy and Social Change in North China*. Stanford: Stanford University Press.

Hussain, Syed Akmal (1978) "The Impact of Agricultural Growth on the Agrarian Structure of Pakistan." Ph.D. dissertation, University of Sussex.

International Labour Office (1977) *Poverty and Landlessness in Rural Asia*. Geneva: International Labour Office.

Ishikawa, Shigeru (1982) "China's Food and Agriculture: Performance and Prospects," in Erwin M. Reisch, ed., *Agricultura Sinica*. Berlin: Duncker and Humblot.

Kilby, Peter (1969) *Industrialization in an Open Economy: Nigeria 1945-1966*. Cambridge: Cambridge University Press.

Kiyokawa, Yukihiko (1975) "Ideology to site no gijyutsu to keizai hatten" (Technology as Ideology and Economic Development: An Analysis of the Political Economy of Technology Transfer), *Azia Keizai* 16, 4 (April 15).

Kojima, Reiitsu (1982) "Accumulation, Technology and China's Economic Development," in Mark Selden and Victor D. Lippit, eds., *The Transition to Socialism in China*. Armonk, N.Y.: M. E. Sharpe.

Koo, Hagen (1984) "The Political Economy of Income Distribution in South Korea: The Impact of the State's Industrialization Policies," *World Development* 12, 10.

Lardy, Nicholas (1985) "State Intervention and Peasant Opportunities," in William Parish, ed., *Chinese Rural Development*. Armonk, N.Y.: M. E. Sharpe.

————. (1983) *Agriculture in China's Modern Economic Development*. Cambridge: Cambridge University Press.

————. (1978) *Economic Growth and Distribution in China*. Cambridge: Cambridge University Press.

Lee, Eddy (1984) "Employment and Incomes in Rural China," in Keith Griffin, ed., *Institutional Reform and Economic Development in the Chinese Countryside*. Armonk, N.Y.: M. E. Sharpe.

Levy, Marion (1949) *The Family Revolution in Modern China*. Cambridge: Harvard University Press.

Lewis, W. Arthur (1963) "Economic Development with Unlimited Supplies of Labour," in A. N. Agarwala and S. P. Singh, eds., *The Economics of Underdevelopment*. New York: Oxford University Press.

Li, Choh-Ming (1967) "Economic Development," in F. Schurmann and O. Schell, eds., *Communist China*. New York: Vintage Books.

Li, Yuju and Shao Taiyan (1981) "Active and Stable Reform of the Management System of the People's Communes—Investigation of the Reform of the Shibantan Commune System," in China Academy of Agricultural Sciences, Agricultural Economics Research Institute, *Agricultural Economics Reference Materials*, no. 10, pp. 5-11 (in Chinese).

Liang, Wensen (1982) "Balanced Development of Industry and Agriculture," in Xu Dixin et al., *China's Search for Economic Growth*. Beijing: New World Press.

Lin, Zili (1983) "On the Contract System of Responsibility Linked to Production—A New Form of Cooperative Economy in China's Socialist Agriculture," *Social Sciences in China* 4, 1 (March).

Lippit, Victor D. (1982) "Field Notes of a Visit to Three People's Communes Near Shijiachuang, August 1982." Unpublished.

————. (1981) "The People's Communes and China's New Development Strategy," *Bulletin of Concerned Asian Scholars* 13, 3 (July-September).

————. (1978) "Economic Development in Meiji Japan and Contemporary China: A Comparative Study," *Cambridge Journal of Economics* 2.

————. (1977) "The Commune in Chinese Development," *Modern China* 3, 2 (April).

————. (1974) *Land Reform and Economic Development in China*. White Plains, N.Y.: M. E. Sharpe.

Liu, Guoguang (1984) "Some Important Problems in China's Strategy for Economic

Development," *Social Sciences in China* 4, 1 (March).

Liu, Ta-chung, and Kung-chia Yeh (1965) *The Economy of the Chinese Mainland: National Income and Economic Development, 1933–1959*. Princeton: Princeton University Press.

Lockett, Martin, and Craig R. Littler (1983) "Trends in Chinese Enterprise Management," *World Development* 11, 8.

Mao Tse-tung (1974) *Miscellany of Mao Tse-tung Thought (1949–1968) Parts I and II*. Arlington, Va.: National Technical Information Service.

————. (1968) "On Contradiction," in *Four Essays on Philosophy*. Beijing: Foreign Languages Press.

————. (1960) *Analysis of the Classes in Chinese Society*. Beijing: Foreign Languages Press.

Marx, Karl (1967) *Capital*, vol. 1. New York: International Publishers.

————. (1962) *Capital*, vol. 3. Moscow: Foreign Languages Publishing House.

————. (1961) *Capital*, vol. 1. Moscow: Foreign Languages Publishing House.

Muller, Ronald (1973) "The Multinational Corporation and the Underdevelopment of the Third World," in C. K. Wilber, ed., *The Political Economy of Development and Underdevelopment*. New York: Random House.

Murphy, Rhoads (1974) "The Treaty Ports and China's Modernization," in Mark Elvin and G. William Skinner, eds., *The Chinese City Between Two Worlds*. Stanford: Stanford University Press.

Myers, Ramon (1977) "Trends in Agriculture: 1911–1949," paper delivered at the Asian Studies on the Pacific Coast 1977 Conference, Eugene, Oregon, June 18, 1977.

————. (1970) *The Chinese Peasant Economy: Agricultural Development in Hopei and Shantung, 1890–1949*. Cambridge: Harvard University Press.

Myrdal, Jan (1965) *Report from a Chinese Village*. New York: Pantheon.

Naseem, S. M. (1981) *Underdevelopment, Poverty and Inequality in Pakistan*. Lahore: Vanguard Publications.

New York Times (dates indicated).

Nove, Alec (1979) *Political Economy and Soviet Socialism*. London: George Allen & Unwin.

Nurkse, Ragnar (1964) *Problems of Capital Formation in Underdeveloped Countries*. New York: Oxford University Press.

Ogura, Takekazu, ed. (1970) *Agricultural Development in Modern Japan*. Tokyo: Fuji.

Parish, William L., ed. (1985) *Chinese Rural Development*. Armonk, N.Y.: M. E. Sharpe.

Perkins, Dwight (1975) "Growth and Changing Structure of China's Twentieth-Century Economy," in D. Perkins, ed., *China's Modern Economy in Historical Perspective*. Stanford: Stanford University Press.

————. (1969) *Agricultural Development in China 1368–1968*. Cambridge: Harvard University Press.

Polachek, James (1975) "Gentry Hegemony: Soochow in the T'ung-chih Restoration," in F. Wakeman, ed., *Conflict and Control in Late Imperial China*. Berkeley: University of California Press.

Potter, Sulamith (1983) "The Position of Peasants in Modern China's Social Order," *Modern China* 9, 2 (April).

Rawski, Thomas (1980) *China's Transition to Industrialism: Producer Goods and Economic Development in the Twentieth Century*. Ann Arbor: University of Michigan Press.

————. (1979a) "Economic Growth and Employment in China," *World Development* 7, 8/9 (August–September).

————. (1979b) *Economic Growth and Employment in China*. New York: Oxford University Press.

————. (1975) "The Growth of Producer Industries, 1900–1971," in Dwight Perkins, ed., *China's Modern Economy in Historical Perspective*. Stanford: Stanford University Press.

Riskin, Carl (1982) "Market, Maoism and Economic Reform in China," in Mark Selden and Victor D. Lippit, eds., *The Transition to Socialism in China*. Armonk, N.Y.: M. E. Sharpe.

————. (1975a) "Surplus and Stagnation in Modern China," in Dwight Perkins, ed., *China's Modern Economy in Historical Perspective*. Stanford: Stanford University Press.

————. (1975b) "Workers' Incentives in Chinese Industry," in U.S. Congress, Joint Economic Committee, *China: A Reassessment of the Economy*. Washington, D.C.: GPO.

Rudra, Ashok, Utsa Patnaik, et al. (1978) *Studies in the Development of Capitalism in India*. Lahore: Vanguard Books.

Schell, Orville (1984) "A Reporter at Large: The Wind of Wanting to Go It Alone," *New Yorker* (January 23).

Schultz, Theodore (1964) *Transforming Traditional Agriculture*. New Haven: Yale University Press.

Seers, Dudley (1973) "The Meaning of Development," in C. K. Wilber, ed., *The Political Economy of Development and Underdevelopment*. New York: Random House.

Selden, Mark (1982) "Cooperation and Conflict: Cooperative and Collective Formation in China's Countryside," in Mark Selden and Victor D. Lippit, eds., *The Transition to Socialism in China*. Armonk, N.Y.: M. E. Sharpe.

Selden, Mark (1972) *The Yenan Way in Revolutionary China*. Cambridge: Harvard University Press.

Selden, Mark, and Victor D. Lippit (1982) "The Transition to Socialism in China," in Mark Selden and Victor Lippit, eds., *The Transition to Socialism in China*. Armonk, N.Y.: M. E. Sharpe.

Shapiro, Sidney (1981) *Experiment in Sichuan*. Beijing: New World Press.

Shiba, Yoshinobu (1975) "Urbanization and the Development of Markets in the Lower Yangtze Valley," in J. Haeger, ed., *Crisis and Prosperity in Sung China*. Tucson: University of Arizona Press.

————. (1970) *Commerce and Society in Sung China*. Ann Arbor: University of Michigan Center for Chinese Studies.

Shih, Vincent (1967) *The Taiping Ideology*. Seattle: University of Washington Press.

Shue, Vivienne (1984) "The Fate of the Commune," *Modern China* 10, 3 (July).

Spence, Jonathan D. (1975) "Opium Smoking in Ch'ing China," in F. Wakeman, ed., *Conflict and Control in Late Imperial China*. Berkeley: University of California Press.

————. (1974) *Emperor of China: Self-Portrait of K'ang-hsi*. New York: Knopf.

State Statistical Bureau, People's Republic of China (1984) *Statistical Yearbook of China 1984*. Hong Kong: Economic Information & Agency.

————. (1983) *Statistical Yearbook of China 1983*. Hong Kong: Economic Information & Agency.

————. (1979) *Main Indicators, Development of the National Economy of the People's Republic of China (1949–1978)*. Beijing.

Sun, Kungtu C. (1969) *The Economic Development of Manchuria in the First Half of the Twentieth Century*. Cambridge: Harvard University Press.

Sweezy, Paul M., and Charles Bettelheim (1971) *On the Transition to Socialism*, 2d ed.

New York: Monthly Review Press.

Todaro, Michael P. (1977) *Economic Development in the Third World*. New York: Longman.

Trescott, Paul B. (1985) "Incentives Versus Equality: What Does China's Recent Experience Show?" *World Development* 13, 2 (February).

Unger, Jonathan (1985a) "Remuneration, Ideology and Personal Interests in a Chinese Village, 1960–1980," in William L. Parish, ed., *Chinese Rural Development*. Armonk, N.Y.: M. E. Sharpe.

————. (1985b) "The Decollectivization of the Chinese Countryside: A Survey of 28 Villages" (unpublished manuscript).

U.S. Department of Agriculture (1982) *China: Review of Agriculture in 1981 and Outlook for 1982*. Washington, D.C.: U.S. Department of Agriculture.

Wakeman, Frederic E., Jr. (1975a) *The Fall of Imperial China*. New York: Free Press.

————. (1975b) "The Evolution of Local Control in Late Imperial China," in F. Wakeman, ed., *Conflict and Control in Late Imperial China*. Berkeley: University of California Press.

————. (1966) *Strangers at the Gate: Social Disorder in South China 1839–1861*. Berkeley: University of California Press.

Walder, Andrew G. (1983) "Organized Dependency and Cultures of Authority in Chinese Industry," *Journal of Asian Studies* 43, 1 (November).

————. (1982) "Some Ironies of the Maoist Legacy in Industry," in Mark Selden and Victor D. Lippit, eds., *The Transition to Socialism in China*. Armonk, N.Y.: M. E. Sharpe.

Walker, Kenneth (1984) *Food Grain Procurement and Consumption in China*. Cambridge: Cambridge University Press.

————. (1966) "Collectivisation in Retrospect: The 'Socialist High Tide' of Autumn 1955-Spring 1956." *China Quarterly* (April-June).

Wall Street Journal (dates indicated).

Wang, Haibo (1982) "Greater Power for the Enterprises," in Lin Wei and Arnold Chao, eds., *China's Economic Reforms*. Philadelphia: University of Pennsylvania Press.

Watson, Andrew (1983) "Agriculture Looks for 'Shoes that Fit': The Production Responsibility System and Its Implications," *World Development* 11, 8 (August).

Wei, Lin, and Arnold Chao, eds. (1982) *China's Economic Reforms*. Philadelphia: University of Pennsylvania Press.

Wilber, Charles K., ed. (1973) *The Political Economy of Development and Underdevelopment*. New York: Random House.

Wolpe, Harold, ed. (1980) *The Articulation of Modes of Production*. London: Routledge and Kegan Paul.

World Bank (1984) *World Development Report 1984*. New York: Oxford University Press.

————. (1975) *The Assault on World Poverty*. Baltimore: Johns Hopkins University Press.

Wright, Mary C. (1957) *The Last Stand of Chinese Conservatism*. Stanford: Stanford University Press.

Wu, Ching-tzu (1957) *The Scholars*. Beijing: Foreign Languages Press.

Xue Muqiao, ed. (1982) *Almanac of China's Economy, 1981*. Hong Kong: Modern Cultural Co. Compiled by the Economic Research Center, State Council of the People's Republic of China, and the State Statistical Bureau.

————. (1981) *China's Socialist Economy*. Beijing: Foreign Languages Press.

Yang, C. K. (1965) *Chinese Communist Society: The Family and the Village*. Cambridge: MIT Press.

————. (1959) *A Chinese Village in Early Communist Transition*. Cambridge, Mass.: MIT Press.

Yeh, K. C. (1984) "Macroeconomic Changes in the Chinese Economy During the Readjustment," *China Quarterly* 100 (December).

Zhang, Yunling (1985) "The Evolution of China's Agricultural Management System" (unpublished manuscript).

Zhao Ziyang (1984) "Report on the Work of the Government (Delivered at the Second Session of the Sixth National People's Congress on May 15, 1984)," *Beijing Review* (June 11).

Zheng Ji (1982) "Employment, Wages, Workers' Welfare and Labor Protection in China," in Xue Muqiao, ed., *Almanac of China's Economy, 1981*. Hong Kong: Modern Cultural Co.

Index

About the Author

A graduate of Harvard College, Victor D. Lippit received a Ph.D. in Economics from Yale University in 1971. In 1967/68 he was a Research Fellow at Hitotsubashi University in Tokyo, and in 1972/73 he was a Postdoctoral Fulbright Research Fellow at Tokyo University.

A Professor of Economics at the University of California, Riverside, Victor Lippit is the author of *Land Reform and Economic Development in China* (1974) and the co-editor (with Mark Selden) of *The Transition to Socialism in China* (1982). His study "The Development of Underdevelopment in China" appeared in *Modern China* and was republished together with the response it evoked in Philip Huang, ed., *The Development of Underdevelopment in China* (1980).

East Gate Books

Harold R. Isaacs
RE-ENCOUNTERS IN CHINA

James D. Seymour
CHINA RIGHTS ANNALS 1

Thomas E. Stolper
CHINA, TAIWAN, AND THE OFFSHORE ISLANDS

William L. Parish, ed.
CHINESE RURAL DEVELOPMENT
The Great Transformation

Anita Chan, Stanley Rosen, and Jonathan Unger, eds.
ON SOCIALIST DEMOCRACY AND THE CHINESE LEGAL SYSTEM
The Li Yizhe Debates

Michael S. Duke, ed.
CONTEMPORARY CHINESE LITERATURE
An Anthology of Post-Mao Fiction and Poetry

Michiko N. Wilson
THE MARGINAL WORLD OF ŌE KENZABURO
A Study in Themes and Techniques

Thomas B. Gold
STATE AND SOCIETY IN THE TAIWAN MIRACLE

Carol Lee Hamrin and Timothy Cheek, eds.
CHINA'S ESTABLISHMENT INTELLECTUALS

John P. Burns and Stanley Rosen, eds.
POLICY CONFLICTS IN POST-MAO CHINA
A Documentary Survey, with Analysis

James D. Seymour
CHINA'S SATELLITE PARTIES

Victor D. Lippit
THE ECONOMIC DEVELOPMENT OF CHINA